The Public Interest Law Review 1995

Editorial Office

The National Legal Center
for the Public Interest
Suite 301
1000 16th Street N.W.
Washington, DC 20036
(202) 296-1683

Seventeen years ago, when the National Legal Center for the Public Interest was in its formative stages, its founders envisioned the publication of a law review. The 1991 edition of *The Public Interest Law Review* was the first of a series published on an annual basis. We are pleased to offer this, the 1995 edition. The law review will have value not only in the initial reading, but also in the future—as a reference document, reflective of our time, for students of law and government.

The National Legal Center provides this law review as a public service. The Center expresses its gratitude to the contributors, whose original work is their own and does not necessarily reflect the opinions of the directors, officers, or advisers of the National Legal Center for the Public Interest. Finally, we are especially grateful again this year to Leonard A. Leo of the Federalist Society for his skillful work in editing the *Review*.

—Ernest B. Hueter, President

The Public Interest Law Review 1995

EDITED BY
ROGER CLEGG
LEONARD A. LEO

CAROLINA ACADEMIC PRESS

for the

National Legal Center for the Public Interest

The Public Interest Law Review

ISBN 0-89089-896-0

The Public Interest Law Review is an annual publication sponsored by the National Legal Center for the Public Interest with the editorial assistance of the Federalist Society. Volumes may be purchased from Carolina Academic Press, 700 Kent Street, Durham, N.C. 27701, (919) 489-7486. Editorial inquiries should be addressed to *The Public Interest Law Review*, National Legal Center for the Public Interest, Suite 301, 1000 16th Street, N.W., Washington, D.C. 20036, (202) 296-1683.

Printed in the United States of America.

CONTENTS

FROM THE EDITORS

The 1995 edition of *The Public Interest Law Review* provides, as did its predecessor volumes, a needed outlet for conservative and libertarian legal scholarship, often ignored or slighted in other law journals.

The articles section of the 1995 *Review* focuses principally on significant recent decisions by the United States Supreme Court. The articles are grouped in pairs: the first two are on First Amendment issues, the next two on the dormant Commerce Clause, and the last two on civil rights. The last article, by Professor Thernstrom, is not about any recent Supreme Court decision, but its critique of the work of the District of Columbia Circuit's Task Force on Gender, Race, and Ethnic Bias is of critical importance for all levels of the judiciary.

As in years past, we also review a number of books on assorted legal topics. At the end of this section, we also print a response by Harry Jaffa to Charles Cooper's piece in last year's *Review* on Mr. Jaffa's book, *Original Intent and the Framers of the Constitution.*

This volume again achieves a noteworthy "diversity," to borrow from today's politically correct jargon. Among its contributors, there is a remarkable balance of academics and practitioners, government or former government officials and residents of think tanks, and lawyers and nonlawyers. There is, accordingly, a true diversity of experience and perspective, rather than of more superficial characteristics.

We welcome any ideas, comments, and suggestions. Letters may be sent to the National Legal Center for the Public Interest in Washington, D.C., which sponsors the *Review*. Copies of this volume as well as the 1991, 1992, 1993, and 1994 volumes may be purchased from Carolina Academic Press in Durham, North Carolina.

ROGER CLEGG
LEONARD A. LEO

The Public Interest Law Review 1995

ARTICLES

HENRY MARK HOLZER

Sauce for the Goose: The Left, the Right, and Free Speech

Introduction

Even today, when informed people should know better, there is a widespread belief that the Left leads the fight for civil liberties. Indeed, in a perverse use of language, the Left's preeminent legal action organization is named the American Civil Liberties Union. Unfortunately, regarding the ACLU in particular and the Left in general, the perception that they are today's guardians of Americans' civil liberties could not be more mistaken. The truth of the matter is that the Left long ago abdicated any claim to stand for the protection of civil liberties, especially when it began trying (and succeeding) to achieve its political goals not through the accountable political branches of government, but through the courts.

What have the Left's efforts spawned? Supposedly in the name of civil liberties[1] ("the right to choose"), a woman now has the constitutional right to destroy her unwanted fetus. Supposedly in the name of civil liberties ("leveling the playing field"), a black now has the constitutional right to benefit from a racial quota. Supposedly in the name of civil liberties ("freedom of religion"), a prisoner now has the constitutional right to order special meals. Supposedly in the name of civil liberties ("a jury of one's peers"), a prosecutor is now constitutionally prohibited from exercising race- and gender-based preemptory challenges. Supposedly in the name of civil liberties ("preventing self-incrimination"), a rapist now has the constitutional right to be told that he has a right to remain silent. And more.

1. Although in some contexts the distinction is important, this paragraph will not distinguish between the concepts "civil liberties" (often understood to include Bill of Rights–type guarantees) and "civil rights" (often understood to embrace political-legislative guarantees, many with a racial flavor, like voting rights).

Although these newly discovered constitutional "rights" are constitutionally and intellectually indefensible, the Left has fought hard for them as an article of unshakable faith—just as it once went to the wall on behalf of the First Amendment's freedom of speech guarantee.

If there is any single area where one can applaud, even respect, the prodigious legal efforts of the Left, it is with regard to free speech in America. The devil is entitled to her due! Sometimes the Left won, sometimes it lost, but usually it fought. The names come wafting back to us across time: Schenck and Abrams, the World War I protestors; Debs, the socialist; Gitlow, the anarchist; Whitney, Dennis, and the other communists; Bridges, the unionist; Hess, the antiwar activist; Cohen, the antidraft protester; Near, the publisher; Ginzburg, the pornographer; and scores of others, too many to mention—school teachers, public employees, politicians, military personnel, authors.

Despite its admirable track record, however, the Left's support for free speech was never wholly unstinting (of course, as we shall see, neither was the Right's). Indeed, as far back as half a century ago the Left's selective focus could be discerned in cases involving what came to be called "commercial speech." It is in the commercial speech cases—beginning with *Valentine v. Chrestensen*,[2] and running through to the more modern *Virginia State Board of Pharmacy v. Virginia Citizens Consumer Council, Inc.*[3]—that one can perceive how the Left's supposed fealty to freedom of expression was rooted not in the universal principle that Americans have the inalienable right to speak freely, but rather in the case-specific social ends to be achieved by whatever speech the Left sought to protect.

For example, pharmacists in Virginia were prohibited from advertising the price of prescription drugs. The law was challenged constitutionally, but not by muzzled pharmacists invoking their right to free speech. The challengers were prescription drug *consumers*, represented and supported by a coalition of Left organizations, who claimed that since prescription drug prices varied widely, consumers would benefit greatly if advertising were freely allowed because they could then shop around for the lowest price. Although the issue for the Supreme Court was whether the Virginia law was constitutional, the Court's formulation of that issue was noteworthy: "Our question is whether speech which does 'no more than propose a commercial transaction' is so removed from any 'exposition of ideas' and from '"truth, science, morality, and arts in general, in its diffusion of liberal sentiments on the administration of government,"' that it lacks all protection."[4]

---

2. 316 U.S. 52 (1942).
3. 425 U.S. 748 (1976).
4. *Id.* at 762–63 (citations omitted).

The implications of this formulation went far beyond the limited subject of commercial speech then before the Court. The formulation suggests a rationale—latent in the Left's earlier First Amendment jurisprudence, but soon to be adopted by it explicitly in aid of two of the Left's contemporary political goals—for separating protected from unprotected speech: *its social utility*. On this principle, whether commercial speech generally, or any specific manifestation of it, is or is not protected is relatively unimportant compared to the socially based criterion by which protection is to be judged. *That* the *Virginia Pharmacy* case protected the advertising of prescription drug prices, and perhaps all truthful commercial speech, is not nearly as significant as *why* it did. As to that, the Court was quite explicit. Yet its reasons noticeably had little to do with the *pharmacists'* free speech.[5] Focusing not on *their* rights, but rather on *consumer needs*, the Court candidly admitted that:

> As to the particular consumer's interest in the free flow of commercial information, that interest may be as keen, if not keener by far, than his interest in the day's most urgent political debate. [The consumers'] case in this respect is a convincing one. Those whom the suppression of prescription consumer drug prices hits the hardest are the *poor*, the *sick*, and particularly the *aged*. A disproportionate part of their income tends to be spent on prescription drugs; yet they are the least able to learn, by shopping from pharmacist to pharmacist, where their scarce dollars are best spent. When drug prices vary as strikingly as they do, information as to who is charging what becomes more than a convenience. It could mean the alleviation of physical pain, or the enjoyment of basic necessities.
>
> Generalizing, *society also may have a strong interest* in the free flow of commercial information. . . .[6]

In short, the *needs* of the poor, sick, and aged (as well, of course, as the interests of "society" generally) were the Court's yardstick for measuring what was, and was not, allowable free speech. The inalienable First Amendment *right* of the pharmacists freely to communicate (or not, as they wished) was not even an issue. That the former's needs justified the latter's speech was—*is*, especially today—a very dangerous notion. To make social utility (i.e., who needs how much of what) the criterion for free speech is to place it under government control and, worse, to place it *in the service of others*. It is too easy for government to decide that no need exists for consumers to hear about a wide variety of topics, and from there to decide that no right exists to speak about them. It is too easy for

5. Of course, one cannot know whether the absent pharmacists were ever interested in asserting a right freely to advertise prescription drug prices.

6. 425 U.S. at 763–64 (emphasis added).

government to assert that the needs of the poor, the sick, the aged—indeed, the needs of "society" itself—have changed, thus allowing still other speech to be silenced. It is too easy for government to conclude—as today the Left, regrettably with some success, is urging the government to conclude—that certain kinds of speech victimizes, and inhibits the conduct of, certain special classes of people: *those who have a "need" to be protected from mere words*. The result? To hell with free speech. And, at the same time, to hell with any further pretense that the Left cares about *that* particular First Amendment civil liberty—especially when normal application of the First Amendment would act to frustrate the Left in achieving two goals high on its current political agenda: succoring "victimized" minorities and protecting abortion "rights." Indeed, the Left's moral, intellectual, and philosophical bankruptcy is nowhere more evident than when it confronts this frustration.

Hate Speech

Whatever the sociopolitical cause(s), it is fair to say that in today's popular culture there exists a degree of militancy never before experienced. Many blacks, homosexuals, feminists, old people, handicapped, and other discrete so-called minority groups and their spokesmen, all claiming some sort of victimhood and each with a sociopolitical agenda of their own, agitate in the culture for acceptance, privilege, and what they see as their slice of the pie.

Not surprisingly, the victims' victims—the white male discriminated against by racial quotas; the heterosexual, denied a promotion; the boss, too-easily charged with sexual harassment; the young, burdened with government-imposed care of the elderly; the employer, wasting money to accommodate disabled employees—have spoken out in self-defense. Sometimes their words have been intemperate, even including old or new epithets: "nigger," "fag," "feminazi," "wetback," "cripple."

As offensive as this kind of language is, the virulent nature of the Left's counterreaction—in a nation which for over 200 years has prided itself on enshrining freedom of speech as perhaps the preeminent constitutional value—would have been hard to predict. Professor Peter Linzer of the University of Houston Law Center wrote in 1991 that he had been informed that more than 100 American universities had promulgated some form of regulation of racist speech.[7] Examples of these regulations, as applied, are enough to make a true civil libertarian's hair stand on end. The vice chancellor of the University of California at Riverside decides that a t-shirt

7. Peter Linzer, *White Liberal Looks at Racist Speech*, 65 ST. JOHN'S L. REV. 187 (1991).

printed by a fraternity is "politically incorrect" because of an alleged anti-Mexican bias; the fraternity is banned from the campus. A University of Michigan student is forced to write and publish a "confession" of political error for merely raising in a classroom discussion the question of whether homosexuality is moral. A Sarah Lawrence student is charged with "inappropriate laughter"(!) for chuckling at *someone else's* joke about gays.

These examples can be multiplied many times over, revealing a systematic attack of unprecedented magnitude on the First Amendment. Worse is that this assault on free speech had its genesis in the fertile minds of those whom many would expect to be most solicitous of the First Amendment, and who, until their own oxen were gored, actually purported to be champions of free speech: left-wing law school professors.

The seminal law review article that gave birth to the hate speech movement was written by Richard Delgado, now the Charles Inglis Thompson Professor of Law at the University of Colorado. In his article, Professor Delgado enlightened the academic, legal, and judicial communities concerning what speech would be acceptable to the thought police, and what would be unacceptable:

> [A]n epithet such as "You damn nigger" would almost always be found actionable, as it is highly insulting and highly racial. However, an insult such as "you incompetent fool," directed at a black person by a white, even in a context which makes it highly insulting, would not be actionable because it lacks a racial component. "Boy," directed at a young black male, might be actionable, depending on the speaker's intent, the hearer's understanding, and whether a reasonable person would consider it a racial insult in the particular context. "Hey nigger," spoken affectionately between black persons and used as a greeting, would not be actionable. An insult such as "You dumb honkey," directed at a white person, could be actionable... but only in the unusual situations where the plaintiff would suffer harm from such an insult.[8]

Delgado's assault on the First Amendment was followed by a second wave launched by Professor Mari Matsuda, who went Delgado one better by proposing that "a range of legal interventions, including the use of tort law *and criminal law* principles, is appropriate to combat racist hate propaganda."[9] Then came Professor Charles Lawrence, who put a hate-speech spin on *Brown v. Board of Education* that not even the creative

---

8. Richard Delgado, *Words that Wound: A Tort Action for Racial Insults, Epithets, and Name-Calling*, 17 HARV. C.R.-C.L. L. REV. 133, 179–80 (1982).

9. Mari Matsuda, *Public Response to Racist Speech: Considering the Victim's Story*, 87 MICH. L. REV. 2320, 2360 (1989) (emphasis added).

mind of Thurgood Marshall could have contemplated, let alone formulated. According to Lawrence,

> *Brown* held that segregated schools were unconstitutional primarily because of the *message* segregation conveys—the message that black children are an untouchable caste, unfit to be educated with white children. Segregation serves its purpose by conveying an idea.... Therefore, *Brown* may be read as regulating the content of racist speech.[10]

Professor Mary Ellen Gale, a chief scrivener of the California American Civil Liberties Union policy on hate speech, has invited us to

> expand our vision of the first amendment beyond the libertarian paradigm—to acknowledge a more complicated world. We can regulate speech to combat the harms done when speakers themselves perpetuate prejudice and repression: silencing the voices of targeted victims, undermining equality, and decreasing both individual liberty and democratic dialogue. A more complex theory of free speech, *informed by social context and lived experience*, can take the harms of racist speech seriously and allow us to weave a remedy into our continuing constitutional story of individual rights.[11]

While the national ACLU itself long fudged the unambiguous question of whether the First Amendment can abide *any* restrictions on hate speech,[12] its California affiliates have promulgated a policy which flatly endorses censorship. After considerable doublespeak about competing ideas, the value of speech, and the protection of repugnant values, the California ACLU, often in the vanguard of using the courts to promote a left-wing sociopolitical agenda, flatly endorsed the censorship of repugnant speech:

> Campus administrators may not... enact campus codes of conduct prohibiting discriminatory harassment of students, faculty, administrators and staff on the basis of speech or expression *unless* at a minimum all of the following conditions are met:
>
> 1. The code of conduct reaches only speech or expression that:
>
> a) is specifically intended to and does harass an individual or specific individuals on the basis of their race, sex, religion, sexual orientation, national alienage, or ethnic origin; and
>
> b) is addressed directly to the individual or individuals whom it harasses; and

10. Charles Lawrence, *If He Hollers Let Him Go: Regulating Racist Speech on Campus*, 1990 DUKE L.J. 431, 439–40.

11. Mary Ellen Gale, *Reimagining the First Amendment: Racist Speech and Equal Liberty*, 65 ST. JOHN'S L. REV. 119, 184 (1991) (emphasis added).

12. American Civil Liberties Union, Policy Statement on Free Speech and Bias on College Campuses (Oct. 13, 1990).

> c) creates a hostile and intimidating environment which the speaker knows or reasonably should know will seriously and directly impede the educational opportunities of the individual or individuals to whom it is directly addressed....[13]

When one reads the extensive legal and nonlegal literature on hate speech there is a single dominant theme, whether expressed in terms of victimhood, oppression, inequality, exploitation, underdogism, inferiority, subordination, or whatever: *"words that wound" must be eliminated from our vocabulary, and if uttered they must then be punished by administrative, tort, and criminal law.*

This startling proposition rests on the utterly untenable, indeed ridiculous, premise that there exists in the to-be-protected groups a "right," constitutional or otherwise, not to hear words which disparage their race, religion, ethnicity, gender, sexual preference, mental and physical condition, and so forth. Coming from those on the Left—who have long believed that antiwar protesters had the First Amendment right to undermine this nation's war efforts, that pornographers had the First Amendment right to purvey filth which especially degraded women and even children, that Nazis in Skokie had the First Amendment right to flaunt genocidal history in the faces of Holocaust survivors—it is not easy to understand fully the hate-speech movement's solicitude for the feelings of those who hear "words that wound." But there is an explanation, and it is the same one which accounts for the Left's willingness to suppress abortion protest.

Abortion Protest

Before one can understand the willingness, indeed driving need, of the Left to suppress abortion protest, it is necessary first to recall the political and legal history of abortion itself in this country, and to realize that no public issue since slavery has more riven America's social fabric. It has fostered deep animosities, ruptured long-standing relationships, influenced national political debate, even spawned murder.

Prior to 1973 the political branches of every state in the union had placed some legal inhibition on the practice of abortion. Then, in that year, the Left won a tremendous victory when the Supreme Court of the United States rendered its constitutionally indefensible decision in *Roe v. Wade.*[14] By convincing merely six Justices that the ersatz "right of privacy" concocted by Justice Douglas in *Griswold v. Connecticut*[15] extended

13. ACLU of California, Policy Concerning Harassment on College Campuses (1990).
14. 410 U.S. 113 (1973).
15. 381 U.S. 479 (1965).

to the "right" to destroy a fetus, the Left succeeded in accomplishing what until then the core principles of federalism and separation of powers (let alone rational constitutional interpretation) had prevented: nullification of the political will of the people in America's fifty states concerning the practice of abortion.

The next assignment for the Left was to protect that victory at all costs, even at the expense of further corruption of the Court's jurisprudence. Nearly a decade ago, in *Thornburgh v. American College of Obstetricians and Gynecologists*, when Justice O'Connor noted that the Court's abortion decisions had even then "worked a major distortion in the Court's constitutional jurisprudence" and that "[t]oday's decision goes further, and makes it painfully clear that no legal rule or doctrine is safe from ad hoc nullification by this Court when an occasion for its application arises in a case involving state regulation of abortion,"[16] she probably could not have predicted that the Left's constitutional distortion would eventually see it attempting to censor speech and, worse, the Court readily acceding. Yet, that is exactly what has now happened.

Last Term's *Madsen v. Women's Health Center, Inc.*[17] pitted the pro-abortion ("pro-choice" is a misleading euphemism) Left against the anti-abortion Right, and the latter lost. So did free speech.[18]

What the plurality did in *Madsen* is easily understood. It approved a state-court injunction which, as Justice Scalia explained in dissent, created "a 36-foot zone in which only a particular group [anti-abortion protesters], which had broken no law, cannot exercise its rights of speech, assembly, and association, and [which enacted] a noise prohibition, applicable to that group and that group alone...."[19] *How* the plurality managed to accomplish that feat in light of what had previously appeared to be the Court's pro-free-speech injunction jurisprudence is a tale worth elaborating, but beyond this article's scope.[20] For our purposes, the real

16. 476 U.S. 747, 814 (1986) (dissenting opinion).

17. 114 S. Ct. 2516 (1994).

18. Further evidence of the Left's intention to suppress even the communicative aspects of anti-abortion protest is found in parts of the federal Freedom of Access to Clinic Entrances Act of 1994 (FACE), recently enacted by the Democrats who then controlled the legislative and executive branches of the national government. On August 12, 1994, the U.S. District Court for the District of Arizona held that, while protestor plaintiffs challenging FACE presented a justiciable controversy, they failed to state a claim upon which relief could be granted. Intervenors included several Planned Parenthood affiliates. *See also* American Life League Inc. v. Reno, 47 F.3d 642 (4th Cir.), *cert. denied,* 64 U.S.L.W. 3223 (U.S. Oct. 3, 1995) (No. 94-1867) (upholding FACE's constitutionality).

19. 114 S. Ct. at 2535.

20. Suffice to say that, in essence, the plurality created and then applied a new, less stringent, standard (dubbed by Justice Scalia as "intermediate-intermediate" scrutiny) by which

story in *Madsen* is *why* the plurality accepted the Left's invitation to turn its constitutional back on the First Amendment.

Part of the reason—though not the most fundamental—lies in what has been touched on above: the abortion controversy has skewed constitutional decisionmaking and distorted basic constitutional principles. First came *Griswold*, where Justice Douglas and his Warren Court colleagues somehow glimpsed in the "penumbras" and "emanations" of legitimate Bill of Rights guarantees the building-block "right to privacy" upon which *Roe* later would be erected. Next came the infamous *Roe* itself in which a narrow majority of the Court's Justices, the judicial branch, crafted a *federal* anti-anti-abortion statute out of nonprecedential thin air. Indeed, Justice White later observed in *Thornburgh* that in *Roe* the Court had "essentially created something out of nothing."[21] In *Thornburgh* itself, the Court held that the "Court of Appeals correctly invalidated the specified provisions of Pennsylvania's 1982 Abortion Control Act"[22] even though, as Justice O'Connor pointed out, "[i]n so doing, the Court prematurely decide[d] serious constitutional questions on an inadequate record, in contravention of settled principles of constitutional adjudication and procedural fairness."[23] The engine of these decisions—from *Griswold's* contraceptives in the drug stores of Connecticut, to *Madsen's* protests on the streets of Florida—was found not in law, but rather in social policy and judicial arrogance. While it is doubtless true that the states' anti-abortion laws had been animated in part by religious belief, moral code, and ethical scruple, as well as by scientific, economic, social, and other considerations, it is also true that those laws were the product of the democratic, federalism-based, separation-of-powers process that is at the heart of the American constitutional system.

There was, then, the obvious need to protect the jerry-rigged jurisprudence of *Roe* and its progeny from the new threat posed by the First Amendment. But is there an even more fundamental reason to explain six Justices' assault on free speech in *Madsen*? There is, and that reason is suggested by the voting lineup of the Justices in *Madsen*. Although conservative Justices Scalia and Thomas, and "moderate" Justice Kennedy, dissented on the First Amendment issue, conservative Chief Justice Rehnquist joined with liberal Justices Blackmun, Stevens, and Ginsburg and with "moderate" Justices O'Connor and Souter to suppress the abortion protesters' speech. Although superficially this mix might seem incongruous, even con-

---

to judge injunctive restrictions on speech, ignoring in the process both sound policy and judicial precedent.

21. 476 U.S. at 813–14.

22. *Id.* at 772.

23. *Id.* at 815.

tradictory, there is a single principle which unites all six Justices and explains what happened in *Madsen*.

Altruism, Collectivism, Statism

It is no secret that the constitutional guarantee of free speech in America has been more the exception than the rule.[24] What is not so well known, however, is the reason: *Just as America's inner contradiction has lain in altruist-collectivist ethics,*[25] *it has been those ethics and their political corollary, statism, which has animated naturally every Supreme Court decision dealing with speech.*

"Altruism" is popularly understood to mean nothing more than simply being "nice"—supporting the arts, helping the less fortunate, contributing money to medical research. The actual meaning of altruism ethically, however, is far different and much more ominous. *Webster's New World Dictionary* defines altruism as "the doctrine that the general welfare of society"—not one's own happiness—"is the proper goal of an individual's action."[26] And closely related to altruism is the concept of "collectivism," which "holds that the individual has no rights, that his life and work belong to the group (to 'society,' to the tribe, the state, the nation) and that the group may sacrifice him at its own whim to its own interest."[27]

Because altruism and collectivism are ethical doctrines, and because the only way to implement them is by force, they necessarily have a familiar political corollary: "statism," which is "the principle or policy of concentrating extensive economic, political, and related controls in the state at the cost of individual liberty."[28] In her essay on "Man's Rights," Ayn Rand wrote:

> The dominant ethics of mankind's history were variants of the altruist-collectivist doctrine which subordinated the individual to some higher authority, either mystical or social. Consequently, most political systems were variants of the same statist tyranny, differing only in degree, not in basic principle, limited only by the accidents of tradition, of chaos,

---

24. All sorts of speech can be suppressed: seditious speech, commercial speech, hostile speech, dirty speech, defamatory speech, sexually harassing speech.

25. Ayn Rand, The Virtue of Selfishness 127 (1965) ("Man's Rights").

26. Rand's elaborated definition of altruism is more explicit: "the ethical theory which regards man as a sacrificial animal, which holds that man has no right to exist for his own sake, that service to others is the only justification of his existence, and that self-sacrifice is his highest moral duty." *Id.* at 32–33 ("The Objectivist Ethics").

27. *Id.* at 175 ("Racism").

28. American College Dictionary 1181 (1970 ed.).

> of bloody strife and periodic collapse. Under all such systems, morality was a code applicable to the individual, but not to society. Society was placed *outside* the moral law, as its embodiment or source or exclusive interpreter—and the inculcation of self-sacrificial devotion to social duty was regarded as the main purpose of ethics in man's earthly existence.
>
> Since there is no such entity as "society," since society is only a number of individual men, this meant, in practice, that the rulers of society were exempt from moral law; subject only to traditional rituals, they held total power and exacted blind obedience—on the implicit principle of: "The good is that which is good for society (or for the tribe, the race, the nation), and the ruler's edicts are its voice on earth."
>
> This was true of all statist systems, under all variants of the altruist-collectivist ethics, mystical or social. "The Divine Right of Kings" summarizes the political theory of the first—"*Vox populi, vox dei*" of the second. As witness: the theocracy of Egypt, with the Pharaoh as an embodied god—the unlimited majority rule or *democracy* of Athens—the welfare state run by the Emperors of Rome—the Inquisition of the late Middle Ages—the absolute monarchy of France—the welfare state of Bismarck's Prussia—the gas chambers of nazi Germany—the slaughterhouse of the Soviet Union.[29]

That the social variant of the altruist-collectivist ethics—on which today's proscriptions of hate speech rest—has infected the free-speech principle from the founding of the United States, and that that variant has animated Supreme Court decisionmaking in free-speech cases since that time, is evident from even a modest perusal of history and of Court opinions. Of all the constitutional guarantees found in our Bill of Rights, the First Amendment's protection of freedom of speech is probably the best known. Unfortunately, it is also the least understood. Contrary to popular belief, the First Amendment was never intended by some to allow, nor has it ever allowed, truly free speech in America.

For example, although the Massachusetts constitution of 1780—adopted only a few years after our Declaration of Independence—contained a free-speech guarantee, at least three political libel convictions were obtained in that commonwealth between 1799 and 1803. Both the Pennsylvania constitution of 1790 and the Delaware constitution of 1792, enacted at virtually the same time as the federal Bill of Rights, expressly imposed liability for "abuse" of the right of free speech. Even Virginia—home of Washington, Jefferson, Madison, Patrick Henry, and John Marshall—enacted a law in 1792 dealing with the "abusive" exercise of speech.

Some of the Founding Fathers were not advocates of fully free speech. For example, Thomas Jefferson was not a free-speech absolutist. When, in a letter to Abigail Adams, Jefferson condemned the notorious Sedition

29. Rand, *supra* note 25, at 123.

Act of 1798—which had crudely punished certain political speech and sent not a few anti-Federalist editors to jail—his opposition was based on a "state's rights" position, not on any belief in an unconditional right of free speech. On the contrary, Jefferson contended only that "[t]he First Amendment... reflected a limitation upon *Federal* power, leaving the right [sic] to enforce restrictions on speech to the States."[30] Jefferson went even further in 1803, writing to the governor of Pennsylvania:

> [T]he federalists having failed in destroying freedom of the press by their gag law, seem to have attacked it in an opposite direction; that is by pushing its licentiousness and its lying to such a degree of prostitution as to deprive it of all credit.... This is a dangerous state of things, and the press ought to be restored to its credibility if possible. The restraints provided by the laws of the States are sufficient for this, if applied. And I have, therefore, long thought that a few prosecutions of the most prominent offenders would have a wholesome effect in restoring the integrity of the presses. Not a general prosecution, for that would look like a persecution; but a selected one.[31]

Thomas Jefferson was not alone in his belief that speech could be censored and that disagreeable speakers should be prosecuted occasionally. The idea persisted. For over a century, the right of free speech was generally regarded as not absolute. Indeed, not until early in the twentieth century did the Supreme Court of the United States first have occasion to address the subject specifically.

During World War I, an antiwar activist named Schenck (and others) produced and distributed an antidraft handbill. One side of it claimed that the Conscription Act constituted slavery and involuntary servitude in violation of the Thirteenth Amendment to the Constitution of the United States:

> In impassioned language it intimated that conscription was despotism in its worst form and a monstrous wrong against humanity in the interest of Wall Street's chosen few. It said, "Do not submit to intimidation," but in form at least confined itself to peaceful measures such as a petition for repeal of the act. The other... side of the sheet was headed "Assert Your Rights." It [claimed that the Constitution was violated by anyone who] refused to recognize "your right to assert your opposition to the draft," and went on, "If you do not assert and support your rights, you are helping to deny or disparage rights which it is the solemn duty

30. Dennis v. United States, 341 U.S. 494, 522 (1951) (emphasis added).

31. The Constitution of the United States of America 864 (U.S. Government Printing Office, 1964).

> of all citizens and residents of the United States to retain."[32] It described the arguments on the other side as coming from cunning politicians and a mercenary capitalist press, and even silent consent to the conscription law as helping to support an infamous conspiracy. It denied the power to send our citizens away to foreign shores to shoot up the people of other lands, and added that words could not express the condemnation such cold-blooded ruthlessness deserves... winding up, "You must do your share to maintain, support and uphold the rights of the people of this country."[33]

As a result of the handbill's distribution, the defendants were charged with conspiring to violate the Espionage Act of June 15, 1917,[34] by attempting to cause, and by causing, insubordination in the military and naval forces and by obstructing the government's recruiting and enlistment efforts. In their defense, Schenck and the others invoked the freedom of speech supposedly guaranteed by the First Amendment's injunction that "Congress shall make no law... abridging the freedom of speech...." Notwithstanding this seemingly clear constitutional prohibition, the defendants were convicted in a Pennsylvania federal court, and their convictions were affirmed by a unanimous opinion of the Supreme Court written by Civil War hero Justice Oliver Wendell Holmes, Jr. After all, said Holmes, "[w]hen a nation is at war many things that might be said in time of peace are such a hindrance to its effort that their utterance will not be endured so long as men fight...."[35]

Schenck was an important decision not only because it held that, in a crunch, even speech could be suppressed for the "common good," but because it became the foundation for the Court's infamous Smith Act decision three decades later. In that case, *Dennis v. United States*, American communists were charged not with actually having committed substantive violent acts, but with having conspired:

> (1) to *organize* as the Communist Party of the United States of America a society... of persons who... *advocate* the overthrow and destruction of... the United States by force and violence, and (2) knowingly and wilfully to *advocate*... the duty and necessity of overthrowing and destroying... the United States by force and violence.[36]

32. If the "deny or disparage rights" and "retained by the people" formulations sound familiar, it is because they are a paraphrase of the Constitution's Ninth Amendment: "The enumeration in the Constitution, of certain rights, shall not be construed to deny or disparage others retained by the people."

33. Schenck v. United States, 249 U.S. 47, 51 (1919).

34. Ch. 30, § 3, 40 Stat. 217, 219.

35. *Schenck*, 249 U.S. at 52.

36. 341 U.S. 494, 497 (1951) (emphasis added).

In upholding their convictions against a First Amendment free-speech defense, Chief Justice Vinson stated categorically that:

> Speech is not an absolute, above and beyond control by the legislature when its judgment, subject to review here, is that certain kinds of speech are so *undesirable* as to warrant criminal sanction. *Nothing is more certain in modern society than the principle that there are no absolutes.*[[37]] . . . To those who would paralyze our Government in the face of impending threat by encasing it in a semantic straitjacket we must reply that *all concepts are relative.*[38]

If from the very first days of this nation restraints on speech were not uncommon, if no less a patriot than Founding Father Thomas Jefferson believed that states could censor speech and that a selective prosecution now and then of an unpopular speaker was desirable, if during World War I antidraft activists could be sent to jail for quoting and arguing from the Ninth and Thirteenth Amendments, if American communists could be imprisoned not for throwing bombs but for merely agreeing to organize and advocate, if there are no absolutes and all concepts—"freedom," "liberty," and "rights" among them—are relative, should anyone be surprised that truly free speech has never existed in our country?

Indeed, even while lauding the great values of the First Amendment, and perhaps elevating them above other constitutional guarantees, in *Thomas v. Collins* the Supreme Court of the United States has simultaneously undercut those values by acknowledging the existence of a supposedly higher interest:

> The case confronts us again with the duty our system places on this Court to say where the individual's freedom ends and the State's power begins. Choice on that border, now as always delicate, is perhaps more so where the usual presumption supporting legislation is balanced by the preferred place given in our scheme to the great, the indispensable democratic freedoms secured by the First Amendment.
>
> . . . .
>
> That priority gives these liberties a sanctity and a sanction not permitting dubious intrusions. . . .
>
> For these reasons any attempt to restrict those liberties must be justified by clear *public interest*. . . .[39]

Schenck, *Dennis*, and *Thomas* illustrate that Americans were long denied the right of truly free speech in the area of political expression. To a lesser extent, the three cases suggest *why*. But for a more thorough under-

37. One wonders if the Chief Justice was absolutely certain of that.
38. 341 U.S. at 508 (emphasis added).
39. 323 U.S. 516, 529–30 (1945) (emphasis added).

standing of the why—and to understand the ethical base of today's hate-speech movement and the motives of those who would silence abortion protest—two other categories of speech must be examined. The first, referred to earlier, is so-called commercial speech, never high on the *Left's* list of protectable values. The other is speech concerning sexual matters, never high on the *Right's* list of protectable values and indeed long a target of its own speech-suppressing ire.

Commercial Speech[40]

The Supreme Court of the United States has long been expert at creating spurious, seemingly antithetical distinctions, such as "personal rights" versus "property rights," "due process" versus "rudimentary due process," "affirmative action" versus "racial quotas." Among these distinctions none has been more spurious than "regular" speech versus "commercial" speech.

An interesting and instructive example of commercial speech arose in *Valentine v. Chrestensen*[41] about fifty years ago. Back in the early 1940s, a New York entrepreneur who owned a submarine wanted to conduct tours of the vessel from a city pier. After the authorities denied him permission, he had handbills printed. One side carried an advertising message promoting the tour, the other a protest against the city's denial of permission to use the pier. The city, attempting to stop the handbilling, invoked a law prohibiting the distribution of any "handbill, circular... or other advertising matter whatsoever in or upon any street."

Eventually, the Supreme Court was confronted with this question: were the handbills a form of protected speech, since they contained a combination of "commercial" and "noncommercial" (i.e., "ideological") matter? The Court held they were not. While conceding that the First Amendment forbade the city's banning of *all* handbilling on public thoroughfares—and even the protest part of the submarine handbills *standing alone*—the Court concluded that the First Amendment imposed "no such restraint on government as respects purely commercial advertising."[42] The *Valentine* decision, which apparently saw the handbills' combined content as being sufficiently commercial to warrant banning, thus creat-

---

40. For a discussion of the *historical* untenability of the commercial/noncommercial distinction drawn by the Supreme Court in its free-speech cases, see RICHARD E. WILEY ET AL., COMMERCIAL SPEECH AND THE FIRST AMENDMENT (1994) (National Legal Center for the Public Interest).

41. 316 U.S. 52 (1942).

42. *Id.* at 54.

ed at least two distinct categories of speech. One could be suppressed by government; the other could not.

The distinction in *Valentine* was underscored by two cases which followed it. In *Martin v. Struthers*[43] the Court held that freedom of speech had been infringed by a municipal ordinance forbidding door-to-door distribution of leaflets publicizing a *religious* meeting, because "no element of the commercial" was involved.[44] Yet in *Breard v. Alexandria*[45] the Court found no freedom of speech violation by an ordinance prohibiting door-to-door solicitation of *magazine subscriptions*. "The selling," the Court reasoned, "brings into the transaction a commercial feature."[46]

The relegation of so-called commercial speech to second-class constitutional status—despite the First Amendment's clear proscription that government "shall make no law . . . abridging the freedom of speech"—was an accepted fact of First Amendment life for more than thirty years.[47] During that period, in which commercial speech was excluded from the protection that the First Amendment afforded to most other types of communication, some Justices, especially the liberal Justice Douglas, were becoming increasingly uncomfortable. Douglas's dilemma—not unlike the Left's dilemma today concerning hate speech and abortion protest—was that, on the one horn, he viewed the First Amendment as an absolute bar to government interference with the highly personal right of speech[48] but that, on the other, his animus toward so-called property rights was deep.[49] So Douglas's problem, fundamentally, was whether commercial speech was commerce or whether it was speech. Was commercial speech merely part of the *marketplace*, where regulation in the public interest was accepted, if not mandatory? Or was it part of the rarefied atmosphere where *ideas* were communicated? Although Douglas had gone along with the majority in *Valentine*, by the time of *Cammarano v. United States*[50] seventeen years later, he was expressing doubts. Those doubts about the commercial-speech doctrine were merely reflective of much deeper questions at the core of all American constitutional law: *How could a supposedly free country be premised on personal sacrifice in the name of*

43. 319 U.S. 141 (1943).

44. Breard v. Alexandria, 341 U.S. 622, 643 (1951).

45. 341 U.S. 622 (1951).

46. *Id.* at 642.

47. *See, e.g.*, Murdock v. Pennsylvania, 319 U.S. 105 (1943); Jamison v. Texas, 318 U.S. 413 (1943); Thomas v. Collins, 323 U.S. 516 (1945); New York Times Co. v. Sullivan, 376 U.S. 254 (1964); Pittsburgh Press Co. v. Human Relations Comm'n, 413 U.S. 376 (1973).

48. *See, e.g.*, Dennis v. United States, 341 U.S. 494 (1951).

49. *See, e.g.*, Village of Belle Terre v. Boraas, 416 U.S. 1 (1974).

50. 358 U.S. 498 (1959).

majoritarian values—i.e., on altruist-collectivist ethics? How could individual rights be subordinated to the *needs* of society? Or, more topically, how could blacks' "need" not to be insulted, or abortionists' "need" not to be condemned, be exalted over the core principle of First Amendment free speech?

The answer given by the Supreme Court, when it finally discarded the harsher aspects of the commercial-speech doctrine, was no cause for celebration.

As noted above, in Virginia pharmacists were prohibited from advertising the price of prescription drugs, and in the mid-1970s the law was challenged constitutionally. But not by muzzled pharmacists, invoking their right to free speech. Interestingly, the attack on the Virginia law came instead from prescription drug *consumers*. They claimed that since prescription drug prices varied widely, they would benefit greatly if advertising were freely allowed, making it possible for them to shop around for the lowest price.[51] The basic issue for the Supreme Court was whether the Virginia law was constitutional, and the significant way in which the Court formulated that issue bears repeating: "Our question is whether speech which does 'no more than propose a commercial transaction' is so removed from any 'exposition of ideas' and from '"truth, science, morality, and arts in general, in its diffusion of liberal sentiments on the administration of government,"' that it lacks all protection."[52] As stated above, the implication of this question transcended the limited subject of commercial speech. The Court's formulation of the question to be decided in the *Virginia State Board of Pharmacy* case itself reveals exactly what will separate protected from unprotected speech: its *social utility*—a principle regrettably long invoked by the Right in its attempt to suppress the expression of sexual material.

Pornography

Just as the strength of steel is best measured under stress, meaningful tests of principle come not over the best of issues but over the worst. One such test assumed the proportions of a major battle in the war between individual rights and the altruism-collectivism-statism of the Right. It has been fought on the grimy field of pornography. But as Ayn Rand once observed, although

51. Virginia State Bd. of Pharmacy v. Virginia Citizens Consumer Council, Inc., 425 U.S. 748 (1976) (citation omitted).

52. *Id.* at 762–63 (citations omitted).

> it is not very inspiring to fight for the freedom of the purveyors of pornography or their customers... in the transition to statism, every infringement of human rights has begun with the suppression of a given right's least attractive practitioners. In this case, the disgusting nature of the offenders makes it a good test of one's loyalty to a principle.[53]

The principle to which Rand referred—the right to the free expression of sexual material, even if society deems it pornographic or obscene—has been under relentless, largely successful, attack by "conservatives" in the Supreme Court of the United States for nearly four decades.

The story, oddly, began in the early 1940s with a Jehovah's Witness in New Hampshire. After calling a policeman "a God damned racketeer" and a "damned fascist," the Witness got into a fight on the sidewalk. Charged with the offense of "fighting words,"[54] a Mr. Chaplinsky was convicted because the New Hampshire court interpreted the law to prohibit "words likely to cause an average addressee to fight," "face-to-face words 'plainly likely' to cause a breach of the peace by the addressee." Believing that Chaplinsky's words were "likely to provoke the average person to retaliation," the Supreme Court of the United States unanimously upheld his conviction in *Chaplinsky v. New Hampshire*.[55]

Putting aside the *Chaplinsky* case's implications for free speech generally, and for the "fighting words" category of political speech in particular, something else of far greater importance emerged from that decision. In the course of his opinion for the Court, Justice Murphy observed in passing that:

> There are certain well-defined and narrowly limited classes of speech, the prevention and punishment of which have never been thought to raise any Constitutional problem. These include the *lewd* and *obscene*, the profane, the libelous, and the insulting or "fighting" words—those by which their very utterance inflict injury or tend to incite an immediate breach of the peace. It has been well observed that such utterances are no essential part of any exposition of ideas, and are of such slight social value as a step to truth that any benefit that may be derived from them is clearly outweighed by the social interest in order and morality.[56]

There were at least two obvious mistakes in Justice Murphy's notion that the prohibition of certain kinds of speech had never bothered anyone. For one thing, it was untrue—there have always been First Amend-

53. *Censorship: Local and Express*, AYN RAND LETTER, Aug. 23, 1973, at 2.

54. "'No person shall address any offensive, derisive or annoying word to any other person who is lawfully in any street or other public place, nor call him by any offensive or derisive name.'" Chaplinsky v. New Hampshire, 315 U.S. 568, 569 (1942).

55. *Id.* at 574.

56. *Id.* at 571–72 (emphasis added).

ment absolutists who read the Constitution's bar of "no law" abridging speech to mean literally just that. Such people have been bothered a lot.[57] For another, Murphy seemed to imply that if no one besides the defendant objected, then preventing and punishing certain speech would be an acceptable practice. This is tantamount to evaluating rights by counting noses.

Much more important, however, is that at the core of Murphy's statement lay three pernicious, though well-entrenched and conservative-accepted, ideas: that morality is defined by societal values; that the only moral utterances are those which are an "exposition of ideas" or "a step to truth"; and that "the lewd and obscene" are beyond the pale. But each of these propositions reduces to a naked statement of the untenable idea that one's rights come from, and are subordinate to, society, and that it is government's proper function to violate individual rights for the common good. And it is only a short step from that premise to censoring hate speech in the name of hurt feelings or abortion protest in the name of free choice.

Such gratuitous observations by the Court about morality, society, and obscenity were wholly unnecessary to the decision in *Chaplinsky* (which was not even an obscenity case), and thus supposedly of no precedential value in any obscenity cases which would later come to the Court. Nevertheless, *Chaplinsky* played an important role when, fifteen years later, the Court did accept an obscenity case for review. The majority opinion in the consolidated cases of *Roth v. United States* and *Alberts v. California*[58] was written by the liberal Justice Brennan. In upholding both anti-obscenity statutes (one federal and one state) he built his opinion on four cornerstones. First, "expressions found in numerous opinions indicate that this Court has always *assumed* that obscenity is not protected by the freedoms of speech and press."[59] Second, in light of American colonial history "it is apparent that the unconditional phrasing of the First Amendment was not *intended* to protect every utterance."[60] Third,

> implicit in the history of the First Amendment is the rejection of obscenity as utterly without redeeming social importance. This rejection for that reason is mirrored in the *universal judgment* that obscenity should be restrained, reflected in the international agreement of over 50 nations,

57. Though Justices Douglas and Black had famous, relatively well-deserved, reputations as First Amendment absolutists, they were members of the *Chaplinsky* majority. Perhaps they viewed it as a mere disorderly *conduct* case, involving speech only tangentially if at all.

58. 354 U.S. 476 (1957).

59. *Id.* at 481 (emphasis added).

60. *Id.* at 483 (emphasis added).

> in the obscenity laws of all of the [then] 48 states, and in the 20 obscenity laws enacted by the Congress from 1842 to 1956.

Fourth, and the nearest the Court could get to precedent, "[t]his is the same judgment expressed by this court in *Chaplinsky v. New Hampshire....*"[61] So, because of repeated "assumptions" by the Court, an analysis of *pre*-constitutional history, an "implic[ation]" in the First Amendment's history and a "universal judgment" condemning obscenity, and the *Chaplinsky* dictum, "obscenity" was held "not within the area of constitutionally protected speech or press."[62]

Defining unprotected "obscene material" as that "which deals with sex in a manner appealing to prurient interest,"[63] the Court in *Roth* was quick to assert that since "sex and obscenity are not synonymous"[64] certain expressions of a sexual nature would be protected—but even then only if certain criteria were satisfied: "All ideas having even the slightest social importance—unorthodox ideas, controversial ideas, even ideas hateful to the prevailing climate of opinion—have the full protection of the [constitutional] guarantees, unless excludable because they encroach upon the limited area of more important interests."[65] Brennan was saying—and the Left-controlled Court was holding—two things: "obscenity" was unprotected speech under any and all circumstances, and all other sexual expression was also unprotected *unless* "society" deemed it of at least some importance. And even then, such semi-important expression could be suppressed if there were "more important" societal interests at stake.

As Justice Douglas was to observe in a later obscenity case:

> In *Roth* v. *United States*... [the Court] ruled that "[o]bscene material is material which deals with sex in a manner appealing to prurient interest." ... Obscenity, it was said, was rejected by the First Amendment because it is "utterly without redeeming social importance." ... The presence of a "prurient interest" was to be determined by "contemporary community standards."[66]

Roth had established that there was a category of unprotected speech called obscenity, which was to be identified by reference to the collectivist sexual premises of one's friends and neighbors. The stage was now set

61. *Id.* at 484.

62. *Id.* at 485.

63. *Id.* at 487. The Court footnoted *Webster's* definition of "prurient": "itching, longing; uneasy with desire or longing."

64. *Id.*

65. *Id.* at 484.

66. Miller v. California, 413 U.S. 15, 37–38 (1973).

for the Supreme Court of the United States to assume the role of High Court of Censorship.

That role has built-in problems—exemplified by a candid observation on the part of Justice Stewart in *Jacobellis v. Ohio*.[67] In that case, though there was no clear-cut majority position, the court did hold that a motion picture was *not* obscene under the *Roth* standard. But it was Justice Stewart who underscored the problems inherent in all obscenity cases. He admitted that the Court was "faced with the task of trying to define what may be indefinable."[68] As for his own test for specific examples of alleged obscenity, the best he could come up with was: "I know it when I see it, and the motion picture involved in this case is not that."[69]

With "I know it when I see it" as more or less the constitutional test for obscenity, the Court next confronted the "Fanny Hill" case, *Memoirs v. Massachusetts*.[70] There, the *Roth* test was reformulated:

> [T]hree elements must coalesce: it must be established that (a) the dominant theme of the material taken as a whole appeals to a prurient interest in sex; (b) the material is patently offensive because it affronts contemporary community standards relating to the description or representation of sexual matters; and (c) the material is utterly without redeeming social value.[71]

Once again, to make the test of free expression depend on whether it affronts, or has value to, others—like minorities or abortion doctors—is explicitly to endorse the altruist-collectivist premise that one's rights are derived from society, and to implement that premise by statism: by government forcing individuals to conform to a social norm.

Memoirs was followed by the Court's infamous 1973 obscenity decisions, *Miller v. California*[72] and *Paris Adult Theater I v. Slayton*.[73] *Miller* again reformulated the obscenity test, this time in the context of an aggressive mass-mailing campaign of pornographic brochures. The most frightening aspect of the new standard was its setting government as the arbiter of whether books, magazines, newspapers, radio, television, and theater have any value at all, let alone "literary, artistic, political, or scientific" value—or, most ominous of all, "serious" value.[74] This was censorship at its worst. How did the Justices attempt to justify it? "The protection

67. 378 U.S. 184 (1964).
68. *Id.* at 197.
69. *Id.*
70. 383 U.S. 413 (1966).
71. *Id.* at 418.
72. 413 U.S. 15 (1973).
73. 413 U.S. 49 (1973).
74. 413 U.S. at 24.

given speech and press was fashioned," asserted the majority opinion, "to assure unfettered interchange of ideas for the bringing about of political and social changes desired by the people." Translation: our right of free speech and press has a strictly pragmatic base—to allow the collective to effect change. "[T]he public portrayal," the Court continued, "of hard-core sexual conduct for its own sake, and for the ensuing commercial gain, is a different matter."[75] "We do not see the harsh hand of censorship of ideas—good or bad, sound or unsound—and 'repression' of political liberty lurking in every state regulation of commercial exploitation of human interest in sex."[76] With this statement, the Court arbitrarily removed obscenity from the realm of ideas and tarred it with the brush of "commercialism."

In the companion case to *Miller*, the theme of commercialism was addressed more fully. When the Paris theater exhibited the films "Magic Mirror" and "It All Comes Out in the End," they ran into censorship trouble from local authorities and ended up in court. The trial judge "assumed 'that obscenity [had been] established,'" but stated that "[i]t appears to the Court that the display of these films in a commercial theater, when surrounded by requisite notice to the public of their nature and by reasonable protection against the exposure of these films to minors, is constitutionally permissible."[77]

The Supreme Court of Georgia disagreed. Though it "assumed that the adult theaters in question barred minors and gave a full warning to the general public of the nature of the films shown," it nevertheless "held that the films were without protection under the First Amendment.... [T]he Georgia court stated that 'the sale and delivery of obscene material to willing adults is not protected under the First Amendment.'"[78] This framed the issue pretty well. *Miller* had reiterated that one category of unprotected speech was obscenity, and in order to define that term had reformulated the earlier *Roth-Memoirs* test. But one thing *Miller* had not explicitly decided was whether the sexual mores of the community could deprive consenting adults of pornographic material which they wanted, sought, and obtained.

Chief Justice Burger's answer for the Supreme Court's majority could not have been clearer:

> We categorically disapprove the theory, apparently adopted by the trial judge, that obscene, pornographic films acquire constitutional immunity from state regulation simply because they are exhibited for con-

75. *Id.* at 34–35.
76. *Id.* at 35–36.
77. 413 U.S. at 53.
78. *Id.*

> senting adults only. This holding [by the Georgia trial judge] was properly rejected by the Georgia Supreme Court. Although we have often pointedly recognized the high importance of the state interest in regulating the exposure of obscene materials to juveniles and unconsenting adults, see *Miller v. California*... this Court has never declared these to be the only legitimate state interests permitting regulation of obscene material.[79]

Georgia's censorship had been upheld. But why? Essentially, wrote Burger and his colleagues, "to protect the weak, the uninformed, the unsuspecting, and the gullible from the exercise of their own volition."[80] When all is said and done, then, the free expression of sexual matter can be suppressed and some people branded criminals and imprisoned, *in order to protect other people from themselves.*

One fascinating aspect of this "weak, uninformed, unsuspecting, gullible" rationale is that it is not an idea which expressly surfaced for the only time in *Paris Adult Theater* or in the obscenity cases generally. The reader will recall, for example, that in *Virginia State Board of Pharmacy* pharmacists could publish their prices only because the poor, sick, and aged would benefit. Indeed, the needs of the allegedly helpless have long served as the justification for all sorts of other anti-individual rights legislation. In fact, conservative Burger took great pains to remind his dissenting liberal colleagues of just that.[81] In Burger's majority opinion, he needled the three liberal dissenters about their seemingly newfound antipathy to government regulation. Burger's references to "state regulation of commercial and business affairs," to "federal securities and antitrust laws and a host of federal regulations," to protecting "the physical environment from pollution," to state "blue sky" laws for regulating "what sellers of securities may write or publish about their wares," to "constitutionally unchallenged laws" prohibiting certain consensual conduct, to regulating "public accommodations," and more, were not-very-subtle reminders to his three dissenting liberal colleagues that, in case after case, *they* had approved of government subordination of the individual to what *they* had perceived as society's greater needs. They too, Burger chided them, had pulled at the "need-over-rights" oars. Twice, Burger reminded the dissenters explicitly:

79. *Id.* at 57.

80. *Id.* at 64 (emphasis added).

81. The voting lineup in both *Miller* and *Paris* was identical. Chief Justice Burger wrote the majority opinion, joined by Justices Blackmun (the author of *Roe v. Wade*), Powell, Rehnquist (the author of *Madsen*), and White. Archliberal Douglas dissented in a separate opinion; Justice Brennan also dissented in a separate opinion, joined by Justices Marshall and Stewart.

> Understandably those who entertain an absolutist view of the First Amendment find it uncomfortable to explain why rights of association, speech, and press should be severely restrained in the marketplace of goods and money, but not in the marketplace of pornography.
>
> . . . .
>
> States are told by some that they must await a "laissez-faire" market solution to the obscenity-pornography problem, paradoxically "by people who have never otherwise had a kind word to say for laissez faire," particularly in solving urban, commercial, and environmental pollution problems.[82]

If government control of the *marketplace* was sauce for the liberal goose, Burger was asking, why wasn't government control of certain forms of *expression* sauce for the liberal ganders? Why, indeed? The Chief Justice's point was unanswerable. The same anti-individual rights values, the same altruism-collectivism-statism, which the liberals had employed over conservative opposition to control individuals in the *marketplace*, now allowed some conservatives, over liberal opposition, to control individuals in the realm of *ideas*. Sauce for the goose was now sauce for the gander.

The principal point that emerges from all this is clear: an anti-individual rights premise makes it possible, indeed inevitable, for government—of the Left or the Right—to control individuals in all ways, and at all times, because that premise cannot differentiate between issues. Indeed, the anti-individual rights premise knows no difference between Justices, all of whom hold it as a basic tenet, as *Madsen* shows—despite the Scalia dissent, which itself seems to subscribe to the Court's general limitations on freedom of speech.

Let us now complete the circle by addressing how the Right's aiding and abetting of this successful historical attempt to suppress pornography bears on the Left's current and near-successful attempt to censor hate speech and abortion protest.

Conclusion

Generally speaking, *opposition* to speech codes and to the suppression of abortion protest comes from the Right. Ironically, it includes the same folks who brought us limitations on free speech such as "contemporary community standards," "prurient interest," "redeeming social importance," "patent offensiveness," "serious literary, artistic, political, or scientific value," and protection of "the weak, the uninformed, the unsuspecting, and the gullible from the exercise of their own volition." Yet, in opposing speech codes and the suppression of abortion protest, the Right

82. 413 U.S. at 62, 64.

is fighting for free speech. *Or is it?* The question is important because if the Right is disarmed in its opposition to speech codes and the suppression of abortion protest, its efforts will fail and even more pernicious government censorship will restrict our lives.

Regrettably, the answer has long been clear to those who understand the roots of conservative ideas.

Over two decades ago, using the gritty issue of pornography as an example, Ayn Rand identified the cancer at the core of conservative thought, growing from its acceptance of the altruist-collectivist-statist morality:

> The conservatives want freedom to act in the material realm; they tend to oppose government control of production, of industry, of trade, of business, of physical goods, of material wealth. But they advocate government control of man's spirit, i.e., man's consciousness; they advocate the State's right to impose censorship, to determine moral values, to create and enforce a governmental establishment of morality, to rule the intellect.[83]

Rand was writing in the context of the *Paris Adult Theater* case, and one of her overarching points was that, because of the acceptance of the altruist-collectivist-statist morality and its consequential disarming of those who would fight for individual rights, the conservative stance on pornography would eventually disable those on the Right when it came time for *them* to fight censorship of something other than pornography. Over two decades ago, Rand wrote these remarkably prescient words:

> If the [*Paris Adult Theater*] censorship ruling is not revoked, the next step will be more explicit: it will replace the words "marketplace of pornography" with the words "marketplace of ideas." *This will serve as a precedent for the liberals, enabling them to determine which ideas they wish to suppress—in the name of the "social interest"—when their turn comes.* No one can win a contest of this kind—except the State.[84]

That is exactly what has happened. For all the reasons offered by the academic Delgados, Matsudas, Lawrences, and Gales, and by the legislative architects of the Freedom of Access to Clinic Entrances Act, in the name of social utility the Left is making war to suppress hate speech and abortion protest.

The Left is of course wrong, its moral, intellectual, and philosophical bankruptcy nakedly obvious. But the constitutional corruption of the Left on the twin issues of hate speech and abortion protest is not the entire story. As we have seen, the Right has an important part to play in this important battle. In this current Left-Right struggle, there is only one effec-

83. *Censorship: Local and Express, Part III*, AYN RAND LETTER, Sept. 10, 1973, at 4.
84. *Id.* (emphasis added).

tive, let alone moral and constitutional, strategy for the Right to employ. The Right must eschew its "me, too" acceptance of the altruist-collectivist-statist morality which inevitably allows censorship of *every* kind, including hate speech and abortion protest. Then, but only then, will the Right legitimately be able to claim that it consistently opposes the suppression of ideas, and that it supports a consistent view of individual rights. If it does not, then, unfortunately, in issues of free speech there will be little to differentiate Right from Left.

RICHARD KLINGLER*

First Amendment Protection for Electronic Communication: The End of Content Regulation and the Scrutiny of Market Regulation

In *Turner Broadcasting System, Inc. v. FCC*,[1] the Supreme Court returned after nearly a decade to the issue of what First Amendment standards govern the electronic media—specifically, cable television. Although the decision creates considerable uncertainty, it also sets forth important principles that provide broad opportunities for deregulating electronic communication, including broadcasting and aspects of telecommunications services, and for ensuring that the First Amendment applies fully to restrict government interference with the content of speech no matter what medium of communication is employed.

At issue in *Turner* were provisions of an act of Congress mandating that operators of cable television systems retransmit the signals of local commercial and public television stations.[2] Operators of cable television systems argued that these "must carry" provisions violated their First Amendment right to choose the messages disseminated over their cable systems, and cable programmers—which supply programming to cable systems—argued that the statute violated the First Amendment by favoring certain speakers (broadcasters) over them. The government in response relied extensively upon *Red Lion Broadcasting Co. v. FCC*,[3] the principal decision underpinning a broad array of broadcasting regulation. The Court produced a fractured opinion, affirming broad First Amendment interests, describing a range of permissible regulation of electronic media, and remanding the case for further factual development.

---

* The author has participated in several of the proceedings tangentially addressed in this piece as a law clerk to Judge Kenneth W. Starr and to Justice Sandra Day O'Connor, and has participated as an associate at Sidley & Austin in various broadcasting and telecommunications matters, including a brief on behalf of certain appellee broadcasters in *Turner* itself. The views expressed here are solely his own.

1. 114 S. Ct. 2445 (1994).

2. Cable Television Consumer Protection and Competition Act of 1992 (Cable Act), Pub. L. No. 102-385, §§ 4–5, 106 Stat. 1460 (1992) (codified at 47 U.S.C. §§ 534–535).

3. 395 U.S. 367 (1969).

Some might dismiss the opinion as inconsequential. For industry participants, the decision was something of an anticlimax. Only further litigation will resolve the constitutionality of the most important regulatory provisions governing the interplay between two enormous industries, cable television and broadcasting. Certain more general aspects of the opinion, too, are relatively opaque and will require elaboration in subsequent cases.

The decision also may alarm those who maintain a traditional libertarian understanding of the First Amendment. The Court overwhelmingly rejected the broader interpretations of the First Amendment proffered by the cable operators and cable programmers. In certain respects, the decision distinguishes cable television from other media, especially print media, and appears to allow a broad scope for the government to regulate cable television.

This article suggests, in contrast, that the Court's decision is neither inconsequential nor alarming. The decision sets forth fundamental First Amendment principles that will govern the next generation of speech issues arising in various electronic media. Those principles suggest that the decision is hardly as alarming as may first appear: the decision both confirms that content regulation is generally inappropriate for electronic media and provides an initial and partially satisfactory resolution of the emerging conflict between the First Amendment and market regulation. Those underlying principles provide expansive opportunities to apply to the increasingly important electronic media the core libertarian protections afforded to personal communications and to the print media.

Specifically, the decision should serve as the basis for deregulating broadcasting and eliminating the aberration in First Amendment doctrine that allows a considerable range of regulation of the content of broadcast communications. The decision also establishes a presumption against regulation of content for all other electronic media and sets forth the basis for various First Amendment challenges to market regulation. Both of those principles will have important deregulatory consequences for a range of industries, including telecommunications services (or "telephony," which encompasses wire-based and wireless telecommunications services employing the public switched telecommunications network).

The general principles set forth in the decision do not, however, unambiguously accord with the First Amendment's core principles. The decision also contains the basis for arguing that a broad category of government regulation is not designed to influence the content of communications and thus is permissible in any media, including print. To the extent that the decision may support a departure from the traditional understanding of what constitutes impermissible regulation of content, a challenge has arisen to ensure that *Turner* is interpreted and applied in a manner that advances the First Amendment's core values.

Background: Competition in Electronic Media and the Court's Decision

The "must carry" requirements at issue in *Turner* must be understood as part of the complicated and continuing interdependence between the cable television and broadcasting industries that has developed since the 1940s. Originally, cable service developed simply as a means of retransmitting broadcast signals to areas unable to receive the signal directly over the air. For this reason, the service was until the 1970s generally known as community antennae television, or CATV. In the 1960s and early 1970s, the Supreme Court affirmed the power of the Federal Communications Commission to regulate cable television as ancillary to the FCC's statutory authority to regulate (and in practice protect) the broadcasting industry,[4] and the FCC in fact placed severe limitations upon cable television service that limited direct competition between the industries.

Deregulation of the cable television industry in the late 1970s ensured considerable growth of cable television systems and created both a symbiotic and adversarial relationship between the industries. As cable television systems increasingly provided service in areas that overlapped with those served by local broadcasting stations, an increasing proportion of consumers subscribed to cable television and received all their video programming—including broadcast television signals—through their cable service. Relatively few subscribers switched to aerial antennae reception to view locally broadcast programming, but instead chose among the broadcast stations that the cable stations retransmitted (along with various sports, movie, entertainment, and other programming services designed for and available over only cable transmission). By 1994, cable television systems were capable of serving (or "passed") more than ninety-five percent of households with television, and approximately three-fifths of households subscribed to cable services.[5]

These developments made broadcasters dependent upon how and whether cable systems retransmitted their signals, and cable systems continued to rely extensively upon retransmission of broadcast signals to attract and retain subscribers. Particularly popular broadcast stations, often owned or affiliated with the principal television networks, sought to prevent a cable system from repositioning their signals—for example, making a signal avail-

4. *See, e.g.*, United States v. Southwestern Cable Co., 392 U.S. 157 (1968); *see also* United States v. Midwest Video Corp., 406 U.S. 649 (1972).

5. *See, e.g.*, Implementation of Section 19 of the Cable Television Consumer Protection and Competition Act of 1992, Annual Assessment of the Status of Competition in the Market for the Delivery of Video Programming, 19 F.C.C.R. 7442, ¶¶ 18–19 (1994); BROADCASTING & CABLE, Aug. 15, 1994, at 56.

able by antennae reception as "channel 7" available over the cable system as "channel 24"—and eventually would seek compensation for the retransmission of their signals. Less popular stations, often including smaller independent and public television stations, most feared being displaced from the cable system altogether, and feared channel repositioning as well. Broadcasters claimed that cable stations, as competitors with them for advertising, had an economic incentive to displace or reposition their signals. Cable television system operators, in turn, asserted their right to arrange their programming selections as they wished, especially as an increasing number of programmers vied for the often limited capacity available on cable systems.

In the late 1970s and early 1980s, the FCC repeatedly sought to intervene in this dispute by imposing upon cable television operators a duty to retransmit the signals of local television broadcast stations. In attacking these regulations, cable system operators and programmers pointed out, correctly, that every channel reserved for particular uses through regulation was one fewer channel subject to the cable operator's programming selection. Without definitively resolving the underlying First Amendment issue, the D.C. Circuit set aside the FCC's efforts.[6]

As one part of the 1992 Cable Act, which imposed a series of rate and practice limitations upon cable television system operators, Congress reimposed the "must carry" obligation (after overriding a presidential veto). The Act requires cable television systems to retransmit the signals of local commercial and public television stations without charge and without altering or repositioning the signal.[7] Broadcasters could elect not to be beneficiaries of this regime, and instead to enter into commercial negotiations with cable operators for the right to retransmit the broadcast signal.[8] The Act limits the percentage of channel capacity that need be set aside to meet this obligation, depending upon the overall capacity of various cable systems. This obligation alone might consume a significant number of channels on a cable system, and other regulatory requirements might require that additional channels be set aside for other purposes (for example, for public, educational, or governmental—or "PEG"—channels).

Cable operators and cable programmers challenged various provisions of the 1992 Act on First Amendment grounds. The Act provided for separate judicial review of the must-carry provisions, which thus separated consideration of those provisions from consideration of other, potentially even

---

6. *See* Quincy Cable TV, Inc. v. FCC, 768 F.2d 1434 (D.C. Cir. 1985); Home Box Office, Inc. v. FCC, 567 F.2d 9 (D.C. Cir. 1977).

7. *See generally* 47 U.S.C. §§ 534–535 (1988 & Supp. IV 1993).

8. *See id.* § 536.

more troublesome provisions of the Act.[9] A three-judge federal district court for the District of Columbia initially considered and upheld the must-carry provisions (through Judges Jackson and Sporkin, with Judge Williams dissenting).[10]

The cable operators and cable programmers pressed their challenge on direct appeal to the Supreme Court, as provided for in the Act. The cable system operators asserted that they possessed the same First Amendment right that newspaper publishers have to control the editorial content of their information product, and that the must-carry regulations directly infringed that right by requiring that they present broadcasters' speech rather than the video programming of their choosing (including programming they may have produced). Cable programmers principally asserted that the must-carry provisions violated the First Amendment by favoring one class of speakers (broadcasters) over another (cable programmers). In defending the Act, the government relied extensively upon *Red Lion*,[11] which supports extensive government oversight of broadcasting, to argue that a special First Amendment standard for cable television was appropriate. Broadcasters principally argued that Congress had legitimately applied general antitrust principles to respond to cable operators' anticompetitive conduct. Self-styled consumer and public-interest groups asserted that the relevant First Amendment right lay in cable subscribers rather than cable operators, and that the Congress had actually advanced First Amendment interests.

The Supreme Court ultimately remanded the case for further consideration by the district court but addressed the appropriate standard of review at length. It held that the cable operators and programmers possess a clear First Amendment interest by virtue of their production and editorial control of speech.[12] (Only the public-interest groups had contested this point.) *Red Lion* and the diminished level of First Amendment protection that accompanies it were inapplicable, the Court held, because the rationale of a "scarcity" of electromagnetic spectrum that supposedly distinguishes broadcasting from other media does not exist for cable television.[13] At the same time, the Court expressly declined to reconsider *Red Lion*'s validity.

The appropriate standard of review, the Court determined, depended upon whether the challenged measure was "content based": whether it was designed to alter the substantive balance or content of communications.[14]

---

9. For the initial consideration of certain of these related issues presented by the 1992 Cable Act, see Daniels Cablevision, Inc. v. United States, 835 F. Supp. 1 (D.D.C. 1993).

10. *See* 819 F. Supp. 32 (D.D.C. 1993).

11. *See infra* pp. 38–39.

12. *See Turner*, 114 S. Ct. at 2456.

13. *See id.* at 2456–58.

14. *See id.* at 2458–59.

Strict scrutiny traditionally applies to governmental measures designed to alter the substance of communications or range of public debate, and permits such restrictions only in the narrowest circumstances. At the same time, a less rigorous First Amendment standard applies to measures designed to advance government objectives unrelated to that content. Government measures may incidentally restrict speech so long as they sufficiently directly advance important government interests that are in this sense "content neutral." This distinction is part of traditional First Amendment doctrine and applies equally to speakers that do not employ electronic media.

The Court, in a decision for five Justices on this point, concluded that the Act's must-carry provisions "are not designed to favor or disadvantage speech of any particular content" but "are meant to protect broadcast television from what Congress determined to be unfair competition."[15] The Court concluded that the Act reflects an effort to remedy the abuse of crucial "bottleneck" cable facilities that cable operators had an incentive to manipulate to harm their competitor broadcast stations. The four dissenting Justices disagreed principally with this characterization of the Act, and concluded instead that Congress in fact sought impermissibly to alter the content of communications, and to favor certain types of speech over others, through the benefits afforded to broadcasters.[16]

At the same time, the Court was unable to conclude that the Act satisfied even the less rigorous First Amendment standard appropriate for content-neutral government regulations. A plurality indicated that that standard required, in this context, a showing that Congress had addressed a problem that was "real" rather than "conjectural" and had not unduly burdened the cable operators' speech interests in seeking to redress that problem.[17] The Court could not reach a conclusion on these points on the record before it, and remanded the case to the three-judge district court for further proceedings to resolve those issues.

Turner's Treatment of Principle: The Limitation of Content Regulation of Electronic Media and the Collision of the First Amendment and Market Regulation

The Court in *Turner* addressed two related and fundamental First Amendment issues that extend considerably beyond regulation of cable television systems. First, *Turner* addressed when, if ever, First Amendment standards

15. *Id.* at 2464.
16. *See id.* at 2470–72 (O'Connor, J., dissenting).
17. *See id.* at 2470–71.

should be varied to permit content regulation based upon the nature of the communication medium at issue. Courts have permitted extensive and intrusive regulation of broadcasting, for example, but we've seen that *Turner* declined to extend that analysis to cable television. Indeed, it did so in a manner that may radically transform regulation of traditional and emerging information services.

Second, *Turner* may be at least as important for its treatment of the increasing conflict between market regulation and the First Amendment. Many of the most highly regulated industries, especially telecommunications, increasingly engage in protected-speech activities. The Court had in many previous decisions established that an entity's speech activities were virtually irrelevant to application of generally applicable antitrust laws, but had provided little guidance regarding laws purporting to regulate competition specifically in industries engaged in protected speech. *Turner* provides an only partially satisfactory initial resolution of that issue, but one that will be of vital importance to the core First Amendment principles likely to be at the forefront of litigation in the coming years.

To understand the Court's treatment of each of these issues, it is necessary first to examine certain of the principal First Amendment doctrines designed to ensure that government is not "abridging the freedom of speech."[18] Traditionally, courts evaluate First Amendment challenges to government measures according to an underlying libertarian conception of the relative competence of private actors over government officials to order private and, ultimately, public affairs, as well as of the particular importance of preventing officials from attempting to shape debate over public affairs or the expression or substance of individual conscience. In this way, the First Amendment requires the greatest judicial hostility when government officials seek to restrict speech based upon disagreement with or disapproval of the message communicated, or when they seek to alter the balance or tone of public debate.[19] This particular sensitivity reflects an underlying concern manifested in all the Amendment's clauses: "the very purpose of the First Amendment is to foreclose public authorities from assuming a guardianship of the public mind through regulating the press, speech, and religion."[20]

---

18. U.S. CONST. amend. I.

19. *See, e.g.*, First Nat'l Bank v. Bellotti, 435 U.S. 765, 783 (1978) (government cannot "dictat[e] the subjects about which persons may speak [or] the speakers who may address a public issue"); Buckley v. Valeo, 424 U.S. 1, 48–49 (1978) ("the concept that government may restrict the speech of some elements of society in order to enhance the relative voice of others is wholly foreign to the First Amendment").

20. *See* Thomas v. Collins, 323 U.S. 516, 545 (1944) (Jackson, J., concurring).

In contrast, judicial application of the First Amendment differs considerably when this core interest or purpose is not at stake, even when a law incidentally restricts speech. Even when the opportunity to speak is reduced, the government has somewhat greater latitude in applying laws that are not designed to affect the substance of communication. Trespass or other laws of property may be applied against me if I attempt without consent to write my deepest political convictions upon my neighbor's fence or upon the page proofs of the *Los Angeles Times*. And even if my business is producing and transmitting speech, I generally cannot avoid paying corporate taxes or the reach of the Sherman Act simply because compliance necessarily and often severely reduces my opportunities to speak.

In First Amendment doctrine, these different types of threats to core libertarian values are captured in the distinction between content-based and content-neutral regulations. Traditionally, a reviewing court's "principal inquiry in determining content-neutrality . . . is whether the government has adopted a regulation of speech because of disagreement with the message it conveys."[21] A court may deem a law or regulation to be content based because its terms reflect distinctions based upon which messages are communicated[22] or because its "manifest purpose is to regulate speech because of the message it conveys."[23] As noted, measures found to be content based are subject to stringent judicial scrutiny and upheld only in exceptionally limited circumstances. (What justifications, if any, may exist for such regulations is an issue beyond the scope of this article.) Those regulations or laws that are found not to be designed for or to have the purpose of affecting the content of communications are deemed content neutral and required to satisfy a lesser standard of scrutiny.

Return now to *Turner*'s treatment of this issue. The Court, both majority and dissent (with the possible and ambiguous exception of Justice Stevens), treated the essential issue as whether the Act was content based or content neutral—just as traditional First Amendment doctrine applied in nearly all other contexts would require. But remember, too, that the discussion concerned an *electronic* medium, one that the government and certain "public interest" groups argued should be treated as akin to broadcasting. As discussed in greater detail below, broadcasting is an unfortunate anomaly in First Amendment doctrine because courts currently permit the govern-

21. Ward v. Rock against Racism, 491 U.S. 781, 791 (1989); *see* R.A.V. v. City of St. Paul, 112 S. Ct. 2538 (1992); Texas v. Johnson, 491 U.S. 397 (1989).

22. *See, e.g.*, Burson v. Freeman, 112 S. Ct. 1846 (1992); Boos v. Barry, 485 U.S. 312 (1988) (plurality opinion).

23. *Turner*, 114 S. Ct. at 2461; *see* United States v. Eichman, 496 U.S. 310 (1990); Clark v. Community for Creative Non-Violence, 468 U.S. 288, 293–94 (1984).

ment to engage in a range of content-based regulation without having to proffer a particularly strong justification.

The Court's extension in *Turner* of established First Amendment analysis to cable television—and, by analogy, most other electronic communication—is tremendously important. In the mid-1980s, the Court remanded a case concerning a cable television regulation while expressing uncertainty as to whether traditional First Amendment standards should apply, instead of those developed for broadcasting, or instead of some other standard.[24] In *Turner*, the Court was presented with the opportunity to extend the principles underlying broadcasting regulation to all electronic communications. In a portion of the decision joined by eight Justices (excepting Justice Stevens), the Court firmly rejected that opportunity. It indicated that general First Amendment principles would apply to this electronic medium, and that decisions regarding broadcasting were an anomaly at best rather than a general model.[25]

The distinction between content-based and content-neutral regulations or laws also underlies the second overarching issue addressed in *Turner*: the relation between the First Amendment and regulation of competition. That issue arises whenever competition or competitive behavior might be regulated in industries that produce speech, and that conflict will increase dramatically as traditionally regulated industries—such as telephone companies—become producers, processors, and presenters of information.

As noted, the Court had upheld application of the Sherman Act and other antitrust laws to newspapers and other speakers, even when the ability to speak was consequently considerably curtailed.[26] The Court also had determined that it would carefully scrutinize general regulations, such as tax laws, to ensure that they did not mask government efforts to single out certain speakers or classes of speakers to affect the content of their speech.[27]

Turner presented a different but related issue: how to treat a law specifically addressing an industry engaged in protected speech activities but justified as designed to prevent anticompetitive acts. Here was a statute that was by its terms no general law: it sought to impose particular obligations upon one class of speakers (cable system operators) to benefit another class (broadcasters), and did so in a manner that necessarily diminished the speech opportunities of a third class (cable programmers). At the same time,

---

24. *See* City of Los Angeles v. Preferred Communications, Inc., 476 U.S. 488 (1986).

25. *See Turner*, 114 S. Ct. at 2456–58.

26. *See, e.g.*, Citizen Pub. Co. v. United States, 394 U.S. 131 (1969); Lorain Journal Co. v. United States, 342 U.S. 143 (1951); Associated Press v. United States, 326 U.S. 1 (1945).

27. *See, e.g.*, Leathers v. Medlock, 499 U.S. 439 (1991); Arkansas Writers' Project, Inc. v. Ragland, 481 U.S. 221 (1987); Minneapolis Star & Tribune Co. v. Minnesota Comm'r of Revenue, 460 U.S. 575 (1983).

the Act was justified as addressing issues unrelated to speech and as designed simply to address a traditional antitrust problem created when an entity (here, cable system operators) controlled a source of bottleneck monopoly power through facilities used to harm direct competitors (broadcasters, competitors for advertising) that depended upon access to those facilities.

The Court resolved this issue by adopting a two-step analysis that likely will apply generally to First Amendment challenges to regulations directed to the information industries. First, the Court sought to determine whether the challenged measure was content based.[28] That is, its analysis indicated that even such industry-specific regulations, and even those directly affecting speech rights, could avoid the most stringent judicial review and be defended under the standard traditionally applied to content-neutral regulations—if it could be shown that the regulation truly was designed to shape competition rather than the content of communications or who may participate in public debate.

As a general proposition, both the majority and dissent agreed that this level of scrutiny applied to statutes and regulations actually designed to bar anticompetitive conduct, even if the regulated practice was closely tied to and arose only in industries that engaged in protected speech.[29] The majority and dissent disagreed regarding what government purposes other than preventing anticompetitive conduct could be classified as content neutral (this point is addressed in greater detail below). The two opinions particularly clashed over whether Congress had in the Cable Act designed the must-carry provisions to remedy an anticompetitive practice or to benefit broadcasters, especially public broadcasters, based upon an assessment of the value of those broadcasters' communications.

There is considerable basis for the Court's unanimous conclusion on this general point. Cable operators and programmers were at base seeking a general exemption from regulations that addressed industry-specific competitive problems but that were unrelated to the content of communications. Congress and regulators would have been barred from employing rules to redress anticompetitive actions or the potential for those actions, so long as those rules incidentally affected speech activities (as an increasing percentage of telephony and cable regulations do). It is hardly clear that the alternative—ad hoc enforcement of antitrust or other generally applicable laws—provides any greater protection for First Amendment values, and indeed the threat of selective prosecution or threats of prosecution against prominent

28. *See Turner*, 114 S. Ct. at 2458–64.

29. *See id.* at 2476 (O'Connor, J., dissenting) ("I agree with the Court that some speaker-based restrictions—those genuinely justified without reference to content—need not be subject to strict scrutiny.").

speakers likely poses a greater danger to those values.[30] At the same time, the Court in the formulation of its test and in its statement of the purportedly content-neutral interests that the government may pursue was insufficiently attentive to the heightened dangers that accompany such industry-specific regulations that affect speech.[31] When a regulation is directed only to speech-producing entities, it is far more likely that government officials are masking improper purposes through invocation of competitive or other ostensibly neutral objectives—and, compared to generally applicable rules, far easier for them to do so.

The second step of the analysis required, after a finding that the challenged provision was content neutral, an unusually heavy and detailed showing that the provision was necessary and appropriate.[32] Rather than assess from the statute's terms whether the challenged provisions directly advanced the asserted, legitimate objectives (the traditional approach), a plurality required an empirical showing that Congress had identified a manifest policy problem and had responded in an efficacious manner. It imposed this requirement even though it already had determined the must-carry provisions to be content neutral and even though the Court was reviewing an act of Congress—one that in this case embodied legislative findings supporting the provisions in the statute itself. Applying this second element of its test, the plurality found the record inadequate to assess whether "the economic health of the broadcasting industry is in genuine jeopardy" (which required record support of the percentage of stations that would be denied carriage without the Act, and the economic effect of that denial) and to assess the degree to which the Act actually altered cable operators' choice of programming.[33]

This second portion of the test reflects, at best, an unfortunate misallocation of duties between the judiciary and legislature. Traditional First Amendment doctrine and the Amendment's underlying values suggest that any special showing or burden should be part of the core judicial inquiry regarding whether a challenged measure is designed to shape or alter communications—that is, abridges the freedom of speech. This is particularly true where, as in *Turner*, that risk is increased by regulation that burdens particular speakers while benefiting others. The traditional analysis of the "fit" between the asserted interest and chosen means is best understood as adjunct and integral to the determination of content neutrality: an appar-

30. Precedent also provided support for the focus upon whether a measure was content neutral, even when it differentially regulated classes of speakers. *See* Leathers v. Medlock, 499 U.S. 439 (1991).

31. *See infra* pp. 46–49.

32. *See Turner*, 114 S. Ct. at 2470–72.

33. *Id.*

ent mismatch of means and ends strongly supports an inference that the measure is in fact designed for the alternative, impermissible objective of shaping content.

Instead, the Court imposed its increased burden upon the separate inquiry of the adequacy of Congress's determination of the Act's necessity. The Court defined the task on remand as essentially second-guessing Congress's policy judgment, and required the district court to evaluate the sufficiency of the empirical record before Congress and any record the parties chose to develop to defend or attack the congressional judgment—including, apparently, facts and developments emerging after the Act's passage. (Indeed, the lower courts' initial applications of *Turner* confirm that the decision will have just this effect.[34]) In this way, the Court shifted the judicial role away from its traditional scrutiny of interference with public debate and directed it toward the empirical and policy determinations that are peculiarly beyond the judicial competence and, under traditional principles of separation of powers, committed to the legislature and executive.[35]

The End of Content Regulation of Broadcasting

As noted above, one of the most important aspects of the *Turner* decision was its analysis of cable television regulation in traditional First Amendment terms and its rejection of *Red Lion* as a basis for analyzing the issues or allowing content regulation of communications over cable facilities. The decision ostensibly declines to address *Red Lion*'s continuing validity for broadcasting. Even so, the decision in combination with other recent developments should have the effect of overturning the aberration in First Amendment doctrine that permits extensive regulation of the content of broadcast communications. Once cable television regulation is assimilated within the doctrines that reflect broader First Amendment values, it becomes exceptionally difficult to justify the continuing departure from those underlying libertarian values for broadcasting.

To understand *Red Lion*'s increasing vulnerability, it is necessary to examine that decision's rationale and the basis for the Court's acceptance of content regulation of broadcast communications. The decision upheld the

34. *See, e.g.*, US WEST, Inc. v. United States, 48 F.3d 1092 (9th Cir. 1994); Chesapeake & Potomac Tel. Co. v. United States, 42 F.3d 181 (4th Cir. 1995), *cert. granted*, 115 S. Ct. 2608 (1995) (Nos. 94-1893 & 94-1900).

35. The Supreme Court will have the opportunity to revisit these issues of institutional powers when it considers a Fourth Circuit decision that applied *Turner* to bar enforcement, on First Amendment grounds, of the federal statute that limits telephone companies' provision of video services in their local service areas. *See* United States v. Chesapeake & Potomac Tel. Co., *cert. granted*, 115 S. Ct. 2608 (1995) (Nos. 94-1893 & 94-1900).

FCC's so-called Fairness Doctrine and related rules that required a broadcasting station to permit a right of reply to certain personal attacks or political editorializing. Under traditional First Amendment principles, these requirements clearly would be prohibited as government efforts to shape public discourse; indeed, the political debate encompassed by the rules and the particular political criticism at issue constitute the core of protected speech.[36] Even so, the Court indicated that broadcasting was different. It noted that the possibility of signal interference justified the government's licensing role, and the necessarily limited electromagnetic spectrum limited the number of licenses that could be allocated.[37] In a famous non sequitur, the Court concluded that "[b]ecause of the scarcity of radio frequencies, the Government is permitted to put restraints on licenses in favor of others whose views should be expressed on this unique medium."[38] The government may "requir[e] a licensee to share his frequency with others and to conduct himself as a proxy or fiduciary with obligations to present those views and voices which are representative of his community and which would otherwise, by necessity, be barred from the airwaves."[39]

Critics have lambasted this "spectrum scarcity" rationale. Judge Bork has pointed out that this scarcity is no different in kind from others: "[a]ll economic goods are scarce, not least the newsprint, ink, delivery trucks, computers and other resources that go into the dissemination of print journalism.... Since scarcity is a universal fact, it can hardly explain regulation in one context and not another."[40] Others have elaborated on the insight that the spectrum can be analyzed like any other property regime.[41] And the FCC later abolished the Fairness Doctrine on the grounds, in part, that the doctrine in fact stifled expression regarding controversial issues (because broadcasters naturally avoided regulatory disputes and enormous potential sanctions by avoiding controversy) and that technological developments had eliminated spectrum scarcity.[42]

---

36. As with more recent efforts to revive the Fairness Doctrine, the doctrine in the case before the Court was applied in response to criticism from a conservative political commentator.

37. *Red Lion*, 395 U.S. at 387–89, 396–400.

38. *Id.* at 390.

39. *Id.* at 389.

40. *See* Telecommunications Research & Action Ctr. v. FCC, 801 F.2d 501, 508 (D.C. Cir. 1986).

41. *See, e.g.*, Ronald Coase, *The Federal Communications Commission*, 2 J. L. & ECON. 1 (1959); Mark Fowler & Daniel Brenner, *A Marketplace Approach to Broadcast Regulation*, 60 TEX. L. REV. 207 (1982).

42. *See* Syracuse Peace Council v. FCC, 867 F.2d 654 (D.C. Cir. 1989); Syracuse Peace Council v. Television Station WTVH, 2 F.C.C.R. 5043 (1987), *aff'd*, *id.*; *see also* Inquiry into Section 73.1910 of the Commission's Rules and Regulations Concerning the General

Despite this criticism, extensive regulation designed to shape the content of broadcast communications continues in force. The FCC continues to oversee programming, and specific rules govern children's programming and advertising, "indecent" or "offensive" programming, the timing of network-determined programming, sponsorship identification (especially for political matters), and lottery information.[43] Political candidates' access to and use of stations is highly regulated.[44] Many of the criteria for acquiring and transferring licenses, including minority preferences, have been justified in part by the effect they will have on broadcast content, as have certain of the restrictions on the dealings of networks and their affiliates.[45] Various FCC policies designed to increase "localism" or responsiveness to community concerns also address broadcast content.

Three recent developments particularly challenge the "spectrum scarcity" rationale and its underlying conception that broadcasting is a unique and uniquely important form of communication that requires extensive government oversight. First, the process of licensing the electromagnetic spectrum has in practice recently been divorced from extensive regulation, and has shifted away from the notion that a licensee is a fiduciary for the public, and more toward a traditional property regime. The lottery system for allocation of the spectrum was an initial step in that direction, but the more recent allocation of certain licenses through an auction process accelerates that movement.[46]

Second, increasing competition in the delivery of video programming has undermined any claim of traditional television and radio broadcasting's

---

Fairness Doctrine Obligations of Broadcast Licensees: Report, 102 F.C.C.2d 143 (1985) (subsequent history omitted).

43. *See, e.g.*, 18 U.S.C. § 1307 (1988 & Supp. IV 1993) (lottery); *id.* § 1464 (offensive programming); 47 U.S.C. §§ 317, 508 (1988 & Supp. IV 1993) (contest regulation and advertising sponsorship); 47 C.F.R. §§ 73.660–73.661 (1993) (children's programming); *id.* § 73.1211 (lottery); *id.* § 73.1212 (sponsorship); *see generally* United States v. Edge Broadcasting Co., 113 S. Ct. 2696 (1993) (lottery); Action for Children's Television v. FCC, 821 F.2d 741 (D.C. Cir. 1989) (programming requirements); Action for Children's Television v. FCC, 58 F.3d 654 (D.C. Cir. 1995) (en banc) (rules governing indecent broadcasts).

44. *See* 47 U.S.C. § 315 (1988 & Supp. IV 1993); Codification of the Commission's Political Broadcast Policies: Report and Order, 7 F.C.C.R. 678 (1991), *recon.*, 7 F.C.C.R. 4611 (1992).

45. *See, e.g.*, Policy Statement on Comparative Broadcast Hearings, 1 F.C.C.2d 393 (1965); Amendment of Section 73.3555 of the Commission's Broadcast Multiple Ownership Rules, Second Report and Order, 4 F.C.C.R. 1741, *recon.*, 4 F.C.C.R. 6489 (1989); *see also* Metro Broadcasting, Inc. v. FCC, 497 U.S. 547 (1990), *overruled*, Adarand Constructors, Inc. v. Pena, 115 S. Ct. 2097 (1995).

46. *See, e.g.*, 47 U.S.C. § 309(j) (1988 & Supp. IV 1993); Implementation of Section 309(j) of the Communications Act—Competitive Bidding, Second Report and Order, 9 F.C.C.R. 2348 (1994); *id.*, Third Report and Order, 9 F.C.C.R. 2941 (1994).

unique character. As discussed above, cable television is now the primary method of delivering video programming, so much so that broadcasters are now dependent upon cable systems for delivery of their programming. "Wireless" cable systems employ the electromagnetic spectrum, but they function like cable television systems rather than over-the-air broadcasters. Satellite-delivered broadcasting is quickly increasing in importance. Telephone companies also are poised to provide widespread distribution of video programming, as well as to produce programming.

Third, it is increasingly recognized that the editorial functions of cable television operators cannot be distinguished from those of broadcasters—and that both are equivalent to newspaper publishers. All three forms of information product—newspapers, television broadcasts, and cable programming—are comprised of three types of information: internally produced material; material secured by the distributor upon payment of a fee (often through syndication); and material secured by the distributor upon receipt of a fee (principally, advertising). And, of course, the First Amendment protects all three types of speech.

Turner accentuates the importance of these three developments and provides a doctrinal basis for overturning content regulation of broadcasting. By pursuing traditional First Amendment analysis rather than an analysis dependent upon *Red Lion*, the Court produced two results. It ensured that *Red Lion* would not and cannot be generalized to electronic media or otherwise provided with a renewed and potentially more defensible rationale. That is, the Court confined *Red Lion* to being an aberration peculiar to broadcasting and eliminated any defenses for it that apply generally to the electronic distribution of video programming.

Second, the Court dramatically increased the burden upon any defenders of *Red Lion* by requiring that cable television, which is in many respects an easier case for regulation, not be subject to content regulation and be analyzed according to general and traditional First Amendment principles. For those who believe that control over video programming distribution justifies extensive regulation, including content regulation, cable television today would, compared to broadcasting, seem a relatively more likely subject of regulation. Cable systems pose a far greater risk than broadcasting stations of "bottleneck" control over distribution of video programming, and cable television operators generally exercise far greater control than any station operator over which programming may be made available to most local viewers. This is so not only because broadcasting stations are dependent upon retransmission by cable television system operators, but also because economies of scale dramatically limit the number of competing cable television operators able to serve a particular area, certainly below the number of potential over-the-air broadcasters that may serve the same area. Nor is there any relevant distinction based upon the government's role in allocating the monopoly: Not unlike the government's role in allocating broadcast licenses, a government franchise policy (often providing for exclusive franchises) established who would serve as the incumbent cable system operator. Despite these relative characteristics, it is now cable television rather than broadcasting that cannot be subjected to content regulation.

Combined with the three recent and more general developments outlined above, these essential aspects of *Turner*—confining rather than generalizing *Red Lion*, and barring content regulation of cable television—place tremendous pressure upon content regulation of broadcasting. Together, they provide a doctrinal as well as factual basis to challenge and overturn *Red Lion* and the related system of content regulation of broadcasting, and make that outcome both considerably more likely and more imminent than before.

The Limits of and Bases for Challenges to Telephony Regulation

Turner's implications for telephony regulation are considerably less one-sided than those for broadcasting, but the decision's treatment of market regulation—especially in subjecting certain market regulation to empirical challenge—may have wide-ranging effects upon aspects of the regulation of telephone companies' operations. This is especially true as telephony companies increasingly seek to produce the information communicated and to control the form in which information, whether produced by the telephone company or others, is presented to consumers.

Telephony regulation remains suspended between an old and a new world. In the new world, telephone companies increasingly seek to be producers and purveyors of information, most prominently video programming but also a range of on-line and other enhanced services. A variety of telephone companies are perhaps among the best positioned of the many types of businesses that are attempting to develop the multimedia and database-centered products that require sophisticated computer programming, billing, customer equipment, customer service, and transmission capabilities; with the exception of the "content" aspect of programming, these are all traditional strengths of telecommunications carriers. Other telephone companies, particularly those that principally provide local exchange and access services, are seeking to provide video programming and delivery services that resemble in many respects traditional cable television services.[47] They are

47. Services and facilities provided as part of the FCC's "video dialtone" regulatory structure are perhaps the most important example of this development. *See* Telephone Company–Cable Television Cross-Ownership Rules, Sections 63.54–58: Second Report and Order, Recommendation to Congress, and Second Further Notice of Rulemaking, 7 F.C.C.R. 5781

undertaking enormous infrastructure investments designed for this purpose and to provide capabilities that support the emerging interactive services. In short, telephone companies are transforming themselves into information companies, and many of their services are clearly speech protected by the First Amendment—whether directly because the companies produce and distribute information, or because their information delivery increasingly includes editorial determinations comparable to other presentations of information encompassed by the First Amendment.

The old world of telephony regulation treats telephone companies as essentially carriers of others' information, and seeks to preserve the separation between that function and the new ventures of telephone companies. There is considerable truth in the assumed role of telephone companies: their principal business remains carriage of others' messages. But the various regulatory separations that may have appeared natural or desirable when enacted often decades ago may make little sense when applied to the new information services. For example, relatively stringent regulations reduce the ability of telephone companies (especially local telephone companies) to combine production and carriage of video programming, to the extent that those companies are allowed to integrate those functions at all.[48] Nearly all distribution of video programming and advanced information products is subject to the various common-carrier obligations developed for traditional telephony, and to additional requirements designed to ensure that carriers afford their affiliates no favoritism.[49] The difference between common-carrier and cable television regulation may be seen perhaps most clearly in the facilities that local carriers are constructing to compete with cable television systems: the systems will serve largely similar functions and indeed likely will increase competition, but the telephone facilities will be

---

(1992); *see also, e.g.*, Application of US WEST Communications, Inc.: Order and Authorization, 9 F.C.C.R. 184 (1993); Application of Chesapeake & Potomac Tel. Co.: Order and Authorization, 8 F.C.C.R. 2313 (1993).

48. *See, e.g.*, Telephone Company-Cable Television Cross-Ownership Rules, Sections 63.54–58, Second Report and Order, Recommendation to Congress, and Second Further Notice of Proposed Rulemaking, 7 F.C.C.R. 5781 (1992).

49. *See, e.g.*, Amendment of Section 64.702 of the Commission's Rules and Regulations, Final Decision, 77 F.C.C.2d 384 (1980) ("Computer II"), *recon.*, 84 F.C.C.2d 50 (1980), *further recon.*, 88 F.C.C.2d 512 (1981), *aff'd*, Computer & Communications Indus. Ass'n v. FCC, 693 F.2d 198 (D.C. Cir. 1982); Separation of Costs of Regulated Telephone Service from Costs of Nonregulated Activities, Amendment of Part 31, the Uniform System of Accounts for Class A and Class B Telephone Companies to Provide for Nonregulated Activities and to Provide for Transactions between Telephone Companies and Their Affiliates: Report and Order, 2 F.C.C.R. 1298 (1987), *recon.*, 2 F.C.C.R. 6283 (1987), *modified*, 3 F.C.C.R. 6701 (1988), *aff'd*, Southwestern Bell Corp. v. FCC, 896 F.2d 1378 (D.C. Cir. 1990).

subject to more extensive, common-carrier regulation (in part because those facilities also are designed for traditional telephone service).

As telephone companies increasingly seek to provide and arrange information, *Turner*'s treatment of market regulation directed to information providers will become considerably more important—both in limiting and providing the basis for First Amendment challenges to industry-specific regulation. Recall *Turner*'s resolution of this point: industry-specific regulation of the information industries that affects speech may avoid strict scrutiny if shown to be designed for a content-neutral purpose (for example, preventing anticompetitive conduct), but the government will have to provide elaborate record support to show the continued existence of the asserted harm and the necessity for the existence and scope of the challenged regulation. Telephone companies can no longer object, as they occasionally have, simply that a restriction upon their speech activities must satisfy strict scrutiny.[50] At the same time, *Turner* provides them with ample basis to challenge the continuing necessity of a range of relatively dated and broad regulatory restrictions upon their activities. For example, *Turner* already has supported successful First Amendment challenges by local telephone companies against statutory restrictions upon their provision of video programming in their local service areas, and the Supreme Court is now considering precisely this issue.[51]

Three issues that will arise as *Turner* is applied in subsequent cases will determine the significance of First Amendment challenges against telephony regulation. One concerns the timing of support for a content-neutral market regulation. Is it sufficient that an empirical basis for a particular type of anticompetitive conduct existed when a regulation was adopted, or should telecommunications companies be able to challenge regulations based upon the current absence of any support for their ongoing enforcement? To allow such challenges creates enormous regulatory uncertainty and invites and accentuates the problem of ongoing judicial oversight of what are essentially policy issues. But to bar them may allow entirely unjustified regulations to remain in force (potentially for reasons related to influencing which entities may participate in public debate), with broad limitations upon protected speech activities. Many of the most important regulatory barriers were designed in the early 1980s or even before and often were adopted without extensive consideration of First Amendment values.

50. *See, e.g.*, US WEST, Inc. v. United States, 48 F.3d at 1098–99; Chesapeake & Potomac Tel. Co. v. United States, 42 F.3d at 193–98.

51. *See* 47 U.S.C. § 533(b) (1988 & Supp. IV 1993); US WEST, Inc. v. United States, 48 F.3d 1092 (9th Cir. 1994); Chesapeake & Potomac Tel. Co. v. United States, 42 F.3d 181 (4th Cir. 1995), *cert. granted*, 115 S. Ct. 2608 (1995) (Nos. 94-1893 & 94-1900).

A second issue, discussed more generally below,[52] concerns the types of interests that the government may invoke to justify a challenged regulation as content neutral. Certain regulations imposed upon telecommunications carriers, like certain of those imposed upon cable television system operators, may be defended as addressing competitive dangers recognized under traditional antitrust doctrine. The more difficult issue arises when government officials purport to address a competitive danger that would not create antitrust liability, or even to achieve a content-neutral objective apart from promoting competition. The scope of potential challenges to regulation will contract to the extent that a wider range of government interests may be invoked in defense of telephony, cable, and other regulations.

A final and related issue is how *Turner* will be applied to common-carrier regulations that limit carriers' activities protected by the First Amendment. Current common-carrier regulations are derived from basic carriage principles developed in the late-nineteenth and early-twentieth centuries for railroad services (and before that as common-law duties), and have been elaborated and expanded for telephony to reflect various market and technological developments.[53] Together, they impose broad limitations upon the terms and conditions of services, including pricing, definition of services, marketing practices, and scope of offerings. Although often developed to further competition, common-carrier regulations have assumed a life of their own and often depart from what traditional antitrust doctrines would require. Their history and application where no protected speech is at issue strongly suggest that they are generally content neutral, but the application of the remainder of *Turner*'s test creates considerable difficulty. Unless the common-carrier duties are recast as and collapsed into competitive considerations, the interests they advance can be characterized quite flexibly as seeking to accomplish various amorphous public policy objectives—which may disguise content regulation and, at a minimum, frustrate the newly mandated assessment of whether the interest is "real" rather than "conjectural" and is directly satisfied by the challenged regulation.

Of course, these points regarding the vulnerability of regulations affecting telephone companies' speech activities apply directly and more obviously to various efforts to regulate the speech activities of cable television system operators. Not only will *Turner* provide the basis to challenge a range of pricing and service regulations ostensibly designed to limit cable operators' anticompetitive activities, but it will even more clearly and categori-

52. *See infra* pp. 46–49.

53. *See, e.g.*, 47 U.S.C. §§ 201–203 (1988 & Supp. IV 1993); *cf.* Time Warner Entertainment Co. v. FCC, 56 F.3d 151 (D.C. Cir. 1995) (First Amendment implications of cable rate regulation).

cally prohibit the varied efforts to apply to cable operators the content regulations applicable to broadcasters.[54] Other traditional aspects of cable television regulation—such as the obligations to carry certain public, educational, and government channels[55]—are also likely to be found to be content based and thus unconstitutional under the *Turner* analysis.

Turner's Threat and Uncertainty

Although *Turner* in many respects advances or accords with core First Amendment principles and values, one aspect of the decision may provide the basis for an unprecedented departure from those values and an expansion of the types of government regulation of speech that receive lesser judicial scrutiny. This difficulty arises in the interests that the Court suggested could be treated as content neutral and thus not subject to strict scrutiny. Obviously, were the Court to treat as content neutral a set of laws and regulations in fact designed to influence the nature of public debate and who may participate in it, that determination would considerably reduce the protection afforded by judicial review to First Amendment values.

Most of the opinion treats the must-carry provisions as content neutral simply because they were designed to prevent anticompetitive activity. As noted, this analysis roughly accords with traditional First Amendment principles and doctrine. Later in the opinion, however, when discussing the relation between Congress's choice of means and its asserted ends, the Court identified *three* government interests that it determined were unrelated to content: "(1) preserving the benefits of free, over-the-air local broadcast television, (2) promoting the widespread dissemination of information from a multiplicity of sources, and (3) promoting fair competition in the market for television programming."[56] Only interest *3* is clearly the traditional government interest in promoting competition that has long been held to be unrelated to the content of communication (although, as noted above, it may pose difficulties in application to particular cases). It is possible to characterize the other two interests as content neutral as well, but only by interpreting them as aspects or consequences of the final interest in preserving competition, rather than independent bases of government action. Thus, enforcing competition laws may, when applied to cable systems' market power, have the effect of preventing anticompetitive harm to those entities dependent upon access to cable facilities. Because it is broadcasters

---

54. *See, e.g., id.* § 315(c)(1) (political broadcasting obligations applied to cable operators); Licensees and Cable Operators Reminded of Lowest Unit Charge Obligations, 4 F.C.C.R. 3823 (1988).

55. *See* 47 U.S.C. § 531 (1988 & Supp. IV 1993).

56. *Turner*, 114 S. Ct. at 2469.

in this case that are most likely subject to cable operators' anticompetitive actions, enforcing competition laws in this context preserves their ability both to provide service (a consequence corresponding to interest *1*) and to continue to add to public debate (a consequence corresponding to interest *2*). The Court has observed that interests *1* and *2* stem from application of the Sherman Act to the press.[57] By linking interests *1* and *2* to interest *3*, it may be possible to characterize those interests as content neutral in a manner consistent with traditional First Amendment doctrine.

This interpretation is, however, relatively strained, and treating the first two interests instead as independent bases of government action (as the decision suggests) creates considerable tension with core First Amendment interests. Interest *1* may readily be characterized as reflecting the peculiar importance of preserving broadcast television because the service provided—the substance of the communications—is important. Interest 2 readily appears to authorize the government to bolster a particular set of speakers because those speakers contribute valuably to the richness of public debate. Either interest, so characterized, would appear to be related to the content of the messages communicated and thus to permit the government to engage in shaping public debate. That role, of course, is the one the First Amendment most clearly prohibits.

For now, this danger is only potential. The elucidation of the two troubling governmental interests is not necessary to the *Turner* decision's holding (because the must-carry provisions can be and were justified as content neutral on the basis of their purpose of preventing anticompetitive conduct), and they are in this limited sense not formally binding precedent. This portion of the opinion is also subject to varying interpretations, and one narrowing construction has been offered above. Even so, this aspect of the decision could serve as the basis for substantial inroads on First Amendment interests and should be the focus of ongoing efforts in subsequent litigation to narrow and limit its scope and effect.

A more recent Supreme Court decision that addressed this aspect of *Turner* only perpetuated the underlying confusion and threat. In *Hurley v. Irish-American Gay, Lesbian and Bisexual Group of Boston*,[58] the Court held that the First Amendment barred application of a local antidiscrimination ordinance that would have required organizers of a parade to include members of a gay and lesbian association. The Court correctly invoked the content-discrimination principle described above, reasoning that the local

57. *See, e.g.*, Citizen Publishing Co. v. United States, 394 U.S. 131, 139–40 (1969); Lorain Journal Co. v. United States, 342 U.S. 143, 155–56 (1951); National Broadcasting Co. v. United States, 319 U.S. 190, 226–27 (1943); Associated Press v. United States, 326 U.S. 1, 20 (1945).

58. 115 S. Ct. 2338 (1995).

government sought to alter the content or balance of messages conveyed through the selection and participation of parade participants.[59] The Court distinguished the government's interest in *Turner* as the important one of "limiting monopolistic autonomy in order to allow for the survival of broadcasters" and of ensuring the "survival of speakers."[60] This formulation is confused in a manner similar to *Turner*'s: it could properly address the non–content-based interest in curbing abuses of monopoly power (with an incidental effect of benefitting persons subject to monopoly abuse who happened to be speakers); or it could suggest that the government has a legitimate and "important" interest in preserving the "survival" of speakers even by limiting others' speech interests—which threatens to permit content-based regulation.

This particular difficulty with the *Turner* decision is an aspect of a broader problem that underlies it and, indeed, runs throughout much of traditional First Amendment doctrine, namely the extent to which government officials may defend rules particularly crafted for the information industries based upon ostensibly content-neutral objectives that depart from those reflected in generally applicable laws. The government may apply generally applicable antitrust or property laws to the information industries, but can it defend rules targeted to the information industries on the ground that they address peculiar or novel competitive injuries or property interests—or any other novel interest that it can show to be unrelated to the content of speech? As noted, the question arises particularly for the various regulations governing telecommunications carriers.

This issue implicates basic constitutional principles. An entirely respectable case, resting upon democratic principles, supports the legislature's and executive's ability to define and pursue a range of objectives without triggering strict scrutiny, so long as those objectives are shown not to be designed to shape public debate. In this view, the peculiarities of the facilities and functions of many of the information industries, particularly telephony, may require peculiar regulatory responses. But a contrary position would focus upon the dangers of regulatory failure and the impulse to regulate communications, as well as the difficulty of distinguishing ostensibly content-neutral measures from masked efforts to shape public discourse. These concerns are especially heightened when the government crafts rules that apply particularly to information services, because the incidental effect upon communications is necessarily great. These concerns could be reflected in heightened scrutiny of the interests asserted as providing the content-neutral justification for an industry-specific regulation. Greater judicial skepticism might greet novel or specifically manufactured objectives, while lesser skep-

59. *See id.* at 2347–48.

60. *Id.* at 2349.

ticism would be applied to asserted objectives that correspond with or implement those reflected in generally applicable laws.

Conclusion

Commentators will continue to debate whether the Court in *Turner* accurately characterized the must-carry provisions before it as unrelated to the content of communications, but in two broader respects the decision will have enduring consequences for the protection of First Amendment values as the Amendment is applied both to existing electronic media and the vast range of emerging information services. First, *Turner* clearly marks the end of content regulation for nearly all electronic media apart from broadcasting, and *Turner* will considerably hasten the approaching end of content regulation of broadcasting. As electronic media become increasingly important sources of information, public debate, and artistic expression, this extension—or return to—the underlying First Amendment tradition will be of enduring importance and value.

In addition, *Turner* marks an important initial attempt to reconcile the First Amendment with regulations designed to check abuses of market power. Although the Court correctly determined that strict scrutiny did not automatically apply whenever a regulation specifically affects an industry's speech activities, the decision in certain respects afforded too little weight to the dangers that such regulations pose to First Amendment values. What additional protections the Court did afford likely will enmesh the judiciary in ongoing oversight of policy determinations that are properly within the province of the legislature and executive. Even so, the decision provides considerable scope for challenges on First Amendment grounds to overbroad or unjustified efforts purportedly undertaken to regulate competition. In this respect, *Turner* will have enduring significance as a basis to limit or at least prompt reassessment of a range of regulations applied to cable television operators, telephone companies, and other industries engaged in the production and presentation of information.

ALBERT G. LAUBER

Barclays Bank: The Mystery of the Sinking Foreign Commerce Clause

Most would agree that *Barclays Bank v. California Franchise Tax Board*[1] was the most significant tax case of the Court's 1993–94 Term. The question presented was obscure even to many tax lawyers—the constitutionality of "worldwide combined reporting," a method formerly used by California and other states to tax multinational corporate income. But despite its esoteric subject matter, *Barclays* excited passion and controversy all around.

The drama had ramifications both foreign and domestic. Worldwide combined reporting as employed by California has always been anathema to America's trading partners, with Britain the most outspoken critic. Some twenty foreign nations appeared as amici in the Supreme Court to oppose California's tax. The British Parliament went so far as to pass retaliatory legislation that aimed to make U.S. companies doing business in Britain the scapegoat for California's perceived sins.

On the domestic front, the revenue consequences for California were enormous. Already reeling from recession and budget woes, the state estimated that a loss in the Supreme Court would trigger potential tax refunds of up to $4 billion. With that many dollars—and California's treasure trove of electoral votes—at risk, worldwide combined reporting made a surprise appearance in the 1992 presidential election campaign. The issue split the conservative camp: "federalist" conservatives supported California and "probusiness" conservatives opposed the tax. And with Republican and Democratic administrations similarly, if oddly, divided, the Solicitor General found himself doing some fancy footwork in a command performance before the Supreme Court.

By a 7–2 vote, the *Barclays* Court sustained California's use of worldwide combined reporting, rebuffing constitutional challenges founded principally on the dormant Foreign Commerce Clause. This closed the book on a fifteen-year saga dating back to *Japan Line, Ltd. v. County of Los Angeles*,[2] where the Court first articulated special protections for foreign

1. 114 S. Ct. 2268 (1994).
2. 441 U.S. 434 (1979).

commerce. The intervening period has witnessed a gradual erosion of that solicitude, to the point where *Barclays* in essence has confined *Japan Line* to its facts. As one astute commentator has written, a "mouse of a doctrine is all that remains of the *Japan Line* whale."[3]

The mystery of the Court's retreat from *Japan Line* has not yet been solved. Some will view *Barclays* as the work of a Court more hospitable to federalism and states' rights; others, as the work of a Court less prone to judicial activism. I would venture a more mundane answer. During its fifteen-year voyage from *Japan Line* to *Barclays*, the Court floated a new doctrine, put it through the test of experience, and—in my view—ultimately discarded the doctrine as unseaworthy. I will try to chronicle the highlights of that voyage, but please bear with me. It is, to complete this overlong nautical metaphor, a choppy trip, made so by actions of the Court itself and of the executive branch.

Japan Line

In *Japan Line*, California attempted to impose a property tax on Japanese-owned cargo containers used exclusively in international commerce. The containers, like the ships that carried them, had their "home ports" in Japan and were subject to Japanese property tax on their full value. California sought to impose an additional, prorated property tax determined by the containers' "average presence" in the state.[4]

While the taxpayer in *Japan Line* had equities in its favor, the constitutional basis for its challenge was not entirely clear. The cargo containers were physically present in California for substantial periods of time, and California plainly had the "minimum contacts" necessary to support a prorated tax under the Court's precedents construing the Due Process Clause. Two years earlier, in *Complete Auto Transit, Inc. v. Brady*,[5] the Court had interpreted the dormant Commerce Clause to impose a four-part framework for testing the validity of state taxes alleged to burden interstate commerce. Besides a trio of due process factors, *Complete Auto* mandated that a state tax "not discriminate against interstate commerce." But the property tax at issue in *Japan Line* clearly satisfied both these due process criteria and the nondiscrimination test, falling evenhandedly on all personalty situated in California, regardless of origin or ownership.

---

3. Charles Rothfeld, *From* Japan Line *to* Barclays*: The Rise and Fall of the Foreign Commerce Clause*, 7 STATE TAX NOTES 367 (Aug. 8, 1994).

4. *See* 441 U.S. at 436–37.

5. 430 U.S. 274 (1977).

The foreign taxpayer's best case was *Hays v. Pacific Mail Steamship Co.*,[6] which held that oceangoing vessels are subject to property tax in their home ports only. But that case had gathered much dust over the years, and its constitutional moorings were suspect. The *Hays* opinion did not rely on the Commerce Clause, nor could it, in 1854, have relied on the Due Process Clause of the Fourteenth Amendment. The "home port doctrine" was basically a creature of federal common law, not the stuff of which modern constitutional challenges are built.

The Solicitor General, filing a brief amicus curiae at the Court's request, opposed California's tax largely on different grounds. He urged that the tax was preempted by the Customs Convention on Containers—a multinational agreement, signed by the United States and Japan, which granted cargo containers temporary admission free of all import duties, taxes, and restrictions.[7] The taxpayer in *Japan Line*, however, had not included a Supremacy Clause challenge in its argument to the California courts. As a rule, a party in the Supreme Court is not allowed to attack the judgment below on a ground not urged below.

As a law clerk during the 1978–79 Term, I was privy, at several removes, to reports of the Justices' conference on *Japan Line*. There was a solid majority to invalidate California's tax, but the theory (unsurprisingly) was neither solid nor clear. A number of Justices were persuaded by the Solicitor General's brief, but were reluctant to premise the opinion on the Supremacy Clause since that argument had not been raised below. Justice Stewart apparently came up with the compromise that guided the opinion's drafting: invalidate the tax under the Commerce Clause, but weave the Container Convention into the Commerce Clause analysis. The opinion was assigned to Justice Blackmun, resident tax expert and author of *Complete Auto*, the Court's most recent pronouncement on Commerce Clause requirements for state taxes.

Justice Blackmun's opinion in *Japan Line* enunciated a new test that distinguished, for the first time, between the scope of Congress's power "to regulate Commerce with foreign Nations" and its power to "regulate Commerce... among the Several States."[8] As he put it:

> An inquiry more elaborate than that mandated by *Complete Auto* is necessary when a State seeks to tax the instrumentalities of foreign, rather than of interstate, commerce. In addition to answering the nexus, apportionment, and nondiscrimination questions posed in *Complete Auto*, a court must also inquire, first, whether the tax, notwithstanding apportionment, creates a *substantial risk of international multiple taxation*, and,

6. 58 U.S. (17 How.) 596 (1855).
7. 441 U.S. at 446 n.10.
8. U.S. Const. art. I, § 8, cl. 3.

> second, whether the tax prevents the Federal Government from *speaking with one voice when regulating commercial relations with foreign governments*. If a state tax contravenes either of these precepts, it is unconstitutional under the Commerce Clause.[9]

The first branch of this new test—the prohibition against "multiple taxation"—had deep roots in the Court's prior jurisprudence. In the case of interstate commerce, this principle usually required no more than that taxes be "fairly apportioned" among the states in which a multistate taxpayer did business.[10] But the Court found the principle to have extra force in foreign commerce, given the Court's inability to police fair apportionment "when one of the taxing entities is a foreign sovereign."[11] And while the Court had tolerated some imperfections in apportionment of interstate taxes, it suggested a stricter standard for the international arena: "Even a slight overlapping of tax—a problem that might be deemed *de minimis* in a domestic context—assumes importance where sensitive matters of foreign relations and national sovereignty are concerned."[12]

The second branch of the Court's new test—the "speaking with one voice" requirement—was borrowed from *Michelin Tire Corp. v. Wages*,[13] a recent precedent construing the Import-Export Clause.[14] The *Japan Line* Court listed various factors tending to show the need for "a uniform national rule" when regulating foreign commerce. In particular, the Court noted the risk that foreign nations disadvantaged by a novel state tax "may retaliate against American-owned instrumentalities present in their jurisdictions."[15]

The Court went on to hold that California's property tax violated both branches of this new test. Because the cargo containers were taxed on their full value in Japan, the Court found that California's levy, though apportioned to reflect the containers' limited presence in the state, nevertheless "produce[d] multiple taxation in fact."[16] And the Court pointed to the Customs Convention on Containers as reflecting "a national policy to remove impediments to the use of containers as instruments of international traffic."[17] While not holding that the Convention literally preempted California's levy, the Court deemed the risk of foreign retaliation acute and con-

---

9. 441 U.S. at 451 (emphasis added).
10. *See Complete Auto*, 430 U.S. at 279.
11. 441 U.S. at 447.
12. *Id.* at 456.
13. 423 U.S. 276, 285 (1976).
14. U.S. CONST. art. I, § 10, cl.2.
15. 441 U.S. at 449–50.
16. *Id.* at 452.
17. *Id.* at 453.

cluded that the tax prevented the United States from speaking with one voice in regulating foreign trade.[18]

"Worldwide Combined Reporting" of Income Tax

Although *Japan Line*'s holding was limited to property taxes on foreign-owned vessels, the Court's new test had great extrapolative possibilities. The principal question was whether the Court would apply the same analysis to income taxes, where the dollars at stake were immeasurably larger. Taxpayers had ample reason to seek a prompt answer.

Most states have long used some kind of "formula apportionment" to ascertain their respective shares of a multistate corporate group's income. The premise of this approach is that separate geographical accounting sheds little light on where income is really earned, since transactions among affiliates are unlikely to be arm's-length. Formula apportionment basically assumes that an integrated corporate group is equally profitable in every state where it does business. The method accordingly assigns income ratably to each state, based on each state's respective share of the group's property, payroll, and sales.

During the 1970s—a decade of vast business expansion overseas—a number of states, led by California, began to apply formula apportionment on a worldwide basis. Assume, for example, an affiliated group of corporations that manufacture and sell pharmaceuticals, detergents, and personal hygiene products worldwide. Assume that the group has a British parent and subsidiaries in sixty-five other countries, and that the group's only contact with the United States is a California subsidiary that sells soap. Finally, assume that the soap company's property, payroll, and sales in California represent, on average, two percent of the group's property, payroll, and sales worldwide. If California determined that the group's operations were sufficiently integrated or "unitary," it would take the total worldwide income of all sixty-six entities, eliminate intercompany profits and dividends, and assign two percent of the balance to California as the soap company's deemed income. California would ignore the soap company's income as reported to the IRS or as shown on its financial statements. This approach came to be known as the "worldwide unitary method" or "worldwide combined reporting."

Most multinational taxpayers strongly opposed this approach, citing first its administrative burdens. Under worldwide combined reporting, the California soap company would have to disclose, then convert into U.S. terms, the balance sheets and income statements of its affiliates in sixty-five for-

18. *Id.* at 452–53.

eign countries. Fluctuating exchange rates, differences in international accounting techniques, and foreign bank secrecy laws could make this data difficult and costly to assemble.

More pointedly, taxpayers argued that worldwide combined reporting produced an unfairly high tax. The premise of formula apportionment is that a group's operations are equally profitable everywhere. Taxpayers urged that this premise was simply untrue in the international context, owing to vastly different wage scales, inflation rates, risks of doing business, and rates of return prevailing in various countries. The California soap company in our example might lose money in a financial and economic sense because of depressed market conditions in California or the high cost of doing business there. But if the worldwide group as a whole had net income—say, because of highly profitable manufacturing operations by affiliates in Asia, or highly profitable pharmaceutical sales by affiliates in Germany—California would assert the right to tax a share of that income.

Drawing on the new framework set forth in *Japan Line*, multinational taxpayers mounted in the lower courts a two-pronged attack under the Foreign Commerce Clause. First, citing the lower costs of doing business overseas, they contended that California was arbitrarily allocating to itself—and taxing a second time—income earned abroad in an economic sense. In other words, by disputing the premise of worldwide combined reporting—that income is earned ratably wherever a multinational group does business—taxpayers hoped to show that California's method caused "multiple taxation" of the same income.

Second, taxpayers contended that worldwide combined reporting prevented the federal government from "speaking with one voice" in foreign affairs. Rather than using worldwide combined reporting, the United States and its trading partners determine the income of multinational affiliates by the so-called arm's-length method. This method attempts to place transactions among affiliates on an arm's-length basis, then computes each entity's discrete income by use of separate financial accounting. Through its program of bilateral income tax treaties, the United States has encouraged other nations to adopt this method. Multinational taxpayers contended that worldwide combined reporting was practically and theoretically incommensurate with the arm's-length method, that it conflicted with the custom of nations and U.S. tax policy, and that it therefore prevented the federal government from speaking with one voice.

From *Chicago Bridge* to *Container Corporation*

The first challenge to worldwide combined reporting that reached the Supreme Court was *Chicago Bridge & Iron Co. v. Caterpillar Tractor Co.*

As the caption suggests, that case arrived in an odd procedural posture: appellant and appellee were both private parties. The Illinois courts held that worldwide combined reporting was authorized by state law and could permissibly be used to determine Caterpillar's tax—a decision with which Caterpillar and Illinois agreed. The only party unhappy with that decision was Chicago Bridge, an intervenor whose tax liability was not before the court.

Despite obvious jurisdictional problems, the Supreme Court in November 1981 noted probable jurisdiction of the appeal.[19] The Solicitor General then weighed in with a brief supporting Chicago Bridge's position, in essence urging that worldwide combined reporting was unconstitutional per se under the Foreign Commerce Clause. The Solicitor General relied heavily—as he had in *Japan Line*—on protests registered by our major trading partners against worldwide combined reporting, suggesting the possibility that they might engage in retaliatory action.

Chicago Bridge was argued in April 1982, at which time the jurisdictional problems became painfully apparent. The Court temporized by ordering the case reargued the following year.[20] On the same day, it noted jurisdiction in *Container Corporation of America v. California Franchise Tax Board*,[21] which presented the foreign commerce question on a fully developed record with no procedural problems.

At that point, something very significant happened, or rather, did not happen. Word of the Solicitor General's filing in *Chicago Bridge*—erstwhile an obscure tax case—finally percolated up to major players at the White House. They were not pleased. The Reagan administration had been a consistent advocate of states' rights and a limited, nonactivist judiciary. For the Solicitor General to urge that a state tax was unconstitutional per se, in a case whose jurisdictional problems made the assertion seem almost gratuitous, was bad enough. Add that President Reagan had served two terms as governor of California—the state that devised worldwide combined reporting, was its principal advocate, and was appellee in *Container Corporation*—and you had the script for a stern conversation. *Container Corporation* proceeded to briefing and oral argument, with nary a peep being heard from the Solicitor General's Office.

In an exhaustive opinion by Justice Brennan, the Court, by a 6–3 vote, rejected the taxpayer's foreign commerce challenge to California's worldwide combined reporting method.[22] Justice Powell, joined by Chief Justice

19. 454 U.S. 1029 (No. 81-349).

20. 456 U.S. 958. *Chicago Bridge* in fact was never reargued, and the appeal was ultimately dismissed for want of a substantial federal question. 463 U.S. 1220–21 (1983).

21. 456 U.S. 960 (1982).

22. 463 U.S. 159 (1983).

Burger and Justice O'Connor, dissented. The majority held that worldwide combined reporting passed muster under both prongs of *Japan Line*'s foreign commerce test. The Court admitted that this method, as applied to Container Corporation, "has resulted in actual multiple taxation," and it grudgingly acknowledged its statement in *Japan Line* that "even a slight overlapping of tax" may suffice to invalidate a state tax where foreign commerce is concerned.[23] The Court then proceeded to strong-arm that dictum, stating that "such an absolute rule is no more appropriate here than it was in *Japan Line* itself, where we relied on much more than the mere fact of double taxation to strike down the state tax."[24]

Container Corporation's proof of multiple taxation, said the Court, had a question-begging quality. It relied on separate geographical accounting to show that formula apportionment caused double taxation; but the basic rationale of formula apportionment was that separate geographical accounting was unreliable to begin with. All of this just served to show that any method of dividing income will be imperfect in some respects. The Court accordingly concluded that "it would be perverse, simply for the sake of avoiding double taxation, to require California to give up one allocation method that sometimes results in double taxation in favor of another allocation method that also sometimes results in double taxation."[25]

Nor in the Court's view did worldwide combined reporting prevent the federal government from "speaking with one voice" in foreign trade. While observing that it had "little competence in determining precisely when foreign nations will be offended by particular acts," the Court discerned little risk that California's tax would "justifiably lead to significant foreign retaliation."[26] And it found no evidence that California's tax violated any "clear federal directive," an inquiry the Court labelled "essentially a species of preemption analysis."[27] Neither the federal tax statutes embodying the "arm's-length" principle nor the bilateral tax treaties executed with foreign nations expressly preempted California's taxing method. Indeed, when given a chance to preempt it, the Senate had refused to do so, declining to approve a proposed U.S.-U.K. tax treaty that would have barred California and other states from using worldwide combined reporting to tax British companies.

The Court's foreign commerce analysis in *Container Corporation* seemed sufficient, on its face, to put to rest for good any question about the constitutionality of worldwide combined reporting. Alas, such was not to be. In a lamentable exercise of the passive virtues, the Court dropped a pair of

23. *Id.* at 187, 189 (quoting 441 U.S. at 456).

24. *Id.* at 189.

25. *Id.* at 193.

26. *Id.* at 194–95.

27. *Id.* at 194.

footnotes that would bedevil the legal community, and prompt continued litigation of this same issue, for the next eleven years.

First, as one of several bases for distinguishing *Japan Line*, the Court noted that the taxpayer in that case had been domiciled abroad, whereas the taxpayer in *Container Corporation*—viz., the parent of the multinational group—was domiciled in the United States. In what would become a much-quoted footnote, the Court then declared that it was not deciding the constitutionality of worldwide combined reporting as applied to "domestic corporations with foreign parents."[28]

As *Barclays* would later make clear, there is virtually nothing in *Container Corporation*'s constitutional analysis to suggest that the taxpayer's domicile should affect the foreign-commerce outcome. The only possible relevance of domicile is that foreign nations might complain more loudly when their own domiciliaries are being directly taxed. And the suggestion that such complaints could be dispositive was doctrinally odd: foreign nations would then become arbiters of the constitutionality of U.S. taxes, and foreign competitors of U.S. corporations would receive a much-desired state-tax advantage. For better or worse, however, the Court's footnote suggested that it was attaching great importance to the frequency and vociferousness of our trading partners' complaints, thus launching the legal community on an extended fool's errand to generate and marshal such evidence.

Second, in deciding whether California's tax prevented the federal government from "speaking with one voice," the Court noted that, "in this case, unlike *Japan Line*, the Executive Branch has decided not to file an *amicus curiae* brief in opposition to the state tax."[29] The dissent pointed out that the Solicitor General had filed a brief in *Chicago Bridge* opposing California's tax; that *Chicago Bridge* was still pending before the Court; and that the Solicitor General had not withdrawn or modified his earlier brief in any way.[30] The majority countered with another footnote.[31] While declining "to speculate as to the reasons for the Solicitor General's decision not to submit a similar memorandum or brief in this case," the majority found "no indication that the position taken by the Government in *Chicago Bridge* still represents its views, or that we should regard the brief in that case as applying to this case."

One suspects that the Justices knew exactly what was going on and were just having some fun at the Solicitor General's expense. If taken seriously, the Court's suggestion was certainly very odd. It is hard to imagine how the mere *filing* of a brief by a political official in the Justice Department could

28. *Id.* at 188–89 & n.26, 195 & n.32.
29. *Id.* at 195.
30. *Id.* at 204.
31. *Id.* at 195 n.33.

have evidentiary weight in determining the constitutionality of a state tax law. Nor is it clear what relevance executive-branch pronouncements of any sort have to the scope of the power "to regulate Commerce with foreign Nations," a power that the Constitution reposes in Congress. But the Court seemed to be sending a strong signal that the Solicitor General's filing of an amicus brief was a crucial determinant of the Commerce Clause outcome. That message was not lost on future litigants (or on their amici).

The Road to *Barclays*

Multinational taxpayers read the tea leaves of *Container Corporation* and headed back to court. Lawsuits were commenced or continued featuring corporate groups headed by foreign parent corporations. A California suit involving a U.S. subsidiary of Barclays Bank (a British company) eventually became the lead case. Diplomatic protests were lodged with the State Department reflecting increasing stridency and heat. The British Parliament passed what might be called contingent retaliatory legislation, designed to spring into effect if the United States failed to solve the problem unilaterally. But the soup was still missing one ingredient—the Solicitor General's cooperation.

The ink had scarcely dried on *Container Corporation* before this last defect was remedied, in a manner that left most contemporary observers flabbergasted. The Reagan administration believed passionately in judicial restraint and states' rights. But President Reagan was also a great admirer and personal friend of Margaret Thatcher, the prime minister of the nation that found worldwide combined reporting most offensive. At some point between 1983 and 1985, President Reagan and Mrs. Thatcher had a heart-to-heart talk.

The conversion that followed was stark as Saint Paul's: the administration that had forbidden the Solicitor General to oppose California's tax regime in *Container Corporation* suddenly became that method's mortal enemy. In November 1985, President Reagan announced that he would introduce legislation barring the states from using worldwide combined reporting. Members of the Reagan and, later, the Bush cabinets sent letters to state governors and Congress expressing the administrations' opposition to that method. And Justice Department lawyers were dispatched to file amicus briefs in state trial and appellate courts, propounding the federal government's position on the issue.

This flurry of diplomatic activity had an effect. Some intermediate California courts—never accused of favoritism toward multinational corporations—actually declared worldwide combined reporting unconstitutional. But the California supreme court stood firm, unanimously upholding the constitutionality of the tax in *Barclays*. Barclays sought certiorari, and the Solicitor General—consistently with the Reagan-Bush policy—filed a brief urging that California's method of taxing foreign-based corporate groups was unconstitutional under the Foreign Commerce Clause. It looked like *Chicago Bridge* all over again, save for the corporate domicile.

Unfortunately for the taxpayer, *Barclays* resembled *Chicago Bridge* in more ways than one: it, too, had a jurisdictional problem. The California supreme court had decided the foreign-commerce issue, but it had remanded for reconsideration of a related due process question, involving Barclays' challenge to the onerousness of complying with California's reporting and recordkeeping requirements. This state of affairs raised a serious question, which the Solicitor General noted, as to whether there existed a "final decision" requisite to Supreme Court jurisdiction. For whatever reason, the Supreme Court denied certiorari in October 1992,[32] and *Barclays I* headed back to California to become *Barclays II*.

Meanwhile, there occurred another of those twists of fate that by now had become commonplace in this seemingly endless litigation. The 1992 presidential campaign was in full swing, and candidate Bill Clinton was eager to lock up California's support, first for his nomination and then for the general election. California for its part was seeking any help it could get in staving off what it estimated to be a $4 billion contingent liability if its tax regime were struck down. It was a marriage made in heaven: Clinton promised that, if elected President, he would support California's position in the *Barclays* case. He was elected.

The California courts were no more hospitable to the due process argument in *Barclays II* than they had been to the foreign-commerce argument in *Barclays I*. The bank sought certiorari a second time in February 1993, this time from an indisputably final judgment. This left the Solicitor General in quite a quandary. The Solicitor General's office prides itself on nothing so much as its reputation for consistent straight-shooting with the Supreme Court, plausibly free of political wind-shifting and intrigue. The office had already filed a brief in *Barclays I* contending that California's tax was unconstitutional. To file another brief taking the opposite position in the very same case was not a strategy calculated to burnish its reputation.

The Solicitor General temporized by doing nothing, hoping the Court would deny certiorari and make the problem go away. No such luck. After three months of anxious waiting by the government, the Court issued the following order on May 17, 1993: "The Solicitor General is invited to file a brief in this case expressing the views of the United States" as to whether

32. 113 S. Ct. 202.

certiorari should be granted.[33] There must have been a few smiles around the Court's conference room when that invitation was issued.

The difficulty of drafting such a brief suggested the wisdom of a negotiated solution. The Clinton administration wasted no time trying to craft one. Several years previously, California had cut back severely on its use of worldwide combined reporting by giving multinational taxpayers an election to have their tax computed on a U.S.-only or "water's edge" basis. A number of allegedly onerous conditions were attached to such elections, however, and Britain in particular had not been mollified. With perhaps some prompting from the Clinton administration, the California legislature rapidly amended its water's-edge provision to soften or eliminate the offending conditions. The British declared themselves, if not elated, satisfied.

This seemed to provide the Solicitor General a way out of his dilemma. In October 1993, he triumphantly filed a brief urging that certiorari be denied. The constitutionality of worldwide combined reporting, the brief explained, was a question of no continuing importance. Bowing to economic pressure from multinationals, most states had abandoned that methodology. California had now perfected its water's-edge election, meaning that no taxpayer would have to endure worldwide combined reporting unless it wanted to. All irritants to America's foreign relations had been removed by a process of negotiation and compromise. All that remained at stake was a little money for past years—not a consideration that typically prompts the Court to grant one of its coveted certiorari slots.

With the filing of the Solicitor General's brief, the smart money was on a rapid denial of Supreme Court review. Wrong again. Not only did the Court grant certiorari in *Barclays II*, it also accepted review of *Colgate-Palmolive Co. v. California Franchise Tax Board*, a case brought by a U.S. taxpayer essentially asking that *Container Corporation* be overruled.

So it was back to the drawing board for the Solicitor General. The brief that ultimately emerged from the office was clever and remarkably candid under the circumstances. Without disavowing the government's prior briefs in *Chicago Bridge* and *Barclays I*, the Solicitor General explained that those briefs had committed one analytical error—they failed to focus on the particular tax years being litigated. For Barclays, the tax year at issue was 1977. As of 1977, the brief explained, there was no expressed federal policy that precluded the states' use of worldwide combined reporting. Subsequent pronouncements by the executive branch were concededly more definitive in asserting that California's taxing formula impeded foreign relations, and the Solicitor General—ever the President's advocate—continued to insist that such executive-branch pronouncements be given weight in the consti-

33. 113 S. Ct. 2330.

tutional calculus. But however relevant these subsequent pronouncements might be in assessing the constitutionality of worldwide combined reporting for later years—a question the brief tactfully did not address—they were assertedly irrelevant in deciding that question for the 1977 tax year involved in *Barclays II*.

The Solicitor General's brief probably made the best of a bad situation. But while his argument had some theoretical appeal, it would have produced, if accepted, a wholly unworkable body of law. Taxpayers would have had to litigate the constitutionality of worldwide combined reporting on a year-by-year basis. Courts would have had to parse subtle annual changes in the executive branch's position, with state tax laws being declared constitutional one year, unconstitutional the next. Statutes would rise and fall with the change of administrations. And the matter would never have been put to rest: litigation by definition would have gone on forever.

Unfortunately for the tax bar, the Supreme Court had the sense to reject this course. In a brief opinion by Justice Ginsburg, the Court unqualifiedly upheld the constitutionality of worldwide combined reporting as applied to foreign-based as well as U.S.-based multinational groups; on the question whether the challenged method prevented the federal government from "speaking with one voice," the Court was unanimous in saying no.[34]

Addressing the "multiple taxation" branch of *Japan Line*, the Court largely reprised its analysis in *Container Corporation*. It noted that any method of dividing income will be imperfect in some circumstances, and it held that the Constitution does mandate a preference for one inevitably imperfect system over another. The Court also concluded that the foreign domicile of the taxpayer (or the taxpayer's parent) made no difference in the constitutional analysis, rejecting the notion that foreign entities need extra protection because they lack access to the U.S. political process:

> [T]he image of a politically impotent foreign transactor is surely belied by the battalion of foreign governments that has marched to Barclays' aid, deploring worldwide combined reporting in diplomatic notes, amicus briefs, and even retaliatory legislation. Indeed, California responded to this impressive political activity when it eliminated mandatory worldwide combined reporting. In view of this activity, . . . we cannot agree that "international practice" has such force as to dictate this Court's Commerce Clause jurisprudence. We therefore adhere to the precedent set in *Container Corporation*.[35]

34. Justice O'Connor, joined by Justice Thomas, dissented as to whether worldwide combined reporting caused international multiple taxation, adhering in that respect to her dissent in *Container Corporation*.

35. 114 S. Ct. at 2281.

Turning to the "speaking with one voice" branch of *Japan Line*, the Court basically consigned that test to the dustbin of history. Even more pointedly than in *Container Corporation*, the Court refused to declare California's tax unconstitutional in the absence of "specific indications of legislative intent to bar the state action."[36] The Court's bottom line was that Congress had multiple chances to preempt the states' use of worldwide combined reporting, but had repeatedly refused to enact legislation that would do so. To the contrary: all available evidence demonstrated "Congress' willingness to tolerate States' worldwide combined reporting mandates, even when those mandates are applied to foreign corporations and domestic corporations with foreign parents."[37]

The taxpayer in *Barclays II* also relied on "a series of Executive Branch actions, statements, and *amicus* filings, made both before and after [the] decision in *Container Corporation*," as evidence of a "clear federal directive proscribing States' use of worldwide combined reporting."[38] The Court had a short answer to that submission: "The Constitution expressly grants Congress, not the President, the power to 'regulate Commerce with foreign Nations.'" Justice Ginsburg concluded as follows:

> Congress has focused its attention on this issue, but has refrained from exercising its authority to prohibit state-mandated worldwide combined reporting. That the Executive Branch proposed legislation to outlaw a state taxation practice, but encountered an unreceptive Congress, is not evidence that the practice interfered with the Nation's ability to speak with one voice.... The Executive Branch actions—press releases, letters, and *amicus* briefs—are merely precatory. Executive Branch communications that express federal policy but lack the force of law cannot render unconstitutional California's otherwise valid, congressionally condoned, use of worldwide combined reporting.[39]

A Post Mortem

What is left of *Japan Line* in the wake of *Barclays Bank*? In my view, not much. *Japan Line* surely remains good law so far as the facts of that case went. Thus, a state tax will still be held to violate the Foreign Commerce Clause if it produces actual double taxation of a ship, aircraft, or other instrumentality of international traffic. But the broader ramifications of *Japan Line*'s "multiple taxation" inquiry, and the entirety of its "speaking with one voice" test, are almost certainly history.

---

36. *Id.* at 2283.
37. *Id.* at 2284.
38. *Id.* at 2285.
39. *Id.* at 2285–86.

In the closing paragraph of her opinion, Justice Ginsburg wrote an epitaph for the expansive scope of protection afforded foreign commerce under *Japan Line*:

> The Constitution does "'not make the judiciary the overseer of our government.'" Having determined that the taxpayers before us had an adequate nexus with the State, that worldwide combined reporting led to taxation which was fairly apportioned, nondiscriminatory, fairly related to the services provided by the State, and that its imposition did not result inevitably in multiple taxation, we leave it to Congress—whose voice, in this area, is the Nation's—to evaluate whether the national interest is best served by tax uniformity, or state autonomy.[40]

This paragraph basically restates the four-part inquiry set forth in *Complete Auto* for testing the constitutionality of state taxes imposed on *interstate* commerce. The only residue of *Japan Line*'s more expansive foreign-commerce test is the requirement that a state tax not "result inevitably" in multiple taxation. That requirement is a pale shadow of *Japan Line*'s inquiry into whether a state tax "creates a substantial risk" of multiple taxation.[41] And the "speaking with one voice" requirement is gone altogether. The only "voice" that counts now is the voice of Congress; and the only way Congress can express that voice is by passing a law specifically preempting a state tax. In that event, of course, there is no need for taxpayers to resort to the Foreign Commerce Clause. The Supremacy Clause will do just fine.

If forced to hazard a guess as to why the Foreign Commerce Clause has suffered this diminution of capacity, I would put four items at the top of my list. First, and most obviously, the Court found that ascertaining the existence of "double taxation" is a much more complicated task when income taxes rather than property taxes are involved. One can feel confident of a conviction that a ship has been taxed twice. Given the bewildering array of income tax credits and deductions that various countries offer—not to mention such arcana as "PFICs" and "Subpart F income"—a conviction that income has been taxed twice will always be more uncertain. And there is an even more fundamental problem: in order to know whether income has been taxed twice, you must first know where the income was earned. But the proper standard for determining where income was earned was itself the subject of the constitutional debate. In a very real sense, the problem was circular.

Second, the Court found it impossible to draw a principled line around the universe of evidence—apart from enactments with the force of law—that courts could consult in deciding whether a state tax prevents the fed-

40. *Id.* at 2286 (citations omitted).
41. 441 U.S. at 451.

eral government from speaking with one voice. In his *Barclays II* brief, the Solicitor General made the best case for giving evidentiary weight to executive-branch pronouncements and other materials lacking the force of law. "[I]n the sphere of foreign relations," he explained, "federal officials are particularly likely to act by methods lacking legal formalities [and] federal policy is especially likely to take the form of informal agreements, understandings, [and] long-term strategies...that have not been codified in a statute or treaty."[42] But the Court was not persuaded. Conscious of the perils of Venetian diplomacy and fearful of the slippery slope, the Court took refuge in the certainty of congressional enactments.

Third, the Court became increasingly aware of how political the "speaking with one voice" inquiry could become. The executive branch changed its position on the issue of worldwide combined reporting no fewer than three times in a single decade. The Justices were willing to defer to the Solicitor General's position in *Japan Line*, perhaps because that position seemed quite noncontroversial, perhaps because the Solicitor General then appeared less partisan than, in the view of some, he later became on this issue. But Justice O'Connor seemed to speak for the entire Court when she wrote in her dissent: "The inconsistent positions taken by the Solicitor General in the course of Barclays' challenge to the California tax illustrate the perils of resting constitutional determinations on such 'evidence.'"[43]

Finally, the Court's doctrine on the subject of preemption has changed somewhat since *Japan Line* was decided. During the 1970s, the Court often invalidated state laws under the Supremacy Clause on the theory that Congress had "occupied the field" in a general sort of way. While not abandoning this doctrine entirely, the Court is now more prone to look for a statute or regulation clearly expressing a preemptive federal intent. This subtle shift in preemption doctrine has a clear echo in *Barclays*' search for "specific indications of congressional intent to bar the state action here challenged."[44]

This echo is not exactly fortuitous. The underlying rationale for *Japan Line*'s speaking-with-one-voice standard was preemption, transmuted into Commerce Clause garb by a procedural quirk in the case. A majority of the Justices in *Japan Line* seemed to think that California's property tax was preempted by the Customs Convention on Containers but, because that issue had not been preserved by the taxpayer's lawyers, the Supremacy Clause argument had to be smuggled into the Court's opinion via the Foreign Commerce Clause. It seems unlikely that today's Justices would agree that the tax in *Japan Line* was preempted: the Court recently held, in similar cir-

42. Br. 16.

43. 114 S. Ct. at 2288.

44. 114 S. Ct. at 2283.

cumstances, that the Customs Convention on Containers does not preempt a state sales tax.[45] Given this shift in the Court's preemption analysis, it is not surprising that the scope of the dormant Foreign Commerce Clause has been diminished as well.

The Court's reasoning and result in *Barclays Bank* are to be applauded. The Court's abandonment of the *Japan Line* framework bears witness to the unworkability of much "dormant Commerce Clause" theory—that is, the constitutional theory that permits invalidation of state laws under the bare language of the Commerce Clause, without Congress's enactment of any law specifically *regulating* commerce.[46] In *Japan Line*, the Court had expanded the scope of protection that the dormant Commerce Clause affords foreign commerce. The basic problem was that the relevant factors under *Japan Line*'s framework—the risk of multiple taxation, the threat of foreign retaliation, the danger of compromising federal diplomatic and trade policy—involved inquiries that are inherently unjudicial.

The Court in *Barclays Bank* wisely decided that it lacked the institutional competence to answer these questions. In effect, it suspended dormant Commerce Clause inquiry and held that specific congressional action was required to invalidate California's tax. That is a victory for those who believe in strict construction of the Constitution and a limited judiciary.

45. *See* Itel Containers Int'l v. Huddleston, 113 S. Ct. 1095 (1993).

46. For a critique of dormant Commerce Clause jurisprudence, see the following article by Professor DeBow. —Editors' note.

MICHAEL DEBOW

Codifying the Dormant Commerce Clause

Introduction

In Article I, Section 8, the Constitution grants authority to Congress to regulate interstate commerce: "The Congress shall have Power... [t]o regulate Commerce with foreign Nations, and among the several States, and with the Indian Tribes...."[1] For approximately the last sixty years, Congress has utilized this grant of authority with great enthusiasm, creating in the process a huge federal regulatory system that touches all aspects of commercial life. In 1937, the Supreme Court in *NLRB v. Jones & Laughlin Steel Corp.*[2] adopted a reading of the Commerce Clause that gave critical support to the growth of the regulatory state. Under this decision and its progeny, Congress's use of its commerce power is constrained only by the easily satisfied requirement that the commercial activity to be regulated have some effect on interstate commerce.[3]

1. U.S. CONST. art. I, § 8, cl. 3.

2. 301 U.S. 1 (1937).

3. Prior to 1937, the commerce power was not understood to extend to manufacturing or commerce that took place within a state's boundaries. The sweeping expansion of Congress's powers came in Supreme Court decisions such as NLRB v. Jones & Laughlin Steel Corp. and Wickard v. Filburn, 317 U.S. 111 (1942), upholding various regulatory aspects of the New Deal against constitutional challenge. In these decisions, the Court upheld sweeping regulatory legislation on the grounds that, when arguably local commercial activity has some effect on interstate commerce, it is consequently within Congress's zone of regulatory authority under the Commerce Clause. For example, in *Wickard*, the Court upheld federal farm price-support legislation against a constitutional challenge by a farmer who had grown wheat on his farm for his own consumption. The Court explained that, even though the farmer did not place his wheat in the "stream of commerce," his consumption of it nonetheless "affected interstate commerce" to the extent of his own consumption and could thus be regulated by Congress.

The Supreme Court's recent decision in United States v. Lopez, 115 S. Ct. 1624 (1995), did strike down for the first time since the 1930s a federal statute on the grounds that it exceeded Congress's authority under the Commerce Clause. At issue was a law making it a federal offense to possess a firearm within 1000 feet of a school. One can hope that a counterrevolution has begun with *Lopez* but, as the Court pointed out in the second sentence of its 5–4 opinion, "The Act neither regulates a commercial activity nor contains a requirement

There is a very good argument that this reading of the Commerce Clause and the expansion of the regulatory state it supported cannot be grounded in the text and history of the Constitution.[4] For numerous reasons, however, it seems very unlikely that we will ever be able to return to anything like the narrower, pre-1937 view of the commerce power—as even the most ardent critics of the present-day Commerce Clause agree.[5] For our purposes the important point is that, rightly or wrongly, the Commerce Clause now vests an essentially unlimited authority in Congress to legislate the details of commercial life.[6]

Given the sweeping nature of Congress's power under the Commerce Clause as currently interpreted, the doctrine known as the "negative" or

that the possession be connected in any way with interstate commerce." Thus, the statute in *Lopez* was exceptional in its lack of a nexus with *any* commercial activity. *Cf.* United States v. Robertson, 115 S. Ct. 1732 (1995) (unanimous, per curiam decision less than a week after *Lopez*, upholding RICO conviction because an Alaska gold mine run by a drug trafficker involved "interstate commerce").

4. *See generally* Gary Lawson, *The Rise and Rise of the Administrative State*, 107 HARV. L. REV. 1231, 1231 (1994) ("The post–New Deal administrative state is unconstitutional, and its validation by the legal system amounts to nothing less than a bloodless constitutional revolution.") (footnotes omitted). For a thorough analysis and critique of the genesis and growth of the post-1937 view of Congress's powers under the Commerce Clause, see Richard A. Epstein, *The Proper Scope of the Commerce Power*, 73 VA. L. REV. 1387 (1987). (A précis of this analysis can be found in Richard A. Epstein, *The Mistakes of 1937*, GEO. MASON U. L. REV., Winter 1988, at 5, 7–12.)

5. *See* ROBERT H. BORK, THE TEMPTING OF AMERICA 158 (1989) ("[I]t is too late to overrule... those decisions validating certain New Deal and Great Society programs pursuant to the congressional powers over commerce, taxation, and spending. To overturn these would be to overturn most of modern government and plunge us into chaos. No judge would dream of doing it."); Lawson, *supra* note 4, at 1249 ("The actual structure and operation of the national government today has virtually nothing to do with the Constitution. There is no reasonable prospect that this circumstance will significantly improve in the near future.").

A very important barrier to a return to the original understanding of the commerce power is the fact that much of the civil rights legislation of the 1960s was grounded in the Commerce Clause. In Heart of Atlanta Motel, Inc. v. United States, 379 U.S. 241 (1964), and Katzenbach v. McClung, 379 U.S. 294 (1964), the Supreme Court upheld the Civil Rights Act of 1964 as a constitutionally valid exercise of Congress's power to regulate interstate commerce. As a result, a serious critique of the current understanding of an essentially limitless congressional commerce power may bring into question much of federal civil rights law. This is as good a reason as any to conclude that there is little chance the original understanding of the Commerce Clause will be recovered and adopted by the federal courts.

6. As Robert Bork explains, "the expansion of Congress's commerce, taxing, and spending powers has reached a point where it is not possible to state that, as a matter of articulated doctrine, there are any limits left." BORK, *supra* note 5, at 158. Indeed, even Justice Thomas recently described the Commerce Clause as conferring on Congress "plenary authority over interstate commerce...." Oregon Waste Sys., Inc. v. Dep't of Envtl. Quality, 114 S. Ct. 1345, 1349 (1994). *But cf. Lopez,* 115 S. Ct. at 1642 (Thomas, J., concurring).

"dormant" Commerce Clause is particularly curious.[7] The doctrine—which I will refer to as the "Dormant Commerce Clause" or "DCC"—is applied in cases where Congress has *not* acted to regulate commerce, but a state government has so acted. To put it simply, the DCC operates to preempt certain forms of state regulation of commerce, even though Congress has not taken any affirmative steps via legislation to preempt the states. Thus, under the Dormant Commerce Clause, congressional inaction may be deemed by the courts to have the same preclusive effect on the states as congressional action. The need for a doctrine to deal with congressional silence about commercial regulation is not immediately obvious, since Congress currently enjoys such extensive powers under the Commerce Clause and has taken the trouble to use these powers on numerous occasions since 1937. The existence of a doctrine to interpret congressional silence in a time when Congress speaks often and with such broad authority is strange, even paradoxical.

But even before 1937—indeed, for most of its 120-plus year history[8]—the Dormant Commerce Clause has troubled judges and other legal scholars, for a number of reasons. Their criticism, which continues in our own time, makes two points. First, there is no basis in the text or history of the Commerce Clause for the DCC. Second, the courts' attempts to flesh out the DCC have been confused and ultimately unpersuasive. Justice Scalia, the most vigorous critic of the doctrine among the current members of the Supreme Court, puts the first point very bluntly: "The historical record provides no grounds for reading the Commerce Clause to be other than what it says—an authorization for *Congress* to regulate commerce."[9] As to the second matter, Scalia offers another blunt assessment: many of the Court's "applications of the doctrine have, not to put too fine a point on the matter, made no sense."[10] The Court itself has characterized much of the DCC

---

7. For an etymology of these terms, see Julian N. Eule, *Laying the Dormant Commerce Clause to Rest*, 91 YALE L.J. 425, 425 n.1 (1982).

8. The Supreme Court first formally adopted the DCC as a constitutional doctrine in Case of the State Freight Tax, 82 U.S. (15 Wall.) 232 (1873). But the idea of a DCC can be found in dicta much earlier, in decisions of the Marshall and Taney Courts. *See* Tyler Pipe Indus., Inc. v. Washington State Dep't of Revenue, 483 U.S. 232, 260 (1987) (Scalia, J., concurring in part and dissenting in part) (noting Gibbons v. Ogden, 22 U.S. (9 Wheat.) 1, 209 (1824), and Cooley v. Board of Wardens, 53 U.S. (12 How.) 299, 313 (1852)). *See also* Martin H. Redish & Shane V. Nugent, *The Dormant Commerce Clause and the Constitutional Balance of Federalism*, 1987 DUKE L.J. 569, 574–80.

9. *Tyler Pipe*, 483 U.S. at 263 (Scalia, J., concurring in part and dissenting in part) (emphasis added). Justice Scalia has restated this belief as recently as the 1994–95 Term, in Oklahoma Tax Comm'n v. Jefferson Lines, Inc., 115 S. Ct. 1331, 1346 (1995) (concurring in the judgment).

10. *Tyler Pipe*, 483 U.S. at 260.

case law as a "quagmire."[11] There is, in addition, a substantial academic literature critical of the DCC, including two recent articles calling for the doctrine to be abandoned.[12] In spite of the considerable intellectual force of this critique—and a preponderance of Republican appointees on the Supreme Court—the Rehnquist Court has not taken any significant steps to rein in the DCC, let alone abandon it.[13] Indeed, in recent Terms the Court has handed down numerous DCC opinions, including one that appears to have *expanded* the reach of the doctrine.[14]

In light of the Rehnquist Court's lack of interest in straightening out the Dormant Commerce Clause, this article will take a simple but nonetheless novel approach: it addresses Congress.[15] I will propose that Congress adopt

---

11. Northwestern States Portland Cement Co. v. Minnesota, 358 U.S. 450, 458 (1959).

12. Redish & Nugent, *supra* note 8; Eule, *supra* note 7.

13. *See generally* David O'Brien, *The Supreme Court and Intergovernmental Relations: What Happened to "Our Federalism"?*, 9 J.L. & Pol. 609, 629–37 (1993) (discussing the Rehnquist Court's DCC decisions). O'Brien concludes that "the Rehnquist Court has not significantly backed away from... imposing its dormant commerce clause power as a limitation on the states." *Id.* at 633. In fact, he demonstrates that "the Rehnquist Court has been even more likely than the Burger Court to preempt state regulations under the dormant commerce clause." *Id.* at 629 (showing that the Burger Court struck down challenged state or local laws in 40% of the 20 Dormant Commerce Clause cases decided between 1969 and 1986, while the Rehnquist Court struck down state or local laws in 56% of the 16 DCC cases decided between 1986 and 1993).

14. The latter decision is West Lynn Creamery, Inc. v. Healy, 114 S. Ct. 2205 (1994), discussed *infra* at 79–80, 84–85. According to Justice Scalia's concurring opinion, the decision may have expanded the DCC to bring into question "a wide variety of state laws that have hitherto been thought permissible." *Id.* at 2219 (Scalia, J., concurring).

In addition to *West Lynn Creamery*, other significant DCC decisions from recent Terms include *Oregon Waste Sys.*, *supra* note 6 (striking down Oregon surcharge on solid waste from out of state); Associated Indus. v. Lohman, 114 S. Ct. 1815 (1994) (state tax case); C & A Carbone, Inc. v. Town of Clarkston, 114 S. Ct. 1677 (1994) (striking down local ordinance requiring solid waste processed within a town to be processed at the town's transfer station); Intel Containers Int'l Corp. v. Huddleston, 113 S. Ct. 1095 (1993) (state tax case); Fort Gratiot Sanitary Landfill, Inc. v. Michigan Dep't of Natural Resources, 504 U.S. 353 (1992) (striking down Michigan statute prohibiting Michigan landfills from accepting out-of-state solid waste); Quill Corp. v. North Dakota, 504 U.S. 298 (1992) (state tax case); Wyoming v. Oklahoma, 502 U.S. 437 (1992) (striking down Oklahoma statute requiring in-state coal-fired electric generating plants to burn coal mixture containing at least 10% Oklahoma-mined coal).

15. To the author's knowledge, only one article previously has suggested that Congress speak to the DCC issue, and that one only in passing. Redish & Nugent, *supra* note 8, at 612. Does this tell us something about the tendency of constitutional scholars to overlook the legislature? In seeking a primary audience that is congressional rather than judicial, this article differs from the numerous law review articles, directed to judges, that explain their authors' views on the proper judicial interpretation of the DCC. Redish and Nugent find this literature "reminiscent of an argument over the proper lapel widths to be placed on the emperor's new clothes." *Id.* at 517. At least this article does not fall into that category.

legislation defining the Dormant Commerce Clause in a way that codifies the portion of the doctrine that deserves to be retained—the prohibition against state statutes that discriminate against out-of-state interests—and otherwise awards the remainder of the field of commercial regulation to the states, unless expressly preempted by later congressional lawmaking. In making this argument, I will draw heavily on the writings of Justice Scalia, who also makes a distinction between the antidiscrimination decisions and other kinds of decisions under the DCC.

The article proceeds as follows. It first considers in more detail the reasons why the Dormant Commerce Clause is so difficult to square with a responsible reading of the text and history of the Constitution. The next section looks at why the DCC is desirable as a policy (rather than a constitutional) matter, which also helps explain why the Court is unlikely to cut back significantly its DCC case law. The following two sections consider the odd position of Congress vis-à-vis the Dormant Commerce Clause, and suggest codification of only the DCC's useful core. The final section summarizes why Congress should act in this area.

The Dormant Commerce Clause Is Bad Constitutional Law

The basic problem raised by the Dormant Commerce Clause is that it has no basis in the text of the Constitution. The Commerce Clause speaks of Congress's "Power... [t]o regulate Commerce...." "On its face," points out Justice Scalia, "this is a charter for Congress, not the courts, to ensure 'an area of trade free from interference by the States.'"[16] And what if Congress is silent as to a subject that it could conceivably address—and under current jurisprudence there are not many subjects that it cannot—under the Commerce Clause? In answering this question, it is important to note that the text does not, by its terms, exclude the states from regulating commerce. The language "gives no indication of exclusivity."[17] Further, one cannot "assume generally that Congress' Article I powers are exclusive; many of them plainly coexist with concurrent authority in the States."[18]

16. *Tyler Pipe*, 483 U.S. at 260 (Scalia, J., concurring in part and dissenting in part) (quoting Boston Stock Exch. v. State Tax Comm'n, 429 U.S. 318, 328 (1977)).

17. *Id.* at 261.

18. *Id.* That federal and state powers are at least presumptively concurrent is the theme of THE FEDERALIST No. 36 (Alexander Hamilton) (Clinton Rossiter ed., 1961). This essay concludes that in the Constitution, "notwithstanding the affirmative grants of general authorities [to the federal government], there has been the most pointed care in those cases where it was deemed improper that the like authorities should reside in the States to insert negative clauses prohibiting the exercise of them by the States." *Id.* at 201. Of course, no such negative clause was inserted with respect to interstate commerce.

Reference to the history behind the Commerce Clause does not help matters much. Justice Scalia has detailed "the overwhelming reality that the Commerce Clause, in its broad outlines, was not a major subject of controversy, neither during the constitutional debates nor in the ratifying conventions."[19] Such a conclusion sounds odd to the reader accustomed to explaining the need for the Constitution, in significant part, by referring to internecine trade disputes among the states during the Articles of Confederation period. But it seems unlikely that, if there were many such disputes, their solution would have provoked little controversy or discussion. And Justice Scalia's revisionist reading of the historical background of the Commerce Clause finds substantial support in Edmund Kitch's landmark study, *Regulation and the American Common Market.*[20] Kitch summarized his findings in a 1982 law review article worth quoting at length:

> I was hardly prepared... for what I found when I turned to the role of the Constitution in protecting freedom of trade in the internal American market. First, when I went back to review the documentation of the claim that the states under the Articles of Confederation had in fact impeded trade among themselves, I found nothing to support the claim. The Federalist papers keep suggesting that this was a serious problem, but if you read carefully you are struck by the consistent failure to give examples and the constant reference to possibilities. It's as if the author did not really believe the charge. This theme of the Federalists was picked up and popularized in a book by John Fiske, whose colorful rhetoric made its way into Supreme Court opinions and from thence into the legal culture. *The problem is that there isn't a shred of evidence to support the claim....* The basic reason why this was not even an issue under the Articles of Confederation was that there simply was very little trade among the states in the eighteenth century. The important interstate commerce that existed occurred within New York Harbor among Connecticut, Manhattan, and New Jersey, and that commerce, aside from one spat over New Jersey's willingness to join the other colonies in sanctions against British shipping, proceeded smoothly and free of regulation throughout the period.[21]

For Justice Scalia, then, the constitutional text and its history provide "no conceivable reason why congressional inaction under the Commerce Clause should be deemed to have the same preemptive effect elsewhere accorded only to congressional action. There, as elsewhere, 'Congress' silence is just

19. *Tyler Pipe*, 483 U.S. at 264.

20. Edmund Kitch, *Regulation and the American Common Market, in* REGULATION, FEDERALISM, AND INTERSTATE COMMERCE 7–55 (A. Dan Tarlock ed., 1981).

21. Edmund W. Kitch, *Regulation, the American Common Market and Public Choice*, 6 HARV. J.L. & PUB. POL'Y 119, 121–22 (1982) (emphasis added).

that—silence. . . .'"[22] Accordingly, Justice Scalia ends his opinion in *Tyler Pipe* with a summary of his indictment of the DCC:

> In sum, to the extent that we have gone beyond guarding against rank discrimination against citizens of other States—which is regulated not by the Commerce Clause but by the Privileges and Immunities Clause, U.S. Const., Art. IV, sec. 2, cl. 1 ("The Citizens of each State shall be entitled to all Privileges and Immunities of Citizens in the several States.")—the Court for over a century has engaged in an enterprise that it has been unable to justify by textual support or even coherent non-contextual theory, that it was almost certainly not intended to undertake, and that it has not undertaken very well.[23]

Some Version of the DCC Is Desirable as a Policy Matter

Nonetheless, the Dormant Commerce Clause lives, and shows no serious signs of decrepitude. How to account for the doctrine's longevity? Supreme Court decisions often invoke the idea that the DCC is vital to the preservation of a common market among the American states, that it is of critical importance in deflecting "the tendencies toward economic Balkanization that had plagued relations among the Colonies and later among the States under the Articles of Confederation."[24] Even if the questionable historical claim is ignored, this view has a good deal to commend it, as many scholars have argued.[25] This view is rooted in the Court's view of the *realpolitik* of state legislation. Simply put, a state legislature should be only too happy to favor in-state interests (who vote and make campaign contributions in the relevant elections) at the expense of out-of-state interests (who do not). If this inclination is not checked, the results would be bad for the public at large, as each state attempted to favor its local interests and restrain competition from out-of-state interests. The Supreme Court has explained this commonsensical notion as follows:

---

22. *Tyler Pipe*, 483 U.S. at 262 (Scalia, J., concurring in part and dissenting in part) (quoting Alaska Airlines, Inc. v. Brock, 480 U.S. 678, 686 (1987)).

23. *Id.* at 265.

24. Hughes v. Oklahoma, 441 U.S. 322, 325–26 (1979).

25. Daniel A. Farber & Robert E. Hudec, *Free Trade and the Regulatory State: A GATT's-Eye View of the Dormant Commerce Clause*, 47 VAND. L. REV. 1401 (1994); Jacques LeBoeuf, *The Economics of Federalism and the Proper Scope of the Federal Commerce Power*, 31 SAN DIEGO L. REV. 555 (1994); 2 RONALD D. ROTUNDA & JOHN E. NOWAK, TREATISE ON CONSTITUTIONAL LAW: SUBSTANCE AND PROCEDURE ch. 11 (2d ed. 1992); Richard B. Collins, *Economic Union as a Constitutional Value*, 63 N.Y.U. L. REV. 43 (1988); Donald H. Regan, *The Supreme Court and State Protectionism: Making Sense of the Dormant Commerce Clause*, 84 MICH. L. REV. 1091 (1986).

> Unrepresented interests will often bear the brunt of regulations imposed by one State having a significant effect on persons or operations in other States. Thus, "when the regulation is of such a character that its burden falls principally upon those without the state, legislative action is not likely to be subjected to those political restraints which are normally exerted on legislation where it affects adversely some interests within the state."[26]

This analysis can be carried a step further. Even if the parochial state legislation has the effect of harming consumers within the state, this group will tend to be large and diffuse, and have relatively little at stake, compared to the in-state business interests which seek passage of the legislation. On the basis of much "public choice" scholarship, we may expect the consumer interest to be relatively underrepresented in the political process and thus to receive less than its due from the legislature.[27] Thus, from a public choice standpoint, the DCC will be directed very often against state statutes that harm the public welfare. This fact doubtless accounts for a significant part of the DCC's staying power.[28]

By the same token, the DCC likely has prevented much balkanization. Professor Kitch's conclusion that the states under the Articles of Confederation did not engage in trade wars does not necessarily lead to the conclusion that such a result would not obtain if the Court were to jettison the DCC tomorrow. It seems likely that the existence of the DCC has had a deterrent effect on the states, helping opponents of bad legislation by giving them a constitutional argument against these measures. If this has happened, then the relative infrequency of interstate trade wars to date—and the arcane subjects of much of the DCC case law[29]—does not tell the whole

---

26. South-Central Timber Dev., Inc. v. Wunnicke, 467 U.S. 82, 92 (1984) (quoting South Carolina State Highway Dep't v. Barnwell Brothers, Inc., 303 U.S. 177, 185 n.2 (1938)).

27. The huge public choice literature on this point can be traced to the work of Mancur Olson. *See* MANCUR OLSON, THE LOGIC OF COLLECTIVE ACTION (1965).

28. In an interesting dissent in West Lynn Creamery, Inc. v. Healy, 114 S. Ct. 2205 (1994), Chief Justice Rehnquist criticizes the majority opinion for its discussion of the interest-group politics that likely generated the statute at issue, which favored Massachusetts dairy farmers over their out-of-state competitors. The majority opinion deals explicitly with the politics of the situation as a reason for its holding. *Id.* at 2215. Chief Justice Rehnquist replies, "Analysis of interest group participation in the political process may serve many useful purposes, but serving as a basis for interpreting the dormant Commerce Clause is not one of them." *Id.* at 2222. Justice Scalia quotes Chief Justice Rehnquist's language approvingly in his concurrence. *Id.* at 2221.

29. The DCC case law is top-heavy with cases from several somewhat odd categories, like milk, mudflaps, and minnows. For example, there are numerous cases dealing with state statutes that regulated the importation of out-of-state agricultural produce, including Dean Milk Co. v. City of Madison, 340 U.S. 349 (1951) (milk); Pike v. Bruce Church, Inc., 397 U.S. 137 (1970) (cantaloupes); Great Atl. & Pac. Tea Co. v. Cottrell, 424 U.S. 366 (1976) (milk); Hunt v. Washington State Apple Advertising Comm'n, 432 U.S. 333 (1977) (apples);

story. In the absence of the DCC, the history of American interstate commerce may well have been substantially different, and worse. The states' recent—and lamentable—passage of stringent antitakeover statutes to protect "local" businesses and "local" jobs stands as a warning of the possibilities for protectionist state legislation in a world without a DCC.[30]

Critics of the DCC tend to dismiss the predictions of economic balkanization as overwrought. Doubtless there are political and economic pressures on the states, as Kitch points out, to open their markets and cooperate with sister states rather than risk retaliatory measures.[31] As the antitakeover example and much of the extant DCC case law demonstrates, however, these pressures to keep domestic markets open do not always prevail. It is not surprising that the courts have been reluctant to cast aside a constitutional doctrine supportive of internal free trade.

Two other critics of the DCC, Martin Redish and Shane Nugent, also discount the possibility of balkanization, but for a somewhat different reason. They argue that "even absent the dormant commerce clause, the Constitution provides a textual structure for the regulation of commerce which can quite effectively prevent an economic Armageddon at the hands of the states."[32] After noting Congress's broad authority under the Commerce Clause, Redish and Nugent—echoing Justice Scalia's opinion in *Tyler Pipe*[33]—conclude that the Privileges and Immunities Clause[34] prohibits economic discrimination by states against nonresidents.[35] Happily, as discussed next,

---

and West Lynn Creamery, Inc. v. Healy, 114 S. Ct. 2205 (1994) (milk). For an explanation of this phenomenon in public choice terms, see Geoffrey Miller, *The Industrial Organization of Political Production: A Case Study*, 149 J. INSTITUTIONAL & THEORETICAL ECON. 769 (1993).

Another significant fraction of DCC cases deals with state attempts to regulate trucking, including Bibb v. Navajo Freight Lines, Inc., 359 U.S. 520 (1959) (Illinois law specifying type of mudflaps to be used in-state); Raymond Motor Transp. v. Rice, 434 U.S. 429 (1978) (Wisconsin regulation banning double trailers more than 65 feet in length); Kassel v. Consolidated Freightways, Inc., 450 U.S. 662 (1981) (Iowa law banning 65-foot trucks).

It is hard to determine the weirdest case in the DCC corpus. Surely two serious contenders are Hughes v. Oklahoma, 441 U.S. 322 (1979), which struck down an Oklahoma law prohibiting the export of minnows grown in-state, and Maine v. Taylor, 477 U.S. 131 (1986), which upheld a Maine statute prohibiting the importation of any live fish to be used as bait in-state.

30. *See generally* Roberta Romano, *The Political Economy of Takeover Statutes*, 73 VA. L. REV. 111 (1987).

31. Kitch, *supra* note 20, at 126–40; Kitch, *supra* note 21, at 124.

32. Redish & Nugent, *supra* note 8, at 605.

33. *See* 483 U.S. at 265 (quoted *supra* p. 75).

34. "The Citizens of each State shall be entitled to all Privileges and Immunities of Citizens in the several States." U.S. CONST. art. IV, § 2.

35. Redish & Nugent, *supra* note 8, at 606–12; *see also* Eule, *supra* note 7, at 446–55.

this is the core principle of the Court's DCC jurisprudence that should be preserved.

What Congress Should Salvage from the Dormant Commerce Clause

Congress should legislate a version of the DCC in order to guard against interstate trade wars, while simultaneously eliminating the uncertainty caused by some aspects of current DCC doctrine, and without exceeding its own constitutionally enumerated powers. This is a tall order. In approaching this task, Congress should pay particular attention to Justice Scalia's critique of the DCC.

There are, to put it simply, two broad categories of DCC case law. The first category deals with statutes that discriminate against interstate commerce; the second category deals with other kinds of state statutes that "burden" commerce. A general DCC statute should retain the doctrine in the first category of cases and reject the doctrine generated by the second.

The first category of DCC cases deals with state statutes that discriminate against out-of-state interests. Justice Scalia explained this category of cases when he wrote for a unanimous Court in *New Energy Co. of Indiana v. Limbach*:

> It has long been accepted that the Commerce Clause not only grants Congress the authority to regulate commerce among the States, but also directly limits the power of the States to discriminate against interstate commerce. This negative aspect of the Commerce Clause prohibits economic protectionism—that is, regulatory measures designed to benefit in-state economic interests by burdening out-of-state competitors. Thus, state statutes that clearly discriminate against interstate commerce are routinely struck down... unless the discrimination is demonstrably justified by a valid factor unrelated to economic protectionism.[36]

In *New Energy*, the State of Ohio awarded fuel dealers a tax credit against the motor-vehicle fuel sales tax for each gallon of ethanol sold (as a component of gasohol). As originally adopted, the credit was available without regard to the source of the ethanol. Later, however, the Ohio legislature limited the credit to ethanol "produced in Ohio or in a State that grants similar tax advantages to ethanol produced in Ohio."[37] Justice Scalia's opinion makes quick work of this problem, holding that the Ohio statute

36. 486 U.S. 269, 273–74 (1988) (citations omitted).
37. *Id.* at 271.

clearly violates the DCC's prohibition of discrimination against interstate commerce.

Justice Scalia has, on several occasions, voiced the opinion that the antidiscrimination case law should be respected, in spite of the constitutional infirmities of the DCC. In his earliest lengthy discussion of the DCC, he stated his view that "a state statute is invalid under the Commerce Clause if, and only if, it accords discriminatory treatment to interstate commerce in a respect not required to achieve a lawful state purpose."[38] Most recently, in *West Lynn Creamery, Inc. v. Healy*, Justice Scalia explained his reasons for wanting to salvage this aspect of DCC case law in terms of stare decisis. The Court has decided "a vast number of negative–Commerce Clause cases, engendering considerable reliance interests."[39] To upset these expectations, at least with regard to the antidiscrimination case law, would be too disruptive.

Congress should reach the same conclusions about the antidiscrimination principle. A codification of the DCC should require simply that state laws not discriminate against out-of-state businesses. Congress clearly has the authority to enact such language under the current understanding of its commerce power, and it seems likely that Congress would have the authority to do so even under the original understanding of the Commerce Clause[40] or, perhaps, the Privileges and Immunities Clause.[41]

In addition to salvaging the antidiscrimination principle, a codified DCC should inter the doctrine generated by the second category of cases. Cases in the second category involve state statutes that do not facially discriminate against interstate commerce. Instead, these statutes typically place some burden on interstate commerce in a way that does not disadvantage or inconvenience out-of-state interests any more than local interests. The classic statement of this requirement is *Pike v. Bruce Church, Inc.*:

> Where the statute regulates even-handedly to effectuate a legitimate local public interest, and its effects on interstate commerce are only incidental, it will be upheld unless the burden imposed on such commerce is clearly excessive in relation to the putative local benefits. If a legitimate purpose is found, then the question becomes one of degree. And the extent of the burden that will be tolerated will of course depend on the nature of the local interest involved, and on whether it could be promoted as well with a lesser impact on interstate activities. Occasionally the Court has candidly undertaken a balancing approach in resolving these issues, but more

38. Bendix Autolite Corp. v. Midwesco Enters., Inc., 486 U.S. 888, 898 (1988) (Scalia, J., concurring).

39. 114 S. Ct. at 2220.

40. For an interesting argument along these lines, see LeBoeuf, *supra* note 25, at 592–607.

41. *See supra* note 34 and accompanying text.

> frequently it has spoken in terms of "direct" and "indirect" effects and burdens.[42]

In *Pike*, the Court struck down a facially neutral Arizona statute regulating the packing of cantaloupes. The *Pike* test has been "applied to a variety of subjects ranging from state corporation laws to highway safety regulations."[43]

The *Pike* balancing approach has received considerable criticism. Justice Scalia famously noted that *Pike* does not really require balancing, because "the scale analogy is not really appropriate, since the interests on both sides are incommensurate. It is more like judging whether a particular line is longer than a particular rock is heavy."[44] Justice Scalia would prefer to "abandon the 'balancing' approach... first explicitly adopted... in [*Pike*] and leave essentially legislative judgments to the Congress."[45] In *West Lynn Creamery*, Justice Scalia nonetheless conceded that he feels constrained to continue to strike down statutes that fall into the second category and are "indistinguishable from a type of law previously held unconstitutional by this Court."[46] He argues that this position is justified on the grounds of stare decisis and settled expectations.[47] He notes that applying this rule

> is not always easy, since once one gets beyond facial discrimination our negative-Commerce-Clause jurisprudence becomes (and long has been) a "quagmire." The object should be, however, to produce a clear rule that honors the holdings of our past decisions *but declines to extend the rationale that produced those decisions any further.*[48]

Whether Congress should adopt prior "second category" case law in this way is deeply problematic. It is conceivable that the stare decisis and settled expectations concerns that Justice Scalia notes may be significant, but this is open to debate.[49] On the other hand, it seems unlikely that statuto-

---

42. 397 U.S. 137, 140 (1970). The seminal category-two decision was Southern Pac. Co. v. Arizona, 325 U.S. 761 (1945). That decision, in turn, relied heavily on a law review article. *See* Noel Dowling, *Interstate Commerce and State Power*, 27 VA. L. REV. 1 (1940).

43. Farber & Hudec, *supra* note 25, at 1414.

44. *Bendix Autolite*, 486 U.S. at 897.

45. *Id.*

46. 114 S. Ct. at 2220.

47. *Id.*

48. *Id.* (emphasis added; citations omitted).

49. Consider the recent overview of the second-category case law:

> In contrast to strict scrutiny [applied to facially discriminatory statutes], the [*Pike*] balancing test in practice seemingly has become rather lax. Indeed, there is some argument that it requires only that the state present *some* evidence of a regulatory benefit, particularly when public health or safety is at stake. Courts have been reluctant to "second guess the empirical judgments of lawmakers concern-

ry language can be drafted that will accomplish this purpose without leaving the courts in the position of making essentially legislative choices in cases of this kind. These Article III problems should trump the stare decisis concerns, particularly since Congress can retain its Commerce Clause authority to legislate with respect to any particular *Pike*-type problem that presents itself.

To summarize, Congress should adopt a statute that retains the antidiscrimination principle outlined in the DCC case law, but cuts off the second branch of existing DCC doctrine.

Why Congress Can Legislate the Contours of the Dormant Commerce Clause

It is odd to speak of Congress overturning nominally constitutional decisions of the Supreme Court via legislation. Yet, as discussed below, Congress has on several occasions done just that, by passing statutes that allow states to regulate commerce in a particular way that had been disapproved by the courts under the DCC. In the odd world created by the Dormant Commerce Clause, this seeming paradox actually makes sense; the courts' presumption of congressional disapproval of state regulation can be rebutted if Congress wakingly regulates by allowing a state role.[50] The only question raised by my proposal is whether Congress may return power to the states in a blanket fashion—by, for example, renouncing the *Pike* balancing test—rather than in a case-by-case fashion.

Congress has overridden DCC decisions in the past. The earliest decision subjected to this treatment appears to be *Leisy v. Hardin*.[51] There, the Supreme Court struck down an Iowa statute prohibiting the sale of liquor. Professors Rotunda and Nowak explain what happened next:

> Congress hastily responded by enacting the Wilson Act subjecting interstate liquor traffic to the laws of the state into which the liquor was import-

---

> ing the utility of legislation." For example, the Second Circuit applied the balancing test to uphold a New York law requiring special signs, notices on menus, and special containers for imitation cheese products. The district judge had found no health justification for this transparently [special interest] law.

Farber & Hudec, *supra* note 25, at 1415 (quoting Kassel v. Consolidated Freightways, Inc., 450 U.S. 662, 679 (1981) (Brennan, J., concurring), and referencing Grocery Mfrs. of America, Inc. v. Gerace, 755 F.2d 993 (2d Cir. 1985)).

On this view, if Congress chooses to do away with the *Pike* balancing precedent, there should be little disruption of settled expectations.

50. For an argument that this is not as strange as it appears, see Rotunda & Nowak, *supra* note 25, at 55–61.

51. 135 U.S. 100 (1890).

> ed. The Wilson Act was sustained by a unanimous Court in the decision of *Wilkerson v. Rahrer* [140 U.S. 545 (1891)]. The Court explained that the subsequent legislation did not represent Congressional delegation to the states of the federal power to regulate commerce, but rather a legitimate manifestation of Congressional power under the Commerce Clause to authorize an acceptable form of state regulation. Congress enacted a federal law and that law incorporated by reference the various laws of the individual states.[52]

More recently, in *Evansville-Vanderburgh Airport Authority District v. Delta Airlines, Inc.*,[53] the Court rejected a DCC challenge to a $1 service fee collected by a municipal airport from each passenger boarding a commercial flight. In response, Congress passed a statute barring states and localities from levying any "tax, fee, head charge, or other charge" on air travel.[54] And, in a 1987 decision, the Court struck down Pennsylvania statutes imposing lump-sum annual taxes on trucks operating on Pennsylvania highways. In a footnote, the Court noted, "If Congress should disagree with this decision, it would, of course, have the power to authorize flat taxes of this kind."[55] Thus, Congress has the authority to strike down individual DCC decisions in spite of the fact that those decisions purport to be based on the requirements of the Constitution.

A question can be raised, however, about Congress's ability to delimit the DCC on a broader basis than a case-by-case reversal of Supreme Court decisions. The most relevant case on this question is *South-Central Timber Development, Inc. v. Wunnicke*.[56] Writing for the majority, Justice White recognized that Congress has the authority to "redefine" state authority over interstate commerce by permitting states to "regulate the commerce in a manner which would otherwise not be permissible" under the DCC.[57] Justice White warned, however, that "for a state regulation to be removed from the reach of the dormant Commerce Clause, congressional intent must be unmistakably clear."[58] He explained the rationale of this statement by first noting the problem, which we have discussed, of one state's desire to bur-

---

52. ROTUNDA & NOWAK, *supra* note 25, at 12.

53. 405 U.S. 707 (1972).

54. 49 U.S.C. app. § 1513(a) (1988) (as described in American Trucking Ass'ns, Inc. v. Scheiner, 483 U.S. 266, 289 n.23 (1987)).

55. *Id.* In his concurring opinion in American Trucking Ass'ns, Inc. v. Smith, 496 U.S. 167, 202–03 (1990), Justice Scalia cites this footnote for the proposition that "state legislation that would (according to our 'negative' Commerce Clause jurisprudence) violate the Constitution can nonetheless be authorized by a federal statute if Congress 'disagree[s]' with our appraisal of the appropriate role of the States in the relevant field."

56. 467 U.S. 82 (1984).

57. *Id.* at 87.

58. *Id.* at 91.

den the residents of other states with the costs of its regulation. He then observed:

> On the other hand, when Congress acts, all segments of the country are represented and there is significantly less danger that one state will be in a position to exploit others. Furthermore, if a state is in such a position, the decision to allow it is a collective one. A rule requiring a *clear expression* of approval by Congress ensures that there is, in fact, such a collective decision and reduces significantly the risk that unrepresented interests will be adversely affected by restraints on commerce.[59]

The scope of the "clear expression" requirement has not been clearly defined. Professors Rotunda and Nowak read *Wunnicke* as requiring that Congress "state[] in legislative actions that the type of state regulation at issue is approved by Congress or . . . [that] the Court otherwise finds that Congressional intent to allow such state regulations of commerce is 'unmistakably clear.'"[60] But it is apparent that Justice White's opinion is concerned with definiteness rather than scope. For the Court to follow a strict Rotunda and Nowak reading of *Wunnicke* that requires a case-by-case limitation on Congress's ability to approve state regulations would surely be too restrictive a view of Congress's ability, after thoroughly airing the question, to take action to define more narrowly the scope of the DCC. The DCC legislation proposed here, which would end *Pike*-type balancing but retain the core antidiscrimination idea of the DCC case law, would be quite definite, and thus consistent with *Wunnicke*.

Moreover, a statutory DCC should include language that recognizes Congress's continuing power, under the Commerce Clause, to preempt state statutes that initially pass inspection under the newly codified (antidiscrimination only) version of the DCC. This is particularly desirable since "second category" state laws will often be economically unsound, but it is not for the federal judiciary, but rather Congress, to make this policy call.

Why Congress Should Codify the Dormant Commerce Clause

Why should Congress turn its attention to the apparently arcane problems posed by the Dormant Commerce Clause? This article has shown that DCC law is not grounded in a legitimate reading of the Constitution, and has generated confusion in those areas not defined by the simple antidiscrimination rule (as outlined by Justice Scalia in *New Energy*). But these problems with the DCC should not obscure the fact that the nation bene-

59. *Id.* at 92 (emphasis added, footnote omitted).

60. Rotunda & Nowak, *supra* note 25, at 14. *See also id.* at 58–59.

fits enormously from a free and open internal marketplace. My modest proposal is that Congress codify the antidiscrimination provisions of the DCC. By doing this, Congress can retain the benefits of the DCC while giving the courts a statutory basis for maintaining the openness of the American common market. Under well-settled doctrine, courts will dispose of a case on statutory rather than constitutional grounds, where both grounds are present.[61] As a result, the codification of the DCC would allow the courts to begin to decide such cases on statutory grounds, with the result that the preexisting DCC case law would fall into disuse and, if you will, dormancy. This chain of events would have the salutary result of reinforcing the importance of sticking to a textual approach to the Constitution. It would also maintain the openness of the American domestic market.

There are three further reasons for Congress to look at the DCC.

First, the DCC case law is sufficiently unstable to pose a continuing threat to the integrity of constitutional law and to federalism. In 1990, Justice Scalia described the *Pike*-type balancing decisions under the DCC as follows:

> [N]o body of our decisional law has changed as regularly as our [DCC] jurisprudence. Change is almost its natural state, as it is the natural state of legislation in a constantly changing national economy....
>
> Because our [DCC] jurisprudence is inherently unstable, it will repeatedly result in the upsetting of settled expectations.[62]

A good example of the arbitrary threat to state legislation posed by current DCC law can be found in the Supreme Court's decision just last year in *West Lynn Creamery*. At issue was a pricing order promulgated by the Massachusetts Department of Food and Agriculture that imposed an assessment on milk sold by dealers to Massachusetts retailers.[63] Approximately two-thirds of the subject milk was produced by out-of-state dairy farmers. The entire amount collected through this assessment was distributed to Massachusetts dairy farmers as a subsidy.[64] Two out-of-state firms challenged the Massachusetts pricing order as violative of the Commerce Clause. The majority opinion struck down the statute in an opinion that deeply troubled Justice Scalia. In his concurrence, he read the majority opinion as announcing "the sweeping principle that the Constitution is violated by any state law or regulation that 'artificially encourages in-state production even when the same goods can be produced at lower cost in other States.'"[65] Indeed,

---

61. Rescue Army v. Municipal Court, 331 U.S. 549 (1947) (citing Ashwander v. TVA, 297 U.S. 288, 347 (1936) (Brandeis, J., concurring)).

62. *American Trucking Ass'ns*, 496 U.S. at 203.

63. For other DCC cases involving milk regulation, see note 29 *supra*.

64. *Id.* at 2209–10.

65. *Id.* at 2219 (quoting the majority opinion, *id.* at 2211).

as Scalia points out, this idea is repeated a number of times in the majority's opinion, and "calls into question a wide variety of state laws that have hitherto been thought permissible."[66] The majority opinion "expressly... reserve[s] the question of the constitutionality of subsidies for in-state industry,"[67] thus calling into question state legislation never before thought to be in any danger under the DCC. Beyond this, Justice Scalia notes:

> The Court's guiding principle also appears to call into question many other garden-variety state laws heretofore permissible under the negative Commerce Clause. A state law, for example, which requires, contrary to industry practice, the use of recyclable packaging materials, favors local non-exporting producers, who do not have to establish an additional, separate packaging operation for in-state sales.[68]

In short, *West Lynn Creamery*'s break with prior case law provides a sufficient reason for Congress to take up the DCC and its implications for federal-state relations at this time.

The second reason for the new Congress to debate the DCC is that it is relatively more conservative in both houses than its predecessors, making this a propitious time to define the proper scope of the DCC. Questions of federalism, and of the relations between the national government and the states' governments, have come to the fore in a way not seen for many years. The political climate seems to favor a return of significant authority to the states and a distrust of power lodged in Washington. So both the dramatis personae and the political realities of the 104th Congress strongly suggest that Congress can adequately debate and draft a statute that narrows and clarifies the scope of the DCC and, at the same time, removes the DCC as a constitutional embarrassment. The 104th Congress should seize this opportunity.

The third reason for Congress to take up the DCC issue is that debate over codifying the DCC would be filled with references to the virtues of free markets and open competition. These ideas cannot get too much exposure, particularly within the halls of government.

And perhaps a debate over the proper scope of state regulation of business would lead to a new and better appreciation of the superiority of markets over politics not only at the state level, but at the national level as well. By the same token, such a debate might force members of Congress to focus on their limited, enumerated powers in Article I, Section 8 of the Constitution—another useful exercise. There seems to be a groundswell of support for the idea that the federal government should both recognize its limits and

---

66. *Id.*

67. *Id.* (citing *id.* at 2214 & n.15).

68. *Id.*

live by the same rules it imposes on the rest of society—as reflected in the recent passage of the Congressional Accountability Act,[69] for example. If the states were constrained by a new statute not to discriminate against the free flow of interstate commerce, this might help so constrain Congress as well. It would be a wonderful irony indeed if a clearer statement of the Dormant Commerce Clause helped rein in Congress's altogether too cavalier attitude toward its commerce power.

69. Pub. L. No. 104-1, 109 Stat. 3 (1995).

NELSON LUND*

Retroactivity, Institutional Incentives, and the Politics of Civil Rights

Introduction

Our courts and legislatures are fundamentally, if imperfectly, distinguished according to the temporal effects of their decisions. Legislatures declare in general terms what the law shall henceforth be, while courts resolve disputes by declaring the specific effects of preexisting general laws. This distinction is significant primarily because it limits the power of two institutions that jointly bring the coercive power of government to bear on individual citizens.

The authority to impose liability for completed conduct is a dangerous tool in the hands of politically responsive institutions. Accordingly, freedom from ex post facto laws and from bills of attainder were the only individual rights that our original Constitution made good against both the federal and state governments. Conversely, requiring judicial bodies to apply the law retroactively restrains judges from two vices that threaten political liberty: a proclivity to invade the legislature's sphere and a willingness to make the law unstable and unknowable by frequent alterations. Retroactive application of new law typically appears unjust. If courts that itch to improve the world by shaking up the law must do so retroactively, the prospect of committing immediate injustices will inhibit their revolutionary impulses.

The importance of the temporal distinction between judicial and legislative acts is not diminished by the exceptions that have arisen. The Ex Post Facto and Bill of Attainder Clauses, for example, have been applied only to penal legislation. This somewhat questionable interpretation of the

* While serving in the White House as Associate Counsel to the President, the author participated in the process that generated the Civil Rights Act of 1991. For helpful comments on an early draft of this paper, the author is grateful to Roger Clegg, Neal Devins, Mara S. Lund, and John O. McGinnis. Special thanks to Glen D. Nager for many helpful conversations about this paper and the issues discussed in it. Generous financial support was provided through the Law and Economics Center at the George Mason University School of Law.

Constitution, however, has been partially counterbalanced with a judicial presumption against the retroactive application of nonpenal legislation, and with a presumption actually favoring the retroactive application of statutes providing *relief* from penal laws. The unchallenged practice of enacting private relief bills is an exception to the general rule of legislative prospectivity, but it is one whose adverse consequences are generally diffused rather than focused on individual citizens. In this respect, private relief bills resemble the executive power of pardon, which exists to correct the occasional injustice of general laws. On the other side of the divide, the traditional rule of retroactivity for judicial decisions can only inhibit, not thwart, disruptive lurches in judicial lawmaking. Such upheavals, however, almost certainly have been less frequent and violent than they would have been without the traditional rule.

With the explosion of judicial activism in the Warren Court era, the basic distinctions between judicial and legislative acts began to collapse. In a series of constitutional decisions dealing with criminal procedure, the Supreme Court began declaring new laws that were given only prospective effect. This practice soon expanded into the civil arena, and the Court developed a mushy "multifactor" test—of the kind too frequently substituted for intelligible rules of law—that was supposed to determine which judicial decisions would apply retroactively and which would not.[1] During the same period, the Court occasionally began to ignore the presumption that statutes do not operate retroactively unless they expressly so provide, substituting for that principle a declaration that courts should ordinarily apply the law in effect at the time of the judicial decision. Both developments were side effects of the Court's increased willfulness, which often converted constitutional adjudication into a legislative process and statutory interpretation into ad hoc judicial policymaking.

In an important series of recent cases, the Supreme Court has begun to restore the traditional restraints that its own activism had loosened. The move to restore the self-restraining rule of retroactivity for judicial decisions became almost complete in *Harper v. Virginia Department of Taxation*,[2] where the Court announced:

> When this Court applies a rule of federal law to the parties before it, that rule is the controlling interpretation of federal law and must be given full retroactive effect in all cases still open on direct review and as to all events,

1. *See* Chevron Oil Co. v. Huson, 404 U.S. 97 (1971). For a critique of the excessive use of such tests, see Antonin Scalia, *The Rule of Law as a Law of Rules*, 56 U. Chi. L. Rev. 1175 (1989).

2. 113 S. Ct. 2510 (1993).

> regardless of whether such events predate or postdate our announcement of the rule.[3]

Justice Scalia's concurring opinion used characteristically colorful language to explain the significance of the Court's ruling:

> Prospective decisionmaking is the handmaid of judicial activism, and the born enemy of *stare decisis*. It was formulated in the heyday of legal realism and promoted as a "techniqu[e] of judicial lawmaking" in general, and more specifically as a means of making it easier to overrule prior precedent.[4]

The Court's newfound devotion to judicial restraint is not without its costs. The rule of retroactivity may discourage but cannot prevent the Court from making sudden changes in the law. Justice O'Connor showed great concern about this in her *Harper* dissent, which emphasized that such unacknowledged shifts are bound to upset reasonable expectations, sometimes with crushing effect on those ensnared by unanticipated decisions from the Supreme Court. Only time can tell whether the self-restraint encouraged by the revival of the traditional rule will prove real or fictive, and thus whether the costs of restoring that rule will be outweighed by its benefits.

Along with the self-restraint on which the Court has evidently resolved, the Justices also have moved to restrain the legislature by restoring the obstacles that once discouraged retroactive applications of ordinary civil legislation. This article will examine that project, and I want to emphasize at the outset that a different sort of judicial resolve is required here than when the Justices discipline only themselves. Because the Court currently has no constitutional doctrine that places meaningful limits on Congress's power to enact retroactive laws outside the context of penal statutes,[5] its efforts to discourage such laws have to operate through the Court's power of statutory construction. Judicial restraint—if understood in its traditional sense

---

3. *Id.* at 2517. This passage appears to indicate that prospective rules can now be offered only as obiter dicta, unless the Court issues advisory opinions that it deems to have the force of law. The passage also implicitly acknowledges that separate questions are raised by remedial issues and by cases that come before the Court on collateral review. *Cf., e.g., id.* at 2519–20; James B. Beam Distilling Co. v. Georgia, 501 U.S. 529, 543–44 (1991) (opinion of Souter, J.); Teague v. Lane, 489 U.S. 288 (1989).

4. 113 S. Ct. at 2522 (Scalia, J., concurring) (quoting Beryl Levy, *Realist Jurisprudence and Prospective Overruling*, 109 U. PA. L. REV. 1 (1960)).

5. The Supreme Court has said that due process would forbid retroactive statutes only if they are "arbitrary and irrational," or unsupported by a "rational legislative purpose." Usery v. Turner Elkhorn Mining Co., 428 U.S. 1, 15 (1976); Pension Benefit Guaranty Co. v. R.A. Gray & Co., 467 U.S. 717, 730 (1984); United States v. Carlton, 114 S. Ct. 2018, 2022 (1994). The Court recently made a small move in the other direction. *See* Plaut v. Spendthrift Farm, Inc., 115 S. Ct. 1447 (1995).

as the faithful implementation of legislative intent or the ungrudging acceptance of a statute's most likely meaning—might simply require courts to apply standard interpretive techniques to decide whether a given new law was meant to be retroactive or not. The Court's recent approach, however, has exhibited something more like hostility to interpreting statutes to allow retroactive application, and this creates a paradox in the Court's attitudes toward the retroactivity of judicial and legislative decisions.

Judicial hostility to applying statutes retroactively has a political dimension that may bring the courts into conflict with the legislature. The potential for such conflict seemed especially acute in the context of the civil rights cases that gave rise to two recent and important retroactivity cases. That potential conflict may throw light on some otherwise very puzzling aspects of the opinions that the Court issued. In brief, I will suggest that the Court had entered the political arena through its civil rights jurisprudence, and that it eventually drew political heat that might have been avoided had the Court confined itself to a properly judicial role from the beginning. Having once been burned, however, the Court may have become overly sensitive to the threat of political criticism, and that sensitivity may have warped its two recent retroactivity opinions.

Retroactivity Disfavored: *Landgraf* and *Rivers*

In 1990, the Court acknowledged an "apparent tension" within its retroactivity jurisprudence.[6] One group of cases, with an ancient pedigree and recent life, holds that new statutes "will not be construed to have retroactive effect unless their language requires this result."[7] Another strand of decisions, however, follows the principle that "a court is to apply the law in effect at the time it renders its decision, unless doing so would result in manifest injustice or there is statutory direction or legislative history to the contrary."[8] These principles conflict in cases where the statute's meaning with respect to retroactivity is unclear. The Supreme Court recently encountered such a statute in two cases arising from the Civil Rights Act of 1991 (1991 Act or CRA '91).

The 1991 Act consists primarily of amendments to the federal statutes that regulate discrimination in the workplace. Many of its most important provisions overruled a series of Supreme Court decisions that had left certain complaining parties with what Congress considered inadequate pro-

---

6. Kaiser Aluminum & Chem. Corp. v. Bonjorno, 494 U.S. 827, 837 (1990).

7. Bowen v. Georgetown Univ. Hosp., 488 U.S. 204, 208 (1988). *See also*, *e.g.*, United States v. Heth, 7 U.S. (3 Cranch) 399, 408 (1806) (Johnson, J.); *id.* at 414 (Cushing, J.).

8. Bradley v. Richmond Sch. Bd., 416 U.S., 696, 711 (1974).

tection.[9] Among these provisions was an amendment to Section 1981 of Title 42, which protects the right to "make and enforce" contracts free from racial discrimination. The Supreme Court had held, in *Patterson v. McLean Credit Union*,[10] that this statute applies to private employers when they "make or enforce" employment contracts, but that it does not cover other discrimination that may occur after the formation of the contract. The 1991 Act expanded the statute to cover all post-hiring discrimination. The 1991 statute also created other new rights that had not been the subject of any Supreme Court decision. The most important change was to make compensatory and punitive damages, and jury trials, available under Title VII of the Civil Rights Act of 1964, which previously had authorized a more limited set of remedies.[11]

In *Landgraf v. USI Film Products*,[12] the Court considered whether the new damages remedy and the accompanying right to a jury trial are available in Title VII cases that were pending on appeal when the 1991 Act became law.[13] In *Rivers v. Roadway Express, Inc.*,[14] the Court faced the same question with respect to a discriminatory-discharge case under Section 1981. In both cases, the governing statutory language in the 1991 Act provided: "Except as otherwise specifically provided, this Act and the amendments made by this Act shall take effect upon enactment."[15]

This general effective-date language is obviously ambiguous.[16] By votes of 8–1, the Supreme Court held that neither the new provision governing

9. Section 3(4) of the 1991 Act lists one purpose of the statute as "respond[ing] to recent decisions of the Supreme Court by expanding the scope of relevant civil rights statutes in order to provide adequate protection to victims of discrimination." 42 U.S.C. § 1981 note.

10. 491 U.S. 164 (1988).

11. Title VII, which regulates employment discrimination on the basis of race, color, sex, religion, and national origin, had previously offered equitable relief (such as declaratory judgments and injunctions) and monetary awards that usually were limited to attorney fees and two years of back pay. The lower courts had held that jury trials were not available under Title VII.

12. 114 S. Ct. 1483 (1994).

13. The district court had found that the plaintiff in this case had been the victim of unlawful sexual harassment. Because the court found that the harassment was not severe enough to constitute a constructive discharge, it awarded her no relief. The plaintiff's appeal from this judgment was pending when the 1991 Act came into force.

14. 114 S. Ct. 1510 (1994).

15. CRA '91 § 402(a), 42 U.S.C. § 1981 note.

16. It could mean that the rights and remedies created by the affected provisions of the 1991 Act apply only in cases arising from conduct that occurred after the statute's date of enactment. Or it could mean that those rights and remedies apply to all cases that had not come to final judgment prior to the date of enactment. Or it could mean that the applicability of the new provisions should depend on the nature of the right or remedy in question and on the procedural posture of particular cases. Perhaps new substantive rights, for example,

post-hiring discrimination under Section 1981 nor the new Title VII provision establishing a damages remedy and a right to jury trials was applicable to cases arising from conduct that occurred prior to the date of the new statute's enactment. Justice Stevens wrote for a five-Justice majority, while Justice Scalia (joined by Justices Kennedy and Thomas) concurred only in the judgments. Justice Blackmun dissented in both cases.

The majority concluded that cases like these, in which a federal statute might be applied to disputes involving events that took place before the statute was enacted, should be analyzed in two steps. First, the court should ask whether Congress has "expressly prescribed the statute's proper reach."[17] If Congress has not done so, then the court should ask "whether the new provision attaches new legal consequences to events completed before its enactment";[18] or, in an alternative formulation, "whether the new statute would have retroactive effect, *i.e.*, whether it would impair rights a party possessed when he acted, increase a party's liability for past conduct, or impose new duties with respect to transactions already completed."[19] Statutes will not be given such retroactive effect, said the majority, "absent clear congressional intent."[20]

Applying this approach, Justice Stevens argued that the text of the statute was inconclusive. He noted the obvious ambiguity of the relevant effective-date language, and rejected a negative inference that might be drawn from the presence in the statute of two other provisions specifically dictating *prospective* operation in certain cases. Stevens also reviewed the legislative history, in which he found no general agreement on the retroactivity issue: "Instead, the history of the 1991 Act conveys the impression that legislators agreed to disagree about whether and to what extent the Act would apply to preenactment conduct."[21]

Having concluded that Congress did not clearly indicate the temporal reach of the general effective-date provision, Stevens turned to the second step of the analysis. In *Landgraf*, he concluded that application of the new

---

should affect only cases in which the defendant's alleged conduct took place after the date of enactment, while new remedies should be available in all cases pending in the courts on that date. Perhaps new procedural rights, such as the right to jury trial, should be available in all pending cases, or perhaps they should be available only in cases in which the old procedure (such as conducting a bench trial) had not yet been applied. None of these possibilities (or others that one might think of) is either specified or excluded by the statute's language. Nor, given the competing strands of case law summarized above, was the proper interpretation dictated by precedent.

17. *Landgraf*, 114 S. Ct. at 1505.

18. *Id.* at 1499.

19. *Id.* at 1505.

20. *Id.*

21. *Id.* at 1496.

damages remedy to pending cases would be retroactive because it would increase a party's liability for past conduct. For that reason, the remedy should not be available. And, since the 1991 Act makes jury trials available only in cases where damages could be awarded, this new procedural right also should be unavailable. In *Rivers*, Stevens concluded that the amendment to Section 1981 imposed new substantive duties on employers, and therefore should not be applied to preenactment conduct. Rejecting the argument that the amendment should be applied to preenactment conduct because it merely "restored" the law as it was understood by Congress and most lower courts prior to the Supreme Court's 1989 decision in *Patterson*, Stevens invoked the principle that underlies the Court's *judicial* retroactivity decisions: *Patterson* conclusively determined that Section 1981 had never covered post-hiring conduct such as discriminatory discharges. Thus, even when such discrimination had been cognizable under the applicable circuit precedent at the time it occurred (as it had been in *Rivers* itself), Stevens concluded that the presumption against the retroactive application of new statutes should govern.

Justice Stevens presented his analysis as a reaffirmation of the Court's traditional approach to retroactivity. In at least two very important respects, that is exactly what it is. First, the Court demonstrated its willingness to resist inconclusive indications that Congress intends its enactments to have retroactive application. There was considerable evidence in the statute and in its legislative history that the Court could easily have seized on to find a congressional "intent" that the 1991 Act apply retroactively. Second, the Court resisted the appeal of fairness arguments in resolving the cases before it. *Landgraf* was a sexual harassment case in which the defendant's conduct was clearly unlawful when it occurred, but the pre-1991 statute denied the plaintiff any relief.[22] And in *Rivers*, the defendant was accused of conduct that was clearly forbidden under Section 1981 according to the governing precedents that were in place at the time the conduct allegedly occurred. That eight Justices repudiated retroactivity in these circumstances suggests that judicial hostility toward retroactive legislation has once again taken deep root in the Court.[23]

22. The district court found that the harassment was severe enough to violate Title VII, but not so severe as to a constitute constructive discharge. Accordingly, although the plaintiff had quit her job after the harassment began, she had not been terminated in violation of Title VII. This made her ineligible for equitable relief or back pay, and Title VII did not authorize other forms of relief.

23. Justice Blackmun, who has since retired, argued in dissent that the "most natural" reading of the statute supported its retroactive application, and that there would in any event be "nothing unjust" about such application.

This might seem to be the end of the story were it not for Justice Scalia's sharply worded opinion concurring only in the judgments.[24] Scalia objected to the majority's approach on three grounds. First, he argued that the traditional rule forbids retroactive application of civil statutes unless the *language* of the statute requires such an application. Stevens' analysis of the 1991 Act's legislative history, which Scalia pointedly characterized as dicta, effectively replaced this simple clear-statement rule with a less disciplined inquiry into legislative intent.

Second, Scalia objected to Stevens' decision to distinguish, and to that extent reaffirm, two prior cases in which the Court had invoked the rule that courts should ordinarily apply the law in effect at the time of the decision. While claiming to "see nothing to be gained by overruling" these two cases, Scalia argued that at least one of them is indefensible.[25]

Finally, in what Scalia regarded as his most significant criticism, he argued that the majority was wrong to define retroactivity by reference to changes in the rights, duties, or liabilities of affected parties. According to Scalia, courts should begin instead by asking what conduct is being regulated by the new statute, and then locate the relevant "retroactivity event" by reference to the purpose of the regulation. Under this approach, a statute imposing new substantive obligations (like the 1991 Act's amendment to Section 1981) would be considered retroactive if applied to conduct predating the statute's enactment. A statute establishing a new rule of evidence, however, regulates the conduct of trials; it would therefore be considered retroactive only if applied to evidence previously admitted or excluded from a trial.

Justice Stevens did not answer Scalia's criticisms directly. This is surprising because recent fashion on the Court has been different. Indeed, the "battles of the footnotes," in which the Justices provide responses and counterresponses to one another's arguments, have become so frequent and intense that some observers have begun to find them tiresome and even unhealthy. As I will try to show, there are plausible reasons that could support the majority's refusal to accept Scalia's position in these cases. Those reasons, however, are political rather than legal in nature. A politically sensitive Court might find such reasons compelling, but for political reasons would not offer them as the basis for decision.

The Legal Dispute between Stevens and Scalia

It would be reckless to advance a political interpretation of a judicial opinion if its legal analysis were otherwise sufficient to explain it. The dispute

24. 114 S. Ct. at 1522.
25. *Id.* at 1523.

between Stevens and Scalia in *Landgraf* and *Rivers*, however, is difficult to explain in purely legal terms.

As is often the case with separate writings, Scalia's concurring opinion in *Landgraf* and *Rivers* offers a more intellectually elegant approach than the majority's. This is perhaps most obvious, and most easily explainable, in Scalia's preference for a clear-statement rule over Stevens' more elaborate investigation of legislative intent. In one sense, this is merely the latest episode in a long-running dispute within the Court (in which Scalia and Stevens have been the most frequent contending spokesmen) about the proper use of legislative history. Scalia's textualist approach to statutory interpretation rarely allows legislative history even to be consulted, while Stevens believes that such extrinsic evidence may sometimes override even the language of the statute.[26] In this case, however, their disagreement goes further. Unlike the majority, Scalia refused to entertain the use of hoary linguistic canons like *expressio unius est exclusio alterius* or the rule that courts should strive to give effect to every provision of a statute: for Scalia, the text must specify retroactive application expressly, or perhaps by *unavoidable* implication.

Scalia justifies his position by citing precedent, and Stevens' opinion is notably devoid of competing citations on this point. The most obvious effect of the majority's apparently novel approach is to weaken the presumption against the retroactive application of statutes. If that presumption can be overcome by ordinary techniques of statutory interpretation (such as evidence from legislative history or the application of canons like *expressio unius*), it runs the risk of becoming just one of several factors that courts can manipulate virtually at will. A clear-statement rule, by way of contrast, would impose much more stringent restraints on the courts' interpretive activity.

No less important, however, Scalia's clear-statement rule would make it more difficult for Congress to effect retroactive application of new statutes. It would, for example, reduce the likelihood of inadvertently retroactive statutes, which can easily result when courts draw negative inferences from statutory language.[27] It would also prevent minority factions from unilaterally inserting retroactive features into statutes through interpretive comments in committee reports and floor statements. Thus, Scalia's approach would be more efficacious than the majority's approach in preventing the retroactive application of statutes. Even apart from the fact that his approach would be easier to apply consistently and would apparently be more faith-

26. *See, e.g.*, INS v. Cardoza-Fonseca, 480 U.S. 421, 432 n.12 (1987) (Stevens, J.); *id.* at 452–55 (Scalia, J., concurring).

27. As Stevens mentioned, there is evidence suggesting that the framers of the 1991 Act gave little attention to the interplay among its several "effective date" provisions. 114 S. Ct. at 1494 & n.11.

ful to the Court's precedents, this is what we might expect from a Justice who previously has expressed his strong distaste for retroactive statutes.[28]

Scalia's second criticism of the majority opinion is more difficult to understand, for it consists of a persuasive objection softened by an unexplained concession. Stevens went to some lengths to reconcile the presumption against retroactivity with *Bradley v. Richmond School Board*[29] and *Thorpe v. Housing Authority*[30]—in which the Court presumed that the law in effect at the time of decision should govern. Scalia criticized Stevens' effort on the ground that it obscured both the novelty of the principle supposedly represented by *Bradley* and *Thorpe* and their "erroneous[ness]." What makes Scalia's own criticism somewhat obscure is his statement that "I see nothing to be gained by overruling" those two cases.[31] Calling *Thorpe*, at least, "really indefensible,"[32] Scalia makes no effort to explain how he could apply his own clear-statement approach without overruling it, whether expressly or sub silentio.[33]

Scalia's failure to demand that *Thorpe* be overruled is puzzling, but the majority's approach is dissembling. At issue in *Thorpe* was a federal directive requiring a local housing authority to provide notice and an opportunity to respond before evicting tenants accused of violating the terms of their leases. *Thorpe* held that this directive was applicable to an eviction proceeding that had been instituted (and upheld by all three levels of the state-court system) before the directive was issued.[34] Under Scalia's approach, *Thorpe*'s application of the directive to invalidate the eviction was, as he

28. *See* Kaiser Aluminum & Chem. Corp. v. Bonjorno, 494 U.S. 827, 855 (1990) (Scalia, J., concurring):

> [A]s an original matter there is nothing to be said for a presumption of retroactivity.... It is contrary to fundamental notions of justice, and thus contrary to realistic assessment of probable legislative intent. The principle that the legal effect of conduct should ordinarily be assessed under the law that existed when the conduct took place has timeless and universal human appeal.

29. 416 U.S. 696 (1974).

30. 393 U.S. 268 (1969).

31. 114 S. Ct. at 1523.

32. *Id.*

33. Scalia may have meant to imply that the holdings in *Thorpe* and *Bradley* could be characterized as rulings that were confined to the particular statutes applied in those cases. If that in turn implies that it would be pointless to overrule the decisions because retroactivity questions could not arise decades after the statutes were enacted, it would also seem to imply the *impossibility* of overruling them in a case arising under a different statute. Scalia, however, clearly implies that overruling *Thorpe* and *Bradley* was an option that could have been exercised in *Landgraf* or *Rivers*.

34. At the time the directive was issued, a constitutional challenge to the eviction was pending before the U.S. Supreme Court on writ of certiorari. 393 U.S. at 272.

says, "plainly retroactive and was wrong."[35] *Thorpe* was just as clearly wrong under the majority's approach, however, for it "impair[ed] rights a party possessed when [it] acted,"[36] and there was no suggestion of a legislative intent to authorize such retroactive effects.

Justice Stevens sought to avoid this conclusion by likening the directive in *Thorpe* to three kinds of cases that traditionally have not been subjected to the presumption against retroactive operation. First, he invoked decisions in which prospective relief (such as an injunction) has been ordered although such relief would not have been available at the time of the transaction giving rise to the litigation. Stevens rested this analogy on the fact that the plaintiff in *Thorpe* had not yet been physically evicted when the federal directive issued. The analogy, however, is fatally and obviously flawed. The federal directive in *Thorpe* did not merely offer a new kind of relief for an act that was illegal when it occurred. On the contrary, the *Thorpe* Court held that the local housing authority was required to comply with prerequisites to eviction that had not been imposed until after the authority ordered the eviction at issue in the case.

Stevens also compared *Thorpe* to cases in which new trial procedures have been used even though they would not have been authorized at the time of the underlying events. Here again, however, the analogy fails, and for the same reason as before: *Thorpe* involved the applicability of *pre-eviction* procedures, not procedures applicable to some sort of later hearing on the validity of an eviction.

Finally, Stevens contended that *Thorpe* is somehow in the tradition that gives retroactive effect to repeals of criminal statutes because the "government should accord grace to private parties disadvantaged by an old rule when it adopts a new and more generous one."[37] This is absurd. Apart from the fact that *Thorpe* bears no resemblance to a criminal case, the presumption of retroactive repeal for criminal statutes applies when a legislature repeals its *own* statute. The federal directive in *Thorpe* did not repeal any prior federal rule, and the party disadvantaged by the new directive was the local housing agency rather than the tenant whom the agency sought to evict.

Scalia's third, and in his view most serious, criticism of the majority involves the definition of retroactivity itself. Stevens' test—which asks whether application of a new statute would impair existing rights, increase liability for past conduct, or impose new duties with respect to completed events—focuses attention on the untoward effects of retroactive statutes on the individuals whose conduct is regulated. It thus takes a kind of "citizen's eye" view of the evils of retroactivity. Scalia's approach adopts a perspective clos-

35. 114 S. Ct. at 1523.
36. *Id.* at 1505.
37. *Id.* at 1503 n.30.

er to the legislature's. By asking what conduct the statute seeks to regulate, and defining retroactivity according to the imputed purpose of the statute, Scalia's approach seems more prone to upsetting citizens' legitimate expectations.

The difference can be illustrated by the one example of a "hard case" that Scalia offers, namely *Bradley*. In that case, the Court awarded attorney fees pursuant to a statute enacted while the underlying case was on appeal. A new attorney fee statute might be meant to discourage certain conduct by making litigation more likely and more expensive for the defendant. If so, then Scalia would find that applying the statute in a case arising from preenactment conduct was retroactive. If, however, the fee statute's purpose is to encourage certain suits, its application would be retroactive only in suits filed before the date of enactment. Or, if the statute's purpose is to facilitate litigation, its application would be retroactive only in suits terminated before enactment. Scalia, who would be very reluctant to consult legislative history, never explains how he would determine which of these was the purpose of the statute. Nor does he explain what the courts should do in the frequent cases where a statute reasonably could be thought to have several different purposes. Nor does he explain how the *possibility* that Congress had a purpose other than to deter certain conduct could be enough to justify imposing attorney fees for preenactment conduct. These defects in Scalia's analysis are much more serious than he suggests when he acknowledges that there may be an occasional hard case.

The majority's analysis of *Bradley* is defective in a different way. Under Stevens' approach, *Bradley* should be no more difficult than *Landgraf* itself. Fee awards, like the damages at issue in *Landgraf*, "increase a party's liability for past conduct."[38] Because fee awards cannot be regarded as a de minimis increase in liability, they must therefore be retroactive if applied in a case involving preenactment conduct. Stevens, however, does not analyze *Bradley* this way. On the contrary, his opinion expressly reaffirms the *Bradley* decision, which applied an attorney fee statute to a case that arose prior to its enactment. The reasons given for this reaffirmation, moreover, are mystifying. Stevens first says that attorney fee determinations are "collateral to the main cause of action,"[39] which may be true but does not alter the fact that they increase a party's liability for past conduct. Stevens then remarks that attorney fees most likely would have been available in *Bradley* under equitable principles even if the new statute had not been applied. This may also be true, and it may mean that applying the new statute did not actually increase the affected party's liability. But it cannot justify the *Bradley*

38. *Id.* at 1505.

39. *Id.* at 1503 (quoting White v. New Hampshire Dep't of Employment Sec., 455 U.S. 445, 451–52 (1982)).

Court's decision to apply the new statute rather than simply allowing the claimant to receive whatever fees were available under equitable principles.

Bradley is not the only precedent with which Stevens' approach runs into difficulty. As Scalia points out, Stevens does not reconcile his approach with the established practice of giving immediate effect to statutes altering a court's jurisdiction. Such statutes certainly can be retroactive in Stevens' sense of the term since they can attach new legal consequences to preenactment events. Stevens' comment that new jurisdictional rules "usually" leave substantive rights unchanged by sending litigants to a different tribunal is patently irrelevant because "usually" is not the same as "always." Stevens might have tried to reconcile his own approach with these prior decisions,[40] and he certainly could have argued that his approach is in general more consistent than Scalia's with the reasoning in prior retroactivity cases.[41] But Stevens made no such arguments. In the end, his response to Scalia seems to be that "retroactivity is a matter on which judges tend to have 'sound... instincts,' and familiar considerations of fair notice, reasonable reliance, and settled expectations offer sound guidance."[42] This conclusion, along with Stevens' failure to respond to Scalia's criticisms, suggests that the majority is not proceeding solely on the basis of a legal theory of retroactivity, whether derived from precedent or from first principles. What remains unclear is what else may be driving the majority.

Scalia's approach, though superficially more consistent with the results in prior cases, has its own internal tensions. The clear-statement prong of his approach would raise the costs of enacting retroactive legislation, and thereby discourage it. Scalia's test for whether a statute has retroactive effect, however, points toward fidelity to legislative purpose and away from what Stevens correctly sees as the underlying threat to the affected citizen. Though not strictly incompatible, these somewhat conflicting tendencies in Scalia's approach are mirrors of the conflict in Stevens' approach, where we find a kind of deference to the legislature softening the traditional clear-statement

40. Cases in which the Court has held that statutes abolishing jurisdiction apply to pending cases were typically decided on the theory that the exercise of judicial power by a court is completely dependent on the existence of a currently operative statutory grant of authority. Congressional intent or expectations have been found irrelevant, which suggests that the theory is rooted in separation of powers principles. *See, e.g.*, Bruner v. United States, 343 U.S. 112, 116–17 (1952); *Ex parte* McCardle, 74 U.S. (7 Wall.) 506, 514 (1869). Under this interpretation of the cases, they would simply stand for the unremarkable proposition that constitutional principles trump the interpretive presumptions that are used in construing ambiguous statutes.

41. Scalia's "retroactivity event" theory apparently had never been articulated before his concurring opinion in these cases.

42. 114 S. Ct. at 1499 (quoting Danforth v. Groten Water Co., 178 Mass. 472, 476 (1901) (Holmes, J.)).

rule, while the test for retroactivity seems to give greater weight to the perspective of those affected by new laws than to the legislature's purpose in adopting them.

The key to understanding these underlying tensions may lie in Justice Scalia's remark that he saw "nothing to be gained by overruling" *Thorpe* and *Bradley*. This is a startling statement because he offers no hint that either his approach or the majority's could honestly be reconciled with *Thorpe* (though he thinks it might be possible to reach the result in *Bradley* under his own approach). Was there something to be lost by overruling those cases, which both the majority and concurring Justices recognized might be significant? What might that be?

I suggest that overruling *Thorpe* or *Bradley* would have heightened the possibility of a congressional reaction against the Court's decisions in *Landgraf* and *Rivers*, and that all eight Justices who voted for the results in those cases may have wanted to avoid that outcome. Those who joined Stevens' opinion, moreover, could have believed it necessary to exercise even more caution than Scalia displayed. To see why these suggestions could account for the otherwise curious features in these opinions, it will be necessary to review in more detail the background to the 1991 Act.

The Supreme Court and the Politics of Civil Rights: 1971–1991

The legislative process that generated the 1991 Act was triggered by seven Supreme Court decisions in 1989, six of which involved interpretations of federal statutes dealing with employment discrimination.[43] The initial proposal, a bill sponsored by Senator Edward M. Kennedy and Representative Augustus F. Hawkins, would have overruled each of the six statutory decisions and made a number of other significant legal changes as well. One striking feature of the Kennedy-Hawkins bill was that it specifically and expressly provided a radical form of retroactivity for the provisions that were aimed at undoing the six decisions from 1989: these provisions were to take effect as of the dates of the various Supreme Court decisions, even though this would have required actually reopening final judgments in some cases.

Although Congress frequently responds to judicial decisions by amending the law so as to overrule them, it very seldom adopts the kind of radical retroactivity provisions that were included in the Kennedy-Hawkins

43. The seventh decision held that some racial quotas in the awarding of government contracts are unconstitutional. City of Richmond v. J.A. Croson Co., 488 U.S. 469 (1989).

bill.[44] This extraordinary slap at the Court was consistent with the overall rhetorical strategy that was employed to push the legislation forward. Many of the matters dealt with in the 1989 cases, and therefore in the Kennedy-Hawkins bill, were highly technical in nature. Faced with the difficult and perhaps hopeless task of winning a public debate about the merits of the matters dealt with in the bill, its supporters mounted an aggressive assault on the Court itself. The Justices were accused of having turned back the clock by overruling decades of settled law—Kennedy-Hawkins, it was said, must be enacted in order to restore the status quo that had existed before the Supreme Court's outrageous burst of reactionary zeal. The executive director of the NAACP, for example, said:

> It is ironic that . . . we find ourselves marching once more to protest the legal lynching of black America's hope for a chance to become full partners in the American dream. The five justices who voted on four separate occasions to roll back the clock on civil rights, by their actions, have unraveled the ropes used by black Americans to climb out of the valleys of economic segregation.[45]

With respect to the 1989 decisions, this political rhetoric was mere political rhetoric. Five of those decisions resolved issues that were ques-

---

44. The Supreme Court recently held that federal statutes requiring courts to reopen final judgments are unconstitutional because they infringe on the judiciary's power to issue conclusive rulings. Plaut v. Spendthrift Farm, Inc., 115 S. Ct. 1447 (1995). This holding, which the Court's precedents did not make easily foreseeable, came in response to a 1991 statute that the Court believed was the first of its kind in the nation's history. Had the 1990 Kennedy-Hawkins bill been enacted in its original form, it would therefore apparently have been without precedent.

45. *Marchers Protest 'Legal Lynching'; NAACP Urges Lawmakers: Counter 4 Top Court Rulings*, CHICAGO TRIB., Aug. 27, 1989, at 1 (quoting Benjamin Hooks). *See also, e.g.*, A. Dahleen Glanton, *PUSH Sends Message on Rights to Bush*, CHICAGO TRIB., June 28, 1989, at 1 (civil rights leader Jesse Jackson "told reporters that the Supreme Court decisions are similar to the position Chinese officials have taken toward those who are fighting for democracy in Beijing"); Reuters News Service, *NAACP to Stage August "Silent March" to Protest Court Rulings*, July 14, 1989 ("'We're not going to let four men and a woman in black robes turn us around, any more than we'll let white robes turn us around,' [NAACP executive director Benjamin] Hooks told the closing session of the NAACP's annual convention . . ."); 136 CONG. REC. S1018–19 (daily ed. Feb. 7, 1990) (remarks of Sen. Kennedy describing the Supreme Court's "abrupt and unfortunate departure from its historic vigilance in protecting civil rights"); S. REP. NO. 315, 101st Cong., 2d Sess. 10–11 (1990) (quoting witnesses who testified that the 1989 Supreme Court decisions "threatened the vitality and enforceability of federal equal employment laws"; constituted "an enormous step backwards"; and caused victims of discrimination to "feel that the clock is being turned back"); 136 CONG. REC. S15,327 (daily ed. Oct. 16, 1990) (remarks of Sen. Kennedy characterizing Kennedy-Hawkins as "legislation to respond to an unfortunate series of recent Supreme Court decisions which have significantly undermined the Nation's civil rights laws banning job discrimination").

tions of first impression in the Supreme Court, and each of the statutory provisions involved had been given conflicting interpretations by various courts of appeals.[46] In one case, moreover, the Supreme Court expressly reaffirmed a particularly outlandish precedent solely on grounds of stare decisis.[47] The sixth decision, a case known as *Wards Cove*,[48] was a little different, and it deserves more attention because it caused the most controversy during the ensuing legislative battle.

Wards Cove was the latest in a long series of cases dealing with the "disparate impact" theory of discrimination under Title VII of the Civil Rights Act of 1964. This theory was created in *Griggs v. Duke Power Co.*,[49] a unanimous 1971 decision holding that employment criteria associated with "underrepresentation" of minorities in a company's workforce can be unlawful even if the employer has not intentionally discriminated against anyone. The disparate impact theory adopted in *Griggs* had no basis in the law, and in fact was incompatible with the statute. Chief Justice Burger's opinion flouted the text of Title VII,[50] distorted and misrepresented the legislative history,[51] and even went so far as to misstate the factual findings of the district court in the *Griggs* case itself.[52]

Apart from being a legislative rather than a judicial exercise, the legislative draftsmanship in the *Griggs* opinion was utterly incompetent. Burger declared that statistical disparities could lead to liability, but he offered no

46. Patterson v. McLean Credit Union, 491 U.S. 164 (1989); Martin v. Wilks, 490 U.S. 755 (1989); Lorance v. AT&T Technologies, Inc., 490 U.S. 900 (1989); Price Waterhouse v. Hopkins, 490 U.S. 228 (1989); Independent Fed'n of Flight Attendants v. Zipes, 491 U.S. 754 (1989).

47. *See* Patterson v. McLean Credit Union, 491 U.S. 164 (1989) (reaffirming Runyon v. McCrary, 427 U.S. 160 (1976)).

48. Wards Cove Packing Co. v. Atonio, 490 U.S. 642 (1989).

49. 401 U.S. 424 (1971).

50. Title VII forbids employers to discriminate against any individual "because of such individual's race, color, religion, sex, or national origin." It is not completely inconceivable that this language could encompass race-neutral practices that have unintended adverse effects on certain racial groups. If that is what the language means, however, the statute must prohibit all such practices that are not covered by one of Title VII's limited exceptions. Burger's opinion in *Griggs* created an exception that cannot be found anywhere in the statute.

51. Burger's mangling of the legislative history of Title VII is discussed in Michael E. Gold, Griggs' *Folly: An Essay on the Theory, Problems, and Origin of the Adverse Impact Definition of Employment Discrimination and a Recommendation for Reform*, 7 INDUS. REL. L.J. 429 (1985).

52. Although the defendant in *Griggs* was held liable for unintentionally discriminating against blacks, Burger's opinion was written in a way that creates the impression that the company had unclean hands. That impression is created largely by several factual assertions that are inconsistent with the factual findings of the district court.

intelligible test either for deciding what statistical comparisons should be used or for deciding how large the disparities must be. Burger's opinion also created a legal defense that employers could use to justify disparities that would otherwise produce liability, but he offered no less than eight different and conflicting formulations of the standard that employment criteria must meet. The hopeless ambiguities and vagueness of *Griggs* launched the Court on a long and difficult search for a manageable set of standards through which the new disparate impact theory could be implemented.

In 1979, the Court decided two cases that would prove to have especially important consequences. In *New York City Transit Authority v. Beazer*,[53] the Court considered a challenge to the Transit Authority's rule against employing methadone users. Although dubious about the plaintiffs' claim that this rule had a strongly disproportionate effect on minority job seekers, the Court held that an employer cannot in any event be liable, no matter what statistical disparities result from its employment criteria, so long as those criteria are "job related."[54] This "job related" standard was extremely generous to employers, for it required only that legitimate employment goals such as safety and efficiency be "significantly served by—even if they do not require" the challenged employment criteria.[55] After *Beazer*, it should have been virtually impossible for a plaintiff to prevail under a disparate impact theory unless the defendant had adopted inexplicably whimsical employment policies.

Perhaps in tribute to the confusion and uncertainty that *Griggs* and other pre-*Beazer* decisions had produced, *Beazer*'s clear holding was frequently ignored by the lower courts. Another 1979 decision, however, got a much

53. 440 U.S. 568 (1979).

54. Although Justice Stevens' opinion belittled the plaintiffs' proof of disparate impact, Justice White's dissent convincingly refuted the majority's argument. Perhaps recognizing the weakness of its position, the majority did not hold the proof inadequate: "At best, [plaintiffs'] statistical showing is weak; even if it is capable of establishing a prima facie case of discrimination, it is assuredly rebutted by [the Transit Authority's] demonstration that its narcotics rule (and the rule's application to methadone users) is 'job related.'" *Id.* at 587 (footnote omitted). The *Beazer* holding is therefore based on the "job related" test, not on the standard governing the prima facie case.

55. *Id.* at 587 n.31. Since the goal of efficiency can cover almost anything, only the most palpably arbitrary employment practices could flunk this test, as *Beazer* itself illustrated. Methadone's effects are to suppress the symptoms of heroin withdrawal and to prevent heroin-induced euphoria, which together make it useful in treating heroin addiction. Despite the drug's salutary effects on the user's behavior, however, the *Beazer* Court held that methadone users could be excluded both from safety-sensitive jobs like driving subway trains *and* from such menial jobs, in which safety was not an issue, as cleaning out buses. *See id.*; *id.* at 576 n.12. *Beazer* therefore cannot be limited to cases where public safety is an issue.

warmer reception. In *United Steelworkers v. Weber*,[56] the Court held that employers were free to use discriminatory racial quotas in order "to eliminate conspicuous racial imbalance in traditionally segregated job categories."[57] As Justice Brennan's majority opinion acknowledged, this decision is impossible to reconcile with the operative text of the statute.[58] And, as Justice Rehnquist's dissent demonstrated in massive detail, it is equally impossible to reconcile with the remainder of the statute or with the legislative history, which contains numerous repudiations of Brennan's theory without providing a single word to support it.

Ignoring Rehnquist's unanswerable critique, the *Weber* majority amended Title VII by fiat. This legislative act, which resembled *Griggs* in its arrogance and dishonesty, also had a deeper connection with *Griggs*. As Justice Blackmun observed in his insightful concurring opinion, employers that used race-neutral hiring criteria (as the *Weber* defendant did before it adopted the challenged racial quota) thereby exposed themselves to liability if such criteria had a disparate impact on minorities. Unless employers were allowed to get their numbers "right" by discriminating against whites, they would be placed in a Catch-22: vulnerable to lawsuits brought by minorities if race-neutral criteria led to disparate effects and liable to whites if they sought to avoid such suits by instituting preferential policies.

By ensuring that this Catch-22 need not arise, *Weber* removed the most likely cause of a congressional attack on *Griggs*. Employers were provided with a comparatively cheap way to avoid liability under the disparate impact theory. This was particularly important for very large employers, who are both the most well-organized politically and the most inviting targets of disparate impact suits.[59] *Weber* also helps these employers satisfy the demands by federal bureaucrats, the press, and organized civil rights lobbies for increased hiring of minorities. Compared with this impressive political coalition, the direct victims of the *Griggs* and *Weber* decisions are only those individuals denied jobs or promotions by employers bent on achieving the approved balance in their workforces. These individuals are, as Justice Scalia would later say, "predominantly unknown, unaffluent, unorganized."[60]

56. 443 U.S. 193 (1979).

57. *Id.* at 209. The Court also said that the devices used to discriminate against whites must not "unnecessarily" trammel their interests. *Id.* at 208.

58. *Id.* at 201–02

59. The rules that eventually evolved in post-*Griggs* cases for establishing the existence of a disparate impact require that disparities be established through relatively large data sets, and it is often quite expensive to collect and analyze the requisite data. And because damages have never been available in such suits, the principal form of relief is a change in the employer's future practices. Thus, large employers can ordinarily be attacked more easily, and injunctive relief granted against them will affect greater numbers of people.

60. Johnson v. Transportation Agency, 480 U.S. 616, 677 (1987) (Scalia, J., dissenting).

The *Griggs* and *Weber* amendments to Title VII could not have been enacted in 1964. They probably could not have been enacted by Congress in later years either, for doing so would have required legislators, at least in the case of *Weber*, to go on record in favor of legalizing discrimination.[61] A vote in favor of employment discrimination would have been difficult for many legislators to defend, and would have provided ammunition for opponents in future campaigns. A vote against the *Griggs* and *Weber* policies, however, would surely have triggered a fierce reaction from the interest groups described above. Thus, once the Court took the initiative, Congress had little incentive to upset the status quo.

In 1988, a somewhat more conservative Court was presented with an opportunity to revisit the *Griggs* doctrine. Until that time, all of the Supreme Court cases dealing with disparate impact had involved objective employment criteria like diploma requirements and written tests. In *Watson v. Fort Worth Bank & Trust*,[62] the Court undertook to resolve a conflict among the lower courts on the applicability of the doctrine to subjective employment practices, such as arrangements under which decisions to hire and promote are left to the unguided discretion of individual supervisors. Writing for a unanimous eight-member Court, Justice O'Connor concluded that disparate impact analysis should be extended to cover such subjective employment practices.

This extension of the doctrine was instituted without a meaningful review of the validity of the disparate impact theory itself.[63] O'Connor did, how-

61. Approving statements about *Griggs* can be found in the legislative history of the 1972 amendments to Title VII, but Congress did not enact the sentiments expressed by some of its members in these statements. The depth of the congressional aversion to addressing the *Weber* issue became clear during the debates in 1990 and 1991. Despite endless discussions about the connection between disparate impact analysis and quotas, there was practically a conspiracy of silence about the preferential policies authorized by *Weber*. When the Counsel to the President circulated a document raising that issue at the very end of the legislative process in 1991, the mainstream press went into a frenzy and President Bush responded by repudiating any opposition to affirmative action. *See, e.g.*, Ann Devroy, *President Signs Civil Rights Bill: White House Disavows Proposed Directive to End Affirmative Action*, WASH. POST, Nov. 22, 1991, at A1; James Gerstenzang, *Bush Drops Repeal of Anti-Bias Rules: Rights Bill is Signed after Fierce Protests Halt a Plan to Scuttle Guidelines Authorizing Affirmative Action: Incident Is Seen as Exacerbating Racial Tensions*, L.A. TIMES, Nov. 22, 1991, at A1.

62. 487 U.S. 977 (1988).

63. In the course of her opinion for the Court, Justice O'Connor suggested for the first time in the Court's history how disparate impact doctrine might be compatible with the statute. Subjective employment practices, she pointed out, may in some cases be infected with "subconscious stereotypes and prejudices." Discrimination based on such prejudices is clearly covered by Title VII, which forbids discrimination "because of [an] individual's race, color, religion, sex, or national origin." Conventional analysis, however, under which plaintiffs are

ever, recognize that the Court's decision could very well lead to enormous new pressures for employers to adopt surreptitious quota systems.[64] In a portion of her opinion representing the views of a four-Justice plurality, she contended that this result would not occur because the law provides employers with ample means to avoid liability when legitimate employment practices are challenged. O'Connor supported this conclusion by pointing to three principal features of disparate impact doctrine.

First, a plaintiff is required to identify specifically the practice that causes a disparate impact. This principle, which had never been challenged even by implication in any of the Court's previous opinions, is important because it helps to prevent employers from being held liable for statistical disparities caused by factors beyond their control.[65] Second, O'Connor reaffirmed the principle adopted in *Beazer*, under which a practice that has a disparate impact is nonetheless permissible if it is based on a legitimate business reason.[66] This was a straightforward reaffirmation of the *Beazer* holding, which in turn was consistent with the language in *Griggs* that had always been accepted as its holding by the Court: a practice is permissible if it has a "manifest relationship to the employment in question." O'Connor was therefore fully justified in insisting that *Beazer* meant what it said and that *Beazer* was the law. Third, O'Connor resolved an ambiguity in prior law by declaring that defendants seeking to show that their practices were based on legitimate reasons need only meet a burden-of-production standard, so that the ultimate burden of persuasion remains with the plaintiff at all times. This was not the most natural reading of the prior cases, and the plurality's willingness to insist on the interpretation more favorable to defendants thus suggested a profound discomfort with disparate impact theory itself.

---

required to prove intentional discrimination, can easily overlook people who are acting on the basis of prejudices that they are aware of only dimly, if at all. O'Connor mentioned this argument, but she declined to pursue its implications. And it is easy to see why. Her theory provided virtually no support for the Court's previous disparate impact decisions, all of which involved objective employment criteria. In fact, it suggests that those decisions actually may have *undermined* the goal of the statute by encouraging employers to replace objective criteria with the kind of subjective criteria that create opportunities for the operation of subconscious prejudices. Inducing employers to shift away from objective tests will, ceteris paribus, almost certainly increase the incidence of illegal discrimination.

64. *See, e.g.*, 487 U.S. at 993 (plurality portion of opinion).

65. The principle is also consistent with Connecticut v. Teal, 457 U.S. 440 (1982), in which the Court held that employers cannot justify the use, as part of a multistage selection process, of a test that has a disparate impact on minorities by including "compensating" components at later points in the process. Thus, even though a multistage selection process has no adverse impact on a minority group, it can violate Title VII if an identifiable part of the process does have such an impact.

66. 487 U.S. at 998.

A year later, by a 5–4 vote, the Court adopted O'Connor's approach in the *Wards Cove* case.[67] Although the burden-of-proof issue was the only respect in which the Court could reasonably be thought to have overruled its previous jurisprudence, *Wards Cove* was immediately caricatured as a dangerous exercise in judicial activism. The Kennedy-Hawkins bill then purported to "restore" prior law by codifying a *truly* radical new approach to disparate impact.

Under Kennedy-Hawkins, plaintiffs could challenge any group of employment practices that results in a disparate impact, without demonstrating which of those practices (if any) caused the disparate impact. There is no case in which the Supreme Court had allowed such a challenge. And, in addition to placing the burden of persuasion on defendants who were faced with the need to justify practices that had a disparate impact, Kennedy-Hawkins redefined the substantive standard that employers must meet. In place of the *Beazer-Watson-Wards Cove* criterion—whether legitimate employment goals are served by the challenged practice—Kennedy-Hawkins adopted a requirement that the challenged practice be "essential to effective job performance." The Supreme Court had never adopted this standard.[68] On the contrary, the Court's pre-*Beazer* descriptions had consistently used the vague and broad phrase "manifest relationship to the employment in question." On its face, of course, this formulation is quite consistent with the *Beazer* and *Wards Cove* language, and utterly different from the Kennedy-Hawkins substitute.

Kennedy-Hawkins might have been swept into law under the banner of "restoring the law," except that the Bush administration was strongly opposed. Defending the Supreme Court's analysis, according to which disparate impact doctrine could easily induce employers to violate Title VII by adopting surreptitious quotas, the administration argued that Kennedy-Hawkins was a "quota bill." The bulk of the Washington business lobby, which objected primarily to provisions in the bill making compensatory and punitive damages available under Title VII, formed a tactical alliance with the Bush administration in opposition to Kennedy-Hawkins.

Although the administration objected to many features in the bill, including its retroactivity provisions,[69] the ensuing debate focused overwhelmingly

67. Justice Kennedy, who was appointed after *Watson* was argued, joined the four-Justice *Watson* plurality to create a majority in *Wards Cove*.

68. The phrase "essential to effective job performance" can be found in Dothard v. Rawlinson, 433 U.S. 321, 331 (1977), where the Court was merely reporting how the *defendant* characterized the challenged practice.

69. When he vetoed the Kennedy-Hawkins bill in 1990, President Bush denounced its "unfair retroactivity rules." *See* Message to the Senate Returning Without Approval the Civil Rights Act of 1990, 26 WEEKLY COMP. PRES. DOC. 1632 (Oct. 22, 1990). A more detailed

on disparate impact. That debate, which was extraordinarily bitter, dealt largely with highly arcane and technical questions raised by the proponents' claim that they were merely restoring the pre–*Wards Cove* law and by the administration's claim that the bill would create a powerful new engine of discrimination. In what must have seemed an almost surrealistic exercise to sensible but nonexpert observers, much of the dispute consisted of competing legal interpretations of the unintelligible *Griggs* opinion and of the subsequent confusion and contradictions that *Griggs* had produced in the courts.

After negotiations among a shifting set of public officials and private lobbyists during the summer of 1990, and the public airing of several proposed compromises, the differences among the interested parties seemed irreconcilable. The negotiations had been punctuated by mutual recriminations and accusations of bad faith, but the issues were so legalistic that no one but a few of the lawyers involved could really have understood what all the fighting was about. Eventually, a slightly modified version of Kennedy-Hawkins passed both houses of Congress by near veto-proof margins. A visibly pained President rejected the bill,[70] and a veto override attempt in the Senate failed by one vote.

More negotiations were conducted the following year, more recriminations were exchanged, and a dizzying array of disparate impact compromises were floated by various parties and would-be mediators. Once again, however, agreement seemed impossible. The House of Representatives passed a bill that was essentially identical to the one Bush had vetoed, but opposition had grown since the previous year.[71] As the session drew to an end,

---

explanation of this objection was provided by the Attorney General, who argued that the bill "unfairly applies the changes in the law... to cases already decided." Memorandum of the Attorney General Accompanying the President's Veto Message.

A few days after the Civil Rights Act of 1991 was enacted, Bush signed an unrelated bill that contained retroactivity provisions which, like those in the original Kennedy-Hawkins bill, required that final judgments be reopened. Although the President's signing statement complained about minor provisions in this bill that purported to interfere with his power to supervise his subordinates, he raised no objection to the radical retroactivity provisions. *See* Statement on Signing the Federal Deposit Insurance Corporation Improvement Act of 1991, 27 WEEKLY COMP. PRES. DOC. 1873 (Dec. 19, 1991).

70. *See* Message to the Senate Returning without Approval the Civil Rights Act of 1990, 26 WEEKLY COMP. PRES. DOC. 1632 (Oct. 22, 1990) ("I am today returning without my approval S. 2104, the 'Civil Rights Act of 1990.' I deeply regret having to take this action with respect to a bill bearing such a title...").

71. The shift in sentiment in the House may have been affected by the fact that the quota issue had played an important part in two well-publicized election campaigns in 1990: the Senate race in North Carolina and the gubernatorial race in California. In both cases, the antiquota candidate had prevailed.

the stage seemed set for another veto by the President, and another failure to override.

Suddenly, just before the House bill was set for floor consideration in the Senate, Senator Dole negotiated a compromise between the administration and Senator Danforth, who represented a group of liberal Republicans that had supported Kennedy-Hawkins in 1990.[72] No doubt recognizing that the Danforth group's defection would doom any chance of overriding a veto, Senator Kennedy went along. The compromise bill passed the Senate and then the House with almost no opposition, and the President signed it into law as the Civil Rights Act of 1991.[73]

The disparate impact provisions of the 1991 Act largely codify *Wards Cove*.[74] This is clearest with respect to whether plaintiffs can challenge groups of employment practices or otherwise avoid the obligation to demonstrate that the employer caused whatever statistical disparities are observed in its workforce. The new statute clearly provides that such evasions of the causation requirement are disallowed.[75] With respect to the employer's ability to justify practices that have a disparate impact, the statute shifts the burden of persuasion to the defendant (overruling *Wards Cove* on this relatively small point[76]), and adopts the following substantive standard: the challenged practice must be "job related for the position in question and consistent with business necessity." This language was drawn from a provision in the Americans with Disabilities Act of 1990,[77] which had been inserted into that statute precisely because it was ambiguous enough to

72. *See* 137 CONG. REC. S15,220 (daily ed. Oct. 25, 1991) (statement of Sen. Dole).

73. For more detailed discussions of the events leading up to the enactment of the 1991 Act, see Neal Devins, *Reagan Redux: Civil Rights Under Bush*, 68 NOTRE DAME L. REV. 955 (1993); Roger Clegg, *A Brief Legislative History of the Civil Rights Act of 1991*, 54 LA. L. REV. 1459 (1994).

74. On most of the other significant issues raised by the Kennedy-Hawkins bill, the Bush administration accepted substantially all of its opponents' demands, thereby violating the principles to which the President had publicly committed himself at the outset of the legislative process in 1990. *See* Nelson Lund, *Congressional Self-Exemption from the Employment Discrimination Laws: A Rational Choice Analysis of the Civil Rights Act of 1991*, 54 LA. L. REV. 1559, 1601 n.128 (1994).

75. Consistent with *Wards Cove*, the statute also provides that "if the complaining party can demonstrate to the court that the elements of [an employer's] decisionmaking process are not capable of separation for analysis, the decisionmaking process may be analyzed as one employment practice."

76. The 1991 Act almost certainly precludes the use of jury trials in disparate impact cases, though juries are now available for other claims under Title VII. *See* CRA '91, § 102, 42 U.S.C. § 1981a. The distinction between the burden of production and the burden of persuasion is less important, as a practical matter, in bench trials than in jury trials.

77. Pub. L. No. 101-326, § 102(b)(6), 104 Stat. 327, 332 (1990) (codified at 42 U.S.C. § 12,112(b)(6)).

avoid triggering the kind of bitter debate that was then taking place over the Kennedy-Hawkins bill.[78] The language, however, is easily compatible with the formulations in *Beazer*, *Watson*, and *Wards Cove*. An employer's "legitimate employment goals" will in almost all cases be job related for the position in question (because "related" is such a broad term) and consistent with business necessity (since a legitimate employment goal could hardly be inconsistent with the needs of a business).

To the extent that there may be doubt about this interpretation, those doubts can be resolved by the "Purposes" section of the statute and by the interpretive memorandum that the statute itself declares to be the only statement that may be used as legislative history.[79] In both places we are told that the statute is meant to codify the concepts of "business necessity" and "job related" enunciated in *Griggs* and the other Supreme Court decisions prior to *Wards Cove*. Because *Beazer* was the authoritative statement of the law and of the proper interpretation of *Griggs* prior to *Wards Cove*,[80] the 1991 Act codified the *Beazer* standard, which is indistinguishable from the *Wards Cove* standard.

Although this is the correct interpretation of the 1991 Act, the ambiguous language used to codify the *Wards Cove* standard ensures that the courts will be urged to read into it the much more stringent requirements that proponents of Kennedy-Hawkins failed to get enacted. And if the Supreme Court resists such blandishments, it may be subjected once again to withering, if misplaced, accusations that it has ignored the will of Congress and turned back the clock on civil rights. The storm cloud created by this possibility hardly could have been invisible to the Justices when they approached the initial cases generated by the 1991 Act.

Law and Politics in *Landgraf* and *Rivers*

The effective-date provision of the 1991 Act, like the disparate impact provisions, is a compromise made possible by its ambiguity. The legislative history shows that each of the three major factions whose agreement was needed for enactment of a bill put a different interpretation on the language.

---

78. Both the Bush administration and the principal proponents of Kennedy-Hawkins strongly supported the Americans with Disabilities Act.

79. See CRA '91, §§ 3(2), 105(b), 42 U.S.C. § 1981 note.

80. Even Justice Stevens' *Wards Cove* dissent acknowledged that "[t]he opinion in *Griggs* made it clear that a neutral practice that operates to exclude minorities is nevertheless lawful if it serves a valid business purpose." 490 U.S. at 665 (Stevens, J., dissenting). This "valid business purpose" test is at least as generous to employers as the *Wards Cove* test, and perhaps more so.

Senator Dole, on behalf of himself, the Bush administration, and thirteen other Republican Senators, cited two then-recent Supreme Court cases to support the proposition that the new statute would not apply to cases arising before its effective date.[81] Senator Danforth and six other liberal Republicans maintained that their intention was to adhere to the principle "followed by the vast majority of Supreme Court cases" under which statutes are not given retroactive effect unless Congress explicitly directs otherwise.[82] Senator Kennedy said that "[i]t will be up to the courts to determine the extent to which the bill will apply to cases and claims that are pending on the date of enactment."[83] Kennedy, however, went on to state his belief that courts ordinarily apply new procedures and remedies to pending cases, and that they do the same with new substantive rules that are "merely a restoration of a prior rule that had been changed by the courts."[84]

From these statements, the Court might well have concluded that it was expected to exercise its own judgment in light of its own interpretation of its own precedents. That understanding would have led easily to the further conclusion that the Court was free to treat *Bradley* and *Thorpe* (which said that courts ordinarily should give effect to whatever rule is the law at the time of the decision) as the anomalies that they are, and apply the traditional presumption against retroactivity in the traditional way. This would have been fully consistent with the Dole and Danforth statements. Senator Kennedy's statement suggests that he might have been disappointed by such an outcome, but his operative words were that it would be "up to the courts" to determine how the new law would affect pending cases.

Justice Stevens deliberately chose not to take this obvious path. Instead, he dismissed all of the legislators' comments about the effective-date provision as "frankly partisan." If this means that the Senators realized that they disagreed with one another, so what? Legislative history often is relied on even when it contains inconsistent statements,[85] and the weight of the

81. 137 CONG. REC. S15,478 (daily ed. Oct. 30, 1991) (citing Bowen v. Georgetown Univ. Hosp., 488 U.S. 204 (1988), and Kaiser Aluminum & Chem. Corp. v. Bonjorno, 494 U.S. 827 (1990)). Senator Dole later said more emphatically that the effective-date provision was "intended" and "designed" to ensure that the statute would not apply to conduct occurring before the date of enactment. *See id.* at S15,953 (daily ed. Nov. 5, 1991).

82. 137 CONG. REC. S15,483 (daily ed. Oct. 30, 1991). Senator Danforth cited the same cases cited by Senator Dole, and Danforth expressly "disapprove[d]" of *Bradley* and *Thorpe*.

83. *Id.* at S15,485.

84. *Id.* In support of his contention, Senator Kennedy cited *Bradley* and several lower court decisions. *See also id.* at S15,963 (daily ed. Nov. 5, 1991) (statement of Sen. Kennedy) (reiterating the same point and citing both *Bradley* and *Thorpe*).

85. *See, e.g.*, Blanchard v. Bergeron, 489 U.S. 87 (1989).

evidence here favored the traditional presumption.[86] Most important, Senator Kennedy acknowledged that it would be "up to the courts" to decide whether *Bradley* or *Thorpe* had altered that presumption, so even *his* "frankly partisan" remarks could have been reconciled with the decision to refuse retroactive application.

For reasons that he did not explain, Stevens chose instead to draw a negative inference from the fact that Congress had *not* accepted two proposals that would have resolved the retroactivity issue clearly. One of those proposals, a provision including explicit retroactivity provisions, was in a bill introduced but not passed in its original form in the House in 1991.[87] The other proposal, which explicitly prohibited retroactive application, was included in the bill that President Bush had proposed in 1991.[88] Together with Stevens' elaborate discussion of events in the *previous* Congress (which enacted nothing), this suggests that his real focus was not on interpreting what was actually said in the relevant legislative history. More likely, his real interest was in evaluating the politics that generated the 1991 Act and the likely political response in Congress to the *Landgraf* and *Rivers* decisions. Because the Court had been the target of extraordinary vitriol throughout the battle in 1990 and 1991, a keen interest among the Justices in the politics of the period would hardly be surprising.

---

86. Justice Stevens created a misleading impression about the weight of the legislative history. He ignored the views offered by Senator Dole, who was the architect of the compromise that became law and who spoke for 14 Senators. Stevens also undercut the significance of the views expressed by Senator Danforth and six other sponsors by quoting Danforth's suggestion (which was made in a different context and at a different time) that courts should be skeptical about interpretive statements offered in the course of the bill's consideration on the floor. *See* 114 S. Ct. at 1495 n.15. Senator Kennedy, whose views were given considerable prominence by Stevens, did not claim to speak for anyone but himself on this issue. In *Rivers*, Justice Stevens also mentioned the conflicting views offered by Representatives Hyde (who echoed Dole) and Don Edwards (who strongly supported retroactive application). 114 S. Ct. at 1517 n.8. Because the House considered the Senate bill under a closed rule (a procedural device disallowing amendments), it is hard to see why Edwards' views add anything significant, or why they should be entitled to more weight than those expressed by President Bush in his signing statement—which Stevens ignored completely.

87. *See* 114 S. Ct. at 1495 & n.14. Stevens misleadingly referred to the original version of this bill, H.R. 1, as "the 1991 bill as originally introduced in the House." The bill that became law was an amendment in the nature of a substitute to S. 1745, a bill originally introduced by Senator Danforth. H.R. 1 was never even considered in the Senate. The version of H.R. 1 that passed the House, moreover, would have made only one of its provisions retroactive, and that provision was not at issue in *Landgraf* or *Rivers*.

88. 114 S. Ct. at 1495 n.14. This footnote contains citations to two unidentified "proposals." If one checks the citations, they turn out to refer to the Bush bill as introduced in the House and in the Senate.

There are additional signs that contribute to this impression. The only references in *Landgraf* to the departed, and therefore politically impotent, Bush administration were an allusion to Bush's veto of the 1990 bill[89] and a footnote dismissing the bill Bush proposed in 1991 as one that "foundered."[90] The views of Senator Dole, who played the key role in devising the final compromise and who introduced an interpretive memorandum on behalf of fourteen Senators and the administration, were cited and ignored. The views of Senator Danforth, who played the most public role in achieving the compromise, but who had announced his retirement from the Senate before *Landgraf* and *Rivers* were decided, were quoted but then undercut. The views of Senator Kennedy, however, who remained a powerful committee chairman when *Landgraf* and *Rivers* were decided, are treated in Stevens' opinion with even more respect than Senator Kennedy himself seemed to demand.

More hints of political sensitivity appear in Justice Stevens' legally irrelevant discussion of the "special concerns" that *Wards Cove* had given rise to in Congress.[91] This discussion was accompanied by a footnote unnecessarily (and somewhat misleadingly) quoting language in the 1991 Act that evinces congressional dissatisfaction with *Wards Cove*.[92] Stevens' gratuitous attention to *Wards Cove* could reflect an acute awareness of the gory details of the rhetorical assaults on the Court that were so prominent in the two-year debate over disparate impact. Such an awareness would hardly be surprising inasmuch as Stevens wrote the principal dissent in *Wards Cove*, in which he called the Court's opinion "this latest sojourn into judicial activism."[93]

Indeed, one cannot help wondering whether Chief Justice Rehnquist deliberately assigned the *Landgraf* and *Rivers* opinions to the author of the principal dissent in *Wards Cove*. If some Justices had been seriously alarmed by the political attacks that *Wards Cove* had provoked, they might have worried that the decisions in *Landgraf* and *Rivers* could lead to new charges that a recalcitrant Court was flouting the congressional will and

89. *Id.* at 1491–92 & n.9.

90. *Id.* at 1495 n.14. Stevens did not bother to identify the bill as Bush's proposal.

91. *Id.* at 1489.

92. Stevens quotes a part of the statute expressing an intent to codify certain concepts "enunciated in 'Supreme Court decisions prior to *Wards Cove*.'" *Id.* at 1489 n.3. This is misleading because the statute actually refers to *Griggs* and "*the* other Supreme Court decisions prior to *Wards Cove*." CRA '91, § 3(2), 42 U.S.C. § 1981 note (emphasis added). By omitting the italicized word at the beginning of the quotation, Stevens creates the impression that Congress might not have intended to codify *Beazer*. This is significant because Stevens' dissenting opinion in *Wards Cove* exhibited considerable discomfort with the opinion that he himself wrote for the Court in *Beazer*.

93. 490 U.S. at 663 (Stevens, J., dissenting).

stubbornly persisting in the same "turn back the clock" mentality that had produced *Wards Cove*. Having the *Landgraf* and *Rivers* majority opinions written by Stevens would make such charges less plausible.

Stevens' rejection of the time-honored rule requiring a clear statement that a statute is to apply retroactively, and his substitution of a new rule requiring clear congressional intent, is obviously consistent with a desire to avoid offending the members of Congress (especially committee chairmen like Senator Kennedy) who control the production of legislative history. Attention to congressional politics could also explain the other puzzling aspects of the *Landgraf* and *Rivers* opinions to which Scalia objected. This is fairly obvious with respect to Stevens' bogus effort to reconcile *Thorpe* and *Bradley* with *Landgraf*'s reaffirmation of the traditional retroactivity presumption. Just as the anti-Court political rhetoric in 1990 and 1991 had focused heavily on the claim that *Wards Cove* and the other 1989 decisions had "overruled" prior law, so Stevens might have been concerned that overruling *Thorpe* or *Bradley* would lead to similar political attacks. Indeed, the Court might have felt more vulnerable in early 1994, when *Landgraf* and *Rivers* were decided, than it had been in 1990 and 1991. During the earlier period, the Bush administration, at least, had defended the Court. By 1994, however, both the Congress and the administration were controlled by the Democrats who had led the earlier attacks on the Court.

It is less obvious how a political motivation might explain Stevens' adoption of the "new legal consequences" definition of retroactivity. Scalia claimed, somewhat dubiously but without rebuttal from Stevens, that this theory is less consistent with precedent than Scalia's own "retroactivity event" analysis. Stevens' theory, however, has the great political advantage that it appeals directly to commonly held intuitive notions of fair play. Unlike Scalia's more legalistic approach, Stevens' theory of retroactivity can be reduced to a comprehensible and attractive sound-bite. And Stevens provided just that sound-bite: "Elementary considerations of fairness dictate that individuals should have an opportunity to know what the law is and to conform their conduct accordingly; settled expectations should not be lightly disrupted."[94]

The apparent inconsistency of Stevens' theory with precedent may even give it a certain political advantage. As Scalia pointed out, Stevens' theory has a kinship with the Court's ex post facto test, under which substantive legal changes may not be applied to events that occurred before the change, although procedural changes may be. But Stevens' exposition adds what Scalia calls "seemingly random exceptions" to that criterion, under which the applicability of procedural rules will depend upon the posture of the case in question.[95] What Scalia deprecates as unprincipled might be seen as

94. 114 S. Ct. at 1497.

95. *See id.* at 1524.

having the practical virtue of flexibility and adaptability. As Stevens acknowledges, his approach does not offer "perfect philosophical clarity."[96] But that very imperfection means that his approach will allow the Court to conform its future decisions with what it perceives as widely held intuitive notions of fairness, and also to avoid placing itself in the path of political locomotives like the one that appeared in 1990. Stevens commented that judges tend to have "sound instincts" about retroactivity,[97] and he might also have thought that judicial instincts would be superior to philosophical clarity in advancing the judiciary's institutional interest in self-protection. Although Scalia's "retroactivity event" theory may be philosophically more respectful of congressional prerogative, Stevens' flexible "instinctual" approach provides a more subtle tool for keeping up the *appearance* of respect for Congress. And, as the Justices are surely aware, appearances are likely to count for more than reality in protecting the Court from congressional assaults.

Conclusion

Judicial restraints on the retroactive application of statutes operate primarily through the constitutional prohibition against ex post facto penal laws and through the traditional presumption that statutes outside that prohibition's reach are meant to have prospective application only.[98] These restraints provide the American citizen with a significant measure of protection from oppressive legislative acts. For that salutary political purpose to be served properly and durably, the judicial doctrines through which it is carried out must generate an appropriate level of institutional competition and conflict. If courts acquiesce too much in legislative willfulness, the restraints will come undone and more willfulness will be invited. But if the restraints are applied without regard to the possibility of willful congressional reactions against the courts themselves, the effort may be self-defeating. Seen in this light, *Landgraf* and *Rivers* might be regarded as an effort at "judicial statesmanship." Such an effort would hardly be surprising from a Court that has lately taken to announcing that its constitutional deci-

---

96. *Id.* at 1499.

97. *Id.*

98. Other constitutional provisions that provide some protection against retroactive legislation include the Due Process Clauses, the Bill of Attainder Clauses, the Contracts Clause, and the Takings Clause. As interpreted by the Supreme Court, however, these provisions add little to the security afforded by the Ex Post Facto Clauses and by the judiciary's traditional reluctance to give retroactive effect to ambiguous statutes.

sions are shaped by a desire to enhance the Court's institutional prestige and to reward those who have refrained from criticizing the Court in the past.[99]

There are, however, at least two reasons not to admire the effort too much. First, the political frenzy that produced the statute at issue in *Landgraf* and *Rivers* had its ultimate source in a political dynamic that the Supreme Court itself had created by its legislative decisions in *Griggs* and *Weber*. And the very possibility of interpreting the 1991 Act to apply retroactively was created mainly by the Court's own decisions in *Bradley* and *Thorpe*. If the Court was confronted with a delicate political problem when it decided *Landgraf* and *Rivers*, that problem was largely of its own making.

Second, it is by no means clear that a straightforward, honest, and doctrinally coherent retroactivity opinion, even one in which *Thorpe* and *Bradley* were expressly overruled, would have created any great risk of a strong congressional counterreaction. The debate over *Wards Cove* in 1990 and 1991 included a good measure of venom against the Supreme Court, but the Court was hardly alone in suffering politically during this episode. Those who supported the Kennedy-Hawkins bill were accused of promoting racial quotas, while those who opposed the bill were denounced as enemies of civil rights. Absorbing inflammatory charges like these may sometimes pay off for politicians who can deliver visible benefits to constituent groups at the end of the process. But the compromise bill enacted in 1991 came nowhere close to meeting that test. At the end of the negotiations, almost everyone went away unhappy, and no one could put in a claim for gratitude with any significant bloc of voters. Politicians don't like outcomes like that, and they will stubbornly resist repeating experiences like the one they had in 1990 and 1991.

For these reasons, Congress was highly unlikely to revisit the deal that was struck in the 1991 Act anytime soon. The strength of the resistance to such a step is confirmed by the fate of an effort to do just that. One of the many compromises in the 1991 Act was to put caps on the new damages remedy that the statute created under Title VII. Such caps inevitably have arbitrary effects, denying some plaintiffs full compensation for proven injuries. The caps in the 1991 statute compound this arbitrary quality by varying the level of the caps according to the size of the employer. Thus, under the new statute, two victims with identical injuries may receive wildly different awards solely because one of them was injured by a large company and the other by a smaller firm. As a compromise between employer interests and those of other powerful constituencies, this scheme may not seem entirely bizarre. But neither is it one that most Democrats could com-

---

99. *See* Planned Parenthood v. Casey, 112 S. Ct. 2791, 2814–16 (1992). *Cf.* Richard A. Posner, *What Do Judges and Justices Maximize? (The Same Thing Everybody Else Does)*, 3 SUP. CT. ECON. REV. 1 (1994).

fortably defend. And yet, despite the election of a Democratic President and Democratic majorities in both houses of Congress in 1992, bills to remove the caps died before reaching the floor in either house. A Congress unwilling to take on this relatively inviting issue likely would not have been provoked into action by an unwelcome Supreme Court decision dealing with the inherently evanescent issue of retroactivity. To suppose otherwise simply strains credulity.

Thus, if the *Landgraf* and *Rivers* opinions were designed to avoid provoking Congress against the Court, the effort seems to have been misplaced. The price paid for the effort may prove small, for the decisions do reaffirm valuable principles that the Court had discarded in *Thorpe* and *Bradley*. And these principles were reaffirmed in circumstances that suggest the current Justices will not be tempted to give any statute an unnecessary retroactive application. The actual price, however, will be determined by future courts, which will get to use their "instincts" (whether sound or unsound) in resolving the questions that Justice Stevens left unanswered. Thus, even if certain features of *Landgraf* and *Rivers* were produced by excessive political timidity, the opinions in those cases leave room for the Court to exercise better, or worse, political and legal judgment in cases yet to come.

STEPHAN THERNSTROM

Critical Observations on the *Draft Final Report of the Special Committee on Race and Ethnicity to the D.C. Circuit Task Force on Gender, Race, and Ethnic Bias*

Are the federal courts in our nation's capital riddled with racial bias? The answer is yes, if you believe a recent report by the Special Committee on Race and Ethnicity of the D.C. Circuit's Task Force on Gender, Race, and Ethnic Bias.[1] The critical reader will find this report of interest not as proof that something is terribly wrong with our judicial system but as an unfortunate exhibit of the affirmative action mentality run amok. Since the Report claims to be the "first in the country to explore the ways in which . . . race and ethnicity may play a role in the workings of federal courts,"[2] it merits close critical scrutiny. If other investigators choose to explore the subject, perhaps they can learn something from the mistakes of these pioneers.

The 500-page volume that contains the Report and various appendices was put together by a group of local civil rights attorneys and a Howard University sociologist. The authors claim that they sought to "obtain balanced data" that would make possible "an objective analysis of the ways in which issues of race and ethnicity . . . arise in the courts of the D.C. Circuit."[3] Unfortunately, the study they have conducted is not marked by either balance or objectivity. The authors obviously began their work with a strong predisposition to find racial and ethnic bias in the operations of the D.C. Circuit court system, so it is not surprising that they found it. The conclusions of the Report will not impress any reader who scrutinizes it with an open mind and some grasp of social science methods. The analysis offered by the authors is partisan, tendentious, and notably lacking in statistical sophistication. At several important points, the statistics con-

1. DRAFT FINAL REPORT OF THE SPECIAL COMMITTEE ON RACE AND ETHNICITY TO THE D.C. CIRCUIT TASK FORCE ON GENDER, RACE, AND ETHNIC BIAS (Jan. 1995) [hereinafter REPORT].

2. *Id.* at 7.

3. *Id.* at 24.

tained in the Report point to conclusions precisely opposite to those drawn by the authors.

The Wrong Pool

The authors of the Report contend that members of racial and ethnic minority groups living in the District of Columbia and its environs are treated unfairly by the D.C. Circuit courts in many ways—indeed in most ways, it would seem. Bias against members of minority groups, they would have us believe, is the rule, not the exception. For example, they assert that minorities have less than their fair share of jobs in the courts of the circuit, particularly of the more desirable jobs.

But a claim of employment discrimination based upon statistical disparities between racial groups cannot be substantiated, of course, without determining both the contours of the labor market in question and the number of minorities in the qualified pool within that labor market. It is necessary to compare "the racial composition of [the at-issue jobs] and the racial composition of the qualified... population in the relevant labor market" to build a convincing discrimination case.[4] Yet the authors make no attempt to assess the educational and other requirements of the various occupations that they discuss, nor to estimate how many members of racial and ethnic minority groups in the Washington area have the necessary qualifications. To ignore the whole question of qualifications is as "nonsensical" as it is to find discrimination in "the selection of accountants, managers, boat captains, electricians, doctors, and engineers... by comparing the number of nonwhites occupying these jobs with the number of nonwhites filling cannery worker positions...."[5]

In a footnote, the authors concede that this is a serious methodological weakness of their study, but they argue that to assess "the qualifications of minorities and non-minorities" in the Washington metropolitan area "would have been a substantial undertaking."[6] Since they had the resources to produce a report that runs over 500 pages, surely a very "substantial" undertaking, it is difficult to see why such an inquiry would have been beyond their capacities. If only "nonsensical" conclusions can be drawn in the absence of information about qualifications, some effort to explore the question was essential if the Report was to be taken seriously.

The authors suggest that the failure to identify the racial and ethnic composition of the qualified pool doesn't really matter, because "no effort

---

4. Hazelwood Sch. Dist. v. United States, 433 U.S. 299, 308 (1977).
5. Wards Cove Packing Co. v. Atonio, 490 U.S. 642, 651 (1989).
6. Report, *supra* note 1, at 31 n.50.

has been made to draw conclusions" from the statistical patterns they find.[7] No conclusions? What an odd and disingenuous disclaimer this is. The authors devote many pages of the Report to an attempt to prove that there are suspicious statistical imbalances in the distribution of the courthouse workforce, without ever stressing—except in a single footnote—that the data they present permit no valid conclusion as to whether the imbalance constituted employment discrimination. Despite this disavowal, the Report is full of "conclusions," and indeed ends with two dozen pages of policy recommendations that supposedly flow from those conclusions. It is impossible to read it without coming away thinking that it concludes very emphatically that the courts of the District of Columbia have had hiring policies strongly biased against minorities, and that prompt and vigorous action is necessary to rectify current injustices.

In an attempt to make their case, the authors offer highly selective and slanted interpretations. When the data they themselves have amassed suggest an absence of bias, for example, or a bias *in favor* of minorities, the authors fail to point it out. Thus we are told that 6 of the 34 Article III judges in the D.C. Circuit are African Americans.[8] That amounts to 17.6%, far above the African American share of the U.S. population (12.6%) and very far above their share of attorneys practicing today (3.4%).[9]

Of course, this is too small a statistical base to take very seriously, though not much smaller than the samples used by the authors to draw conclusions elsewhere. A better basis for generalization may be gained by looking at the 573 judges on the nation's federal district courts. The authors report that 8% of U.S. district court judges are African American and 5% are Hispanic.[10] They fail to notice that if blacks hold 8% of the federal judgeships but comprise only 3.4% of the nation's attorneys, that means that the odds of an African American lawyer getting appointed to the federal bench are more than double those of a white attorney.

This racial imbalance within the judiciary is not confined to the federal courts. The 1990 census indicates the race of the more than 32,000 federal, state, and local judges in the nation. Some 7.0% of all judges in the land were African Americans, again twice as high a proportion as we would expect if the judiciary reflected the racial composition of the bar

7. *Id.*

8. *Id.* at 55.

9. The figure on the African American share of the population in 1995 is from U.S. Bureau of the Census, Statistical Abstract of the United States: 1994, at tbl. 23; data on the black proportion of the legal profession are provided in the Report, *supra* note 1, at app. D, tbl. D1.

10. Report, *supra* note 1, at 17.

as a whole.[11] If we accept the assumption of the authors that statistical disparities constitute prima facie evidence of bias in hiring, this would have to count as proof of problack, not antiblack, bias in the process of appointments to the judiciary.

Similarly, the authors' statistics reveal that Hispanic attorneys have twice as good a chance of becoming a judge as non-Hispanic white attorneys—just 2.5% of all lawyers but 5% of all federal judges are Hispanic[12]—another imbalance they fail to note because it does not square with their preconceived belief that the system is invariably unfair to minorities. The report conveys the false impression that blacks and Hispanics have less than their proper share of seats on the bench, while in fact they have much more than their share when we take into account the composition of the pool of eligibles.

The same predisposition of the authors to assume that there are "not enough" minorities shows up in their approving references to complaints about the "predominantly white makeup" of the District of Columbia federal bench and bar (79% and 88%, respectively). One attorney professes to find it remarkable that when you appear in a D.C. federal court "you'd never believe that you're in a predominantly black city."[13] The authors here ignore the obvious point they themselves had made at the outset—that the subject at hand is not the municipal courts of the District of Columbia but *federal* courts, and indeed federal courts that happen to have "unique statutory responsibilities for review of federal government actions, most of which raise national issues with no local focus."[14]

If we were to expect these national legal institutions to mirror the racial composition of some population, surely it would be the population of the United States, not the population of the District of Columbia or even the far larger population of the Washington metropolitan area. The President of the United States does not confine his attention to residents of the District of Columbia when he makes appointments to the D.C. Circuit courts. The attorneys who appear in those courtrooms are not the equivalent of the bar in Omaha or Little Rock. They belong to a national elite, and are drawn from the nation as a whole, just as the staff of the *Washington Post* is. In fact, the "predominantly white" federal courts of the District of Columbia do mirror the population of the nation as a whole pretty well.

---

11. U.S. Bureau of the Census, 1990 Census of the Population, Supplementary Reports, at 1990CP-S-1 (*Detailed Occupation and Other Characteristics From the EEO File for the United States*, tbl. 1) (1992).

12. Report, *supra* note 1, at 17 & tbl. D1.

13. *Id.* at 58–59.

14. *Id.* at 1.

Eight of ten Americans today do consider themselves white, as do 93% of the members of the bar nationally.

Courthouse Staff

When the authors of the Report look at the ethnic and racial composition of the courthouse workforce below the judicial level, they again convey the misleading impression that members of racial and ethnic minority groups do not have their fair share of positions and thus have not been given a fair shake. They tell us that 44% of the employees at the district court in the District of Columbia and 26% of those at the court of appeals are African Americans.[15] This means that in the district court blacks are actually much more heavily represented than they are in the population of the Washington metropolitan area (29%), and in the court of appeals they are only very slightly underrepresented. The authors never ask why the district court's hiring practices are apparently so biased against whites.

Hispanics and Asians are indeed substantially "underrepresented" in the staff of the court, as the authors claim. But what percentage of these groups has the qualifications for work of this kind? How many of those who are qualified are interested in having such jobs? Consider the case of Asians and Pacific Islanders. The authors assume that the small numbers of Asians employed by the courts represents some cruel rebuff of people whose greatest dream is to work at a federal courthouse. It happens that a great many Asians in the United States today have such strong qualifications for employment of other kinds that they would never consider taking the jobs offered at the courthouse. Although Asians and Pacific Islanders are only 2.9% of the labor force of the United States today, they comprise 11% of the nation's physicians, 7.2% of its college professors, 7.1% of its engineers, 6.7% of its natural scientists, and 6% of its mathematicians and computer scientists.[16] With such enormous concentrations of Asians in very well-paid professional positions like these, Asians will necessarily be underrepresented in many other jobs. Asians in the Washington metropolitan area who are physicians, engineers, and college professors do not have their hearts set on becoming court clerks.

As for Hispanics, they may be underrepresented in such jobs because many are recent immigrants who do not speak or read and write English well enough to do the work satisfactorily.[17] Some positions around the

---

15. *Id.* at 30.

16. *See supra* note 11.

17. Buried away in the Report is the information that only 27% of the adult Hispanic residents of the District of Columbia are citizens of the United States (REPORT, *supra* note 1, at 105 n.180). This is not only a major reason why few Hispanics qualify for jury duty;

courthouse may require citizenship, and Hispanics have the lowest naturalization rate of any American ethnic group today.[18] The authors are silent on what skills are required for such jobs, and do nothing to demonstrate that Hispanics possess them. It may also be that the lower echelons of the court staff are regarded by Hispanics, whether accurately or not, as black turf on which they would not be welcome. An analogy can be drawn here with the U.S. Postal Service. In Los Angeles today, according to the vice chairman of the Postal Service Board of Governors, blacks are 9.6% of the labor force but a remarkable 63% of all postal workers. Latinos are 34% of the labor force but have only 15% of jobs in the post office. In Chicago, likewise, blacks are 18% of the labor force but 80% of the postal workers. Hispanics have far fewer of these positions than their share of the city population.[19] The explanation in these cases may be that informal networks keep blacks informed about tests and hiring, and Hispanics are not part of them.[20] That blacks are part of such informal networks around the courthouse in the District of Columbia and Latinos are excluded from them is a possibility the authors do not entertain and explore.

The core assumption on which this whole analysis rests is that, if ethnic and racial groups are not equally represented at every occupational level at every employment site, something is wrong. Someone must be discriminating against the "underrepresented" groups, and in favor of those "overrepresented" ones. This could be true only if all groups had identical educations, did equally well in school at precisely the same subjects, and had exactly the same job preferences. To spell out these assumptions is to expose their absurdity.

The authors find it anomalous and disturbing that although 43% of staff positions in the courthouses of the District of Columbia are held by minority employees, "principally African Americans," minorities have "only" 32% of supervisory or managerial positions.[21] They are indeed underrepresented—moderately underrepresented—in the higher ranked jobs. The question is why. One obvious explanation for this modest dis-

---

noncitizenship would also disqualify them for many jobs in law enforcement, and is strongly correlated with limited command of English, which would likely bar them from many other positions.

18. For evidence that the various Hispanic groups ranked at or very near the bottom in their naturalization rates as of 1992, see Philip Martin & Elizabeth Midgley, *Immigration to the United States: Journey to an Unknown Destination*, 42 POPULATION BULL. 36 (Sept. 1994).

19. Brian Doherty, *Affirmative Reaction*, REASON, Oct. 1994, at 6–7.

20. *Cf.* Orvis Collins, *Ethnic Behavior in Industry: Sponsorship and Rejection in a New England Factory*, 52 AM. J. SOC. 293 (1946).

21. REPORT, *supra* note 1, at 32.

crepancy is that such supervisory or managerial posts require educational credentials that are not evenly distributed among racial and ethnic groups. Some of these jobs may demand a college diploma, for example, and only 24% of African Americans in the District of Columbia today are college graduates, as compared with some 46% of whites.[22] Given that huge educational gap, one might expect an even larger racial discrepancy among the occupants of supervisory and managerial positions in the courts.

The same failure to take into account group differences in educational background and the educational requirements of various jobs is apparent when the authors report that 80% of minority employees, but "only" half as many nonminority employees, began their courthouse employment at pay-grade-level 9 or below. Conversely, 5% of minorities but 24% of nonminorities began at pay-grade-level 11 or above.[23] An innocent reader might conclude that these disparities reveal terrible bias in the system. We can conclude nothing of the sort, of course, without knowing what the skill requirements are for posts at various pay-grade levels. Is it not true that applicants for the higher pay-grades in federal service must have better educational credentials and more work experience than those at lower pay-grades? And do all racial and ethnic groups have the same level of educational attainment and work experience—as the authors' analysis seems to assume? It is astonishing that the authors seem unaware that these questions must be asked and answered before any conclusions can be drawn about discrimination in hiring. The need to control for education in assessing group differences of many kinds comes early in Sociology 101.

Equally elementary is the point that age and seniority must be held constant when exploring differences in the distribution of groups within the job hierarchy. The authors tell us that "minority women held proportionately fewer supervisory positions in the government"—that 74% of the white male attorneys who worked in the government were supervisors, while minority women "accounted for only 6%" of supervisory government attorneys.[24] This is a misleading and erroneous way of tabulating the data, and in fact is not even a correct description of the numbers.

22. Census data on the educational attainment of the District of Columbia population in 1990 are given in the Report itself (app. C, tbl. C4). That it was so conveniently available makes it all the more distressing that the authors failed to take it into account when discussing ethnic and racial differences in the distribution of the workforce. The figures cited are for the District of Columbia, not for the entire metropolitan area, which would be more appropriate. Such figures also could have been obtained easily by the authors.

23. REPORT, *supra* note 1, at 32–33.

24. *Id.* at 67.

In fact, the evidence shows not that 74% of the white male attorneys working for government were supervisors but that 74% of government supervisor attorneys were white males—a completely different point. The Report contrasts this with the figure for minority women—6%—without noting that the total population of minority women attorneys working for the federal government is small. That is, even if every single minority female employed by government had been a supervisory attorney, they would still comprise only a very modest proportion of the total supervisory population because they are a small share of the total population. The comparison the authors should have made is between the proportions of the government employees in each group who were supervisory attorneys—38% of white men and 18% of minority women, a far smaller gap than the one between 74% and 6%.

The difference between 18% and 38% is no proof that discrimination is at work. To assess that, we would need to know, at a minimum, how long attorney supervisors had typically been working for the government—how much seniority they had acquired. If supervisors had typically been employed by government for two decades, say, the entire difference between the two groups might be attributable to the fact that very few minority women were graduating from law school and entering government service twenty years ago, when the typical white male who is now a supervisor was first hired.

Age and seniority are equally relevant in assessing the validity of another charge the Report makes about the position of minority women in the legal profession—that few are partners in private firms.[25] Partnerships are not awarded to young men and women upon graduation from law school; it typically takes many years to work oneself up to that level. If disproportionate numbers of minority female attorneys have only recently emerged from law school and entered the labor market, we can hardly expect them to have a large share of partnerships.

Clerkships

The share of judicial clerkships going to minority law school graduates is considered by the Report at some length, but its discussion is especially slanted and inept.[26] The authors claim that "only a handful of minority attorneys are receiving federal judicial clerkships in the D.C. Circuit courts, far fewer than their numbers in the law schools and in the profession." "Only a handful," "far fewer than"—this is the kind of

25. *Id.* at 67.
26. *Id.* at 75–79.

sound-bite language that is likely to be featured in the press. That will be regrettable, because the charge is quite simply false. The statistics the authors present do not support it in the least.

Data on the racial and ethnic background of clerks for the district court and the court of appeals were not available for earlier years, but 1993–94 figures show that 4 of the 63 clerkships were held by Asian Americans and 4 by African Americans. Are these numbers "far fewer than their numbers in the law schools and in the profession"? I cannot imagine how the authors could possibly think that this is the case.

The charge is particularly absurd when applied to Asians. According to figures presented in the authors' own Report, just 1.4% of attorneys in the U.S. today are Asians or Pacific Islanders.[27] The Asian share of clerkships, by contrast, is 6.3%, which works out to be four times their share in the profession as a whole. If we take the proportion of Asians receiving law degrees today (3.2%) to be a better basis for comparison—logical because clerks are normally people fresh out law school—Asians still have double their share of clerkships.[28]

Nor is it the case that the 6.3% share of clerkships going to African Americans is below what we might fairly expect them to have. It is in fact a bit higher than their 4.9% share of law degrees currently being awarded. Blacks do not have "far fewer" clerkships than they would have if there were no statistical disparities; they are a shade above statistical parity if our standard of reference is the proportion currently graduating from law school. If the standard is the proportion now in the profession, the other point of reference the authors think is relevant, African Americans have nearly double their 3.4% share.[29]

---

27. *Id.* at app. D, tbl. D1.

28. The latest figures are for 1991–92. NATIONAL CENTER FOR EDUCATION STATISTICS, DIGEST OF EDUCATIONAL STATISTICS: 1994, at tbl. 264 (1994). The authors say that their point of comparison is the racial composition of the nine law schools that are the principal source of law clerks in this circuit. REPORT, *supra* note 1, at 76 n.141. But they are suspiciously vague about the exact numbers. They claim that "minorities comprised from 15% to 36% of all students" at these nine law schools, without further detail as to the share of various minority groups. This is a broad range, and one would like to know the mean figure, which they should have provided, and the breakdown by specific group. Furthermore, clerkships go only to graduates, and there could well be significant group differentials in graduation rates. The authors claim that an ABA publication reports that nationally 19% of all J.D.'s in 1991 went to minority students. But the figures given in the authoritative DIGEST OF EDUCATIONAL STATISTICS, tbls. 264 & 265, show that in 1991–92, non-Hispanic white students were awarded 33,807 of the 38,848 L.L.B.'s or J.D.'s that were reported, leaving a share of 13% for all minority groups combined, about a third below the proportion the ABA estimated. In 1990–1991, the minority share was 12.2%.

29. *Studies Suggest That Minorities Still Lag in Admissions, Tests*, NAT'L L.J., Feb. 24, 1992, at 4.

Despite the striking overrepresentation of Asians in clerkships and a figure somewhat above parity for blacks as well, the discussion of this matter in the Report insinuates that there is something very unfair about the selection process—that a sinister old boy network somehow controls it. For example, the authors assert that some judges "may feel more comfortable" with graduates of certain schools.[30] The implication is that they select clerks not on the basis of their merits but merely because they wear the old school tie. Implicit in this charge is the suggestion that anyone who would let such a trivial consideration as an old school tie influence an important choice like this might also be prone to pick clerks with the same skin color. Without actually having said that any judges currently on the bench are conscious or unconscious racists, this passage leaves us with the suspicion that some must be.

More fundamentally, the authors seem unable to grasp and to give a fair hearing to a perspective that I suspect is the one held by most judges today. This is the meritocratic, color-blind (and gender-blind) view held by those whose sole aim is to select those clerks who have the best legal minds, and who care nothing whatever about the race, ethnicity, religion, gender, or any other extraneous social characteristic of candidates. Many in this camp are convinced, on the basis of long experience, that student grades in law school are the best available measure of the quality of their minds.

This point of view is apparently too old-fashioned for the authors to consider seriously. But any serious inquiry into this topic must ask whether the choice of clerks is in fact governed primarily by meritocratic considerations, as such judges would insist. To determine whether this is just a smoke screen, a mere mask for prejudice, it is necessary to estimate what the racial balance among the clerks would look like if choices were made strictly on the basis of academic merit. The Report evades that crucial question. It concedes that clerks are "usually drawn" from students in the "top tiers" at leading law schools, but claims that figures on how many minority students were at the top of their class were "not available."[31] In the absence of such evidence, though, no valid conclusions can be drawn about the sources of any racial or ethnic "imbalance" that the study purports to find.

Are African Americans and members of other racial and ethnic minorities in fact represented at the top of the class in the nation's top law schools in proportion to their numbers? Such sensitive information is generally kept well hidden from public view, but enough is known to allow a provisional judgment in the case of black students, at least. A large majori-

30. Report, *supra* note 1, at 77.
31. *Id.* at 76.

ty of African Americans enrolled in law schools today have been the beneficiaries of very strong affirmative action preferences. They were admitted with much weaker college records and much lower LSAT scores than their white counterparts. The best evidence is from a recent article by the editor of the *Journal of Blacks in Higher Education*, a strong defender of affirmative action. In arguing *for* preferential admissions, the author points out that in 1992–93 the mean LSAT score at the top twenty law schools was 165.7. The median for all black test-takers was a mediocre 142.4. Only 63 black students in the entire country scored at or above the average level for students at the top law schools in that year. And yet these schools admit about 500 African Americans each year.[32] Eight out of nine black students, therefore, have LSAT scores below those of the average student at the institutions at which they are enrolled. Without a double standard in admissions, the number of African American students in the leading law schools would be very drastically reduced.

Do these very sharp differences in performance disappear, or even shrink notably, over three years of law school? A decade ago, Robert Klitgaard's meticulous survey of tests as predictors of performance in elite educational institutions found no evidence that such was the case in law and medical schools,[33] and I am not aware of subsequent studies that support more optimistic conclusions. It appears that students at the top of the class in all the major law schools are disproportionately white, and those at the bottom are disproportionately black. This is supported by the undeniable fact that most white law graduates pass the bar exam the first time they take it, but most blacks do not. Their failure rate is approximately double that of whites.[34] If we make the reasonable assumption that the criteria that federal judges employ in defining excellence in a clerk correlate fairly well with how students perform on the bar exams, it would follow that proportionally many fewer African American students would win clerkships.

The authors express sympathy with "minority attorneys" who "struggle under the perception that their achievements are not due to ability but

---

32. It is also suggestive and depressing that the median LSAT score for all African Americans taking the test in 1992–93 was lower than the median for enrolled students in all but two of the 176 ranking law schools in the United States, both of which were located in Puerto Rico. Theodore Cross, *What If There Were No Affirmative Action in College Admissions? A Refinement of Our Earlier Calculations*, J. BLACKS HIGHER EDUC., Autumn 1994, at 54.

33. ROBERT KLITGAARD, CHOOSING ELITES (1985).

34. The pass rate on the Florida bar exam in 1991 was 76% for whites, 46% for blacks. In California, in 1988, the gap was even wider—78% for whites versus 38% for blacks. NAT'L L.J., *supra* note 29, at 4.

rather to racial preference, or 'affirmative action.'"[35] They deplore such invidious "perceptions" and imply that they are racist. That follows only if we assume that such "perceptions" are false—that minority achievements are impressive when measured by the same standard applied to everyone. It is not clear that this assumption is correct. Affirmative action as currently practiced entails the use of benign double standards, rewarding people for performances that would not have been good enough had they been of a different race. One of the most unfortunate consequences of such preferential treatment is that it casts suspicion upon the achievements of all members of the group, whether or not they were individually the beneficiaries of affirmative action.[36]

The authors deny that they are recommending that the number of minorities obtaining clerkships be increased by "lowering standards." But they cite with obvious approval judges in the circuit who said that candidates for clerkships should be judged by less "ephemeral" standards than "paper qualifications of high academic achievement." Another judge

35. REPORT, *supra* note 1, at 78. The authors cite the experience of Christine Lee as a case in point. Ms. Lee sought a clerkship on the circuit, and received no interviews from white judges, although she had been on the *Harvard Law Review* (*id.* at 79 n.144). The authors imply that she was obviously qualified to receive interviews, but fail to provide evidence to convince the disinterested observer. They do not tell us what kind of grades Ms. Lee had. She had made the law review, but it is no secret that the *Harvard Law Review* practices affirmative action, electing racial minorities with academic records that would not qualify them for the honor if they were white. Since prospective employers know that a double standard is employed, it would not be surprising if they discounted the achievement. When positions on the law review are not awarded on the basis of academic standing alone, employers who value academic achievement above all else will no longer regard it as an unquestionable sign of intellectual distinction. Ironically, affirmative action policies in choosing students for the law review devalue the credential of being on it *except* in the case of white males, the only group ineligible for affirmative action. Making the law review remains a great achievement for them, indeed a greater one than before, since some reserved seats are now removed from the competition, set aside for those belonging to "underrepresented" groups.

Note that the editors of the *University of Pennsylvania Law Review* are apparently disturbed at the belief that affirmative action appointees to the review are taking places away from nonminorities with better qualifications. To counter that perception, the review has announced that the numerical goals for the racial, ethnic, and gender composition of its staff will henceforth be kept secret, so that "things" will "appear fair." Lisa Anderson, *Law Review Masks Diversity in New Admissions System*, N.Y. TIMES, July 7, 1995, at A17. This is an interesting principle that might have wider applications. The less institutions tell the public about their policies, the more "fair" those policies will "appear" to be. It is a pity that students at Penn law school cannot invoke the Freedom of Information Act to find out how much the editors of the law review have stretched academic standards in their pursuit of racial, ethnic, and gender balance.

36. STEPHEN L. CARTER, REFLECTIONS OF AN AFFIRMATIVE ACTION BABY (1991).

observed that greater diversity would result if judges would, "without sacrificing" standards, "think of a different way to make the choice."[37] What "different way" could there be? If judgments are not made solely on the basis of academic achievement but instead involve additional criteria that lead to decisions different from those that would be made on strictly academic grounds, academic standards *are* sacrificed, except in the rare case in which other criteria are used solely as tie-breakers.

The Report provides no clue as to precisely what qualifications would be less "ephemeral" than a student's academic record in professional school. These vague and mysterious comments, however, likely mean that inherited racial, ethnic, and gender characteristics should be the basis for judgment, at least once a certain minimal academic standard is met. These ascribed characteristics are undeniably deeper and more enduring than mere school performance. If a candidate's academic record is to be regarded as "ephemeral," and if obtaining a "more diverse" group of clerks is the highest goal, it follows that clerkships should be allocated by quota.

It may be that they already are, to some degree. Given the huge racial gap in academic qualifications among law school graduates, it is not surprising that there are not more African Americans getting clerkships in the courts of the District of Columbia—indeed, when intellectual achievement as measured by performance in law school is taken into account, it is surprising that there are as many African American clerks as there are. For blacks to have a little more than parity in the number of clerkships, as they do, some of them must have been given affirmative action points by judges who dismiss academic achievement as "ephemeral."[38]

Committees, Panels, Special Masterships, and Conferences

The Report's discussion of appointments to various court committees, panels, and special masterships reveals the same analytical failings that have been described so far. Many possible criteria for picking attorneys to serve on bodies like these may be imagined, including seniority, specialized knowledge of a particular subject, demonstrated interest, and intellectual distinction. But once again the authors' strategy is merely to provide a crude head count of the number of minorities engaged in these activities, to duck the question of the racial composition of the qualified pool, and to deplore the imbalance.[39]

37. Report, *supra* note 1, at 78.
38. *See id.*
39. *Id.* at 79–90.

The authors' discussion of invitees to the circuit's judicial conference in the years 1988–92 follows the same pattern and is vulnerable to the same criticisms. We are told that minorities constituted 13% of all invitees. Is that a lot or a little? The tone of the discussion certainly implies that 13% is dismayingly low. In fact, it represents a slightly larger share than the minority membership of the bar in the Washington metropolitan area; according to figures given in the Report, only 11.8% of the attorneys in the area are from racial or ethnic minority groups.[40]

It is very revealing that the authors do not provide these figures at this point in the text; the reader must ferret them out from an appendix at the rear. We are never told that minorities are not underrepresented but are actually slightly overrepresented at the circuit's judicial conference. Instead of confronting facts that clash with their preconceptions, the authors offer a string of quotations from judges about the importance of having adequate representation of minorities at such gatherings, including one who declares that "it is just plain ridiculous that we would not have minorities" at the judicial conference. What is "just plain ridiculous" is that the data show that "not having" minorities in attendance is not an issue, that they are in fact more than proportionally represented at the judicial conference. It is absurd that the authors of this document attempt to conceal that fact and to create exactly the opposite impression.[41]

The authors' treatment of the demographic composition of the court's Criminal Justice Act (CJA) panels—set up to provide indigent defendants with attorneys—follows similar lines. The data show that 12% of attorneys on court of appeals CJA panels and 19% of those on similar panels of the district court were minorities.[42] Compared to their share of the membership of the Washington metropolitan area bar, minorities have exact proportional representation in panels chosen by the court of appeals and

40. *Id.* at tbl. D3.

41. Even if it could be shown that the guest list at the judicial conference did not precisely mirror the composition of the bar of the Washington, D.C., area in every demographic characteristic, we would have to ask whether the organizers of the conference were seeking to attract nothing more than a representative cross section of the bar. Was that the aim, or was it to gather together a group of the more influential or promising members of the legal community? It is not clear why such a meritocratic definition of the intended audience would be inappropriate. If one sought not a random sample of the bar but a gathering of leaders of the profession, fledgling attorneys who had entered the profession only recently would undoubtedly be underrepresented. That decision would depress the number of minority attorneys and the proportion of women on the invitation list, because disproportionately large numbers of them would be new to profession. Whether this would be a legitimate source of complaint seems highly debatable.

42. REPORT, *supra* note 1, at 94.

substantially more than proportional representation on district court CJA panels.

You wouldn't know it, though, from reading the Report's text. Once again, there is a radical disjunction between the statistics contained in the Report and the conclusions the authors advance. It would appear that the authors drew their conclusions before they tabulated the data, and decided that no reader would notice if the statistics show the opposite of what they are claimed to show. The authors speak blithely of "the overall low numbers of minority attorneys" on CJA panels, despite the fact that their tables show that the numbers are not low at all relative to any obvious standard.[43] We are told that "some minority attorneys . . . question whether . . . race contributed to the selection decisions."[44] This is evidence of the state of mind of certain minority attorneys, perhaps, but it is not evidence that shows bias in appointments to panels. The statistics collected here show that racial groups are equally represented on court of appeals panels, and distinctly overrepresented on district court panels.

Employment Discrimination and Criminal Cases

Much of the latter part of the Report may be discussed more briefly because it follows a formula, albeit a highly unsatisfactory one. The authors first tell us that they had planned a full study of a complex issue, such as whether the district court handles employment discrimination cases with the proper care and impartiality. They then admit that unfortunately they discovered that "the complexity of the effort, time limitations, and the need to rely almost entirely upon volunteers" made it impossible to do the research that was really needed. They were left, as virtually their only basis for commenting upon the subject, with data from questionnaires and interviews revealing the "perception" of attorneys involved in such cases.[45] Undaunted by their admittedly inadequate evidentiary base, the authors nevertheless proceed to opine at length about the subject and to draw sweeping conclusions about pervasive bias in the system.

For instance, the Report tells us that "a significant percentage" of attorneys who handle employment discrimination cases involving race and ethnicity believe that judges treat such cases as if they were "unimportant or a waste of time."[46] Upon inspection of the data, this "significant" proportion turns out to be fewer than one in five attorneys—14% of the males and 23% of the females. This could be seen not as a strikingly high fig-

43. *Id.* at 99.
44. *Id.*
45. *Id.* at 190.
46. *Id.* at 192.

ure but as a rather low one. Why do the perceptions of the one out of five count for so much in the mind of the authors and those of the remaining four out of five for so little? From the discussion that follows, one would think that the great majority of attorneys have perceptions that are actually confined to a relatively small minority of them.

We are also told that "several" witnesses at a public hearing and participants in focus groups believe that "some" judges in the circuit regard these as "nuisance cases." The authors then go on to report that three trial court judges "spoke unfavorably" about employment discrimination cases and one appellate judge suggested that some of his colleagues believed plaintiffs are usually "disgruntled employees."[47] One wonders just how the crime of speaking "unfavorably" about these cases was defined. What of a statement comparable to what one might hear from a lower court judge about divorce cases—"these are usually very messy and unpleasant"? Would that be classified as "unfavorable"? Would making such a comment really mean that a judge would handle employment discrimination disputes unfairly? The Report is ultimately leveling a very serious accusation against the federal judges of the D.C. Circuit courts—that many of them downplay the significance of racial discrimination in employment and are biased against plaintiffs. The authors advance this grave charge mainly upon the basis of hearsay evidence from largely unknown, interested parties. It never dawns upon them that there could *be* such a thing as a nuisance case, and that members of the federal judiciary who have actually mastered all the details of many employment discrimination cases might know whereof they speak. The authors did not analyze any actual employment discrimination cases litigated in the D.C. Circuit courts—the obvious first step to grasping this subject. They originally understood that close case-by-case analysis was essential, found that they were for some reason unable to carry out the research, and then conveniently forgot why such evidence would be needed at all. Their uninformed opinion is the result of a prior conviction that they brought to the inquiry, a conviction that plaintiffs in such cases are invariably right.

The authors find support for their view that the judges are biased in the fact that some of the attorneys who responded to their survey claim that judges treat their fee petitions in these cases with "disdain," and that it is impossible for them to get "fair compensation."[48] Here is another example of the propensity of the authors to be astonishingly credulous about testimony that squares with their own biases. Before taking this accusation seriously, it should have been determined whether attorneys in other areas of the law make fewer complaints about the fees allowed them by

47. *Id.* at 192–93.
48. *Id.* at 195.

the courts. Perhaps they do, but one wonders. Asking people whether they think they are fairly remunerated is hardly an adequate basis for deciding whether or not they really are. Using the methods of the Report, one probably could "prove" that every single occupational group in the United States—from librarians and bus drivers to brain surgeons and major league baseball players—is underpaid. And even if the level of griping by attorneys in employment discrimination cases could be shown to be higher, that would not be unmistakable evidence that the complaints are true, let alone that the "disdain" is rooted in racism. Another possible explanation for such a pattern would be that this is an area of the law which attracts more than its share of greedy or self-righteous attorneys.

The discussion of bias in the operations of the criminal justice system fits precisely the same mold. We are told that an elaborate study, based upon a variety of sources, was planned but was impossible to execute. Thus the authors had to fall back upon the very slender remaining reed available to them—survey responses and testimony from "various participants in the criminal justice system" that indicate "perceptions."[49] To discover whether black and white defendants truly receive equal justice or not, we would need to look closely at persons of different races accused of the same offense, and see whether at different stages of the process there is disparate treatment that stems from racial considerations. There are many complications involved in assessing bias in legal proceedings, but some model studies demonstrate that it is possible.[50] The authors, on the other hand, demonstrate only that black attorneys and white attorneys tend to disagree on this subject, and that they indeed have very different opinions about the role of racial factors in many corners of the judicial system. These differences in perception are worth knowing about, but they do not tell us what the reality is.

Of course, there is a sense in which perceptions do constitute reality. As a wise sociologist remarked early in this century, "if men define situations as real, they are real in their consequences."[51] But it is essential to note that complaints of unfair treatment coming from members of minority groups cannot be taken as simply true by definition. What is true in people's minds and what is true in the external world are separate questions, and the latter cannot be answered on the basis of information about people's opinions.

---

49. *Id.* at 199–200.

50. *See, e.g.*, STEPHEN P. KLEIN, SUSAN TURNER & JOAN PETERSILIA, RACIAL EQUITY IN SENTENCING (1988).

51. W.I. Thomas, *quoted in* ROBERT K. MERTON, SOCIAL THEORY AND SOCIAL STRUCTURE: TOWARD THE CODIFICATION OF THEORY AND RESEARCH 197 (1949).

Suppose that the authors had conducted a broader survey of the opinions of black and white residents of the District of Columbia about public health as well as legal issues, and had found that 40% of African Americans but only 1% of whites believed that the AIDS virus was invented by Jewish doctors as part of a genocidal plot directed against black people. Now this would be an interesting sociological datum.[52] But would the authors say that this widespread perception on the part of blacks comprised evidence about where AIDS came from? Would they maintain that, while this cannot be viewed as decisive evidence about the actual origins of AIDS, it should at the very least persuade Jewish doctors of the need to examine what aspects of their behavior could have created such a "perception"? This seems to be the logic underlying a Report recommendation that judges address the "perception" problem they face.

A major theme of the Report is that the judges are out of touch with local minority opinion, and that if they only knew what such people felt they would go about judging quite differently. Thus we are solemnly informed that "lawyers and community members alike believe the judges' limited familiarity with the communities of the District of Columbia and of minority communities in general has an impact," presumably not a favorable impact, on the decisions made by the courts.[53] It is not clear just how "community members" know that the familiarity of federal judges with "the communities of the District of Columbia" is "limited." And one wonders if the average member of the local bar is in a better position to make such a judgment. It would not be surprising if the subjects of these remarks found them arrogant and presumptuous, as well as fatuous.

Yet another example of leaping from "perception" to social reality is the use the authors make of their finding that 22% of minority courthouse employees say that "they had been denied promotions because of their race or ethnicity."[54] Is this indubitable evidence of bias in the promotion process, as the authors seem to assume?[55] Hardly. It may show only that a significant fraction of minority employees have an inflated sense of their own abilities, or of others' racism, and fail to grasp that they lacked the qualifications to merit the promotion they sought. After all, we have similar evidence that a good many white males who have received Ph.D.'s in recent years currently believe that *they* have been denied academic jobs on the basis of *their* race—that they have been passed over in favor of

52. *Cf.* Howard Odum, Race and Rumors of Race (1943) (classic examination of bizarre rumors among southern whites of antiwhite conspiracies among blacks).

53. Report, *supra* note 1, at 113.

54. *Id.* at 42.

55. *Id.*

minorities as a result of affirmative action.[56] That they *believe* this to be the case, however, does not make it so, as the authors of the Report would likely point out in this instance. Survey evidence that shows that some people feel aggrieved and mistreated is not necessarily compelling evidence that they actually have been mistreated. It can be a useful starting point for an inquiry, but the Report treats it uncritically, as the inquiry's end.

Conclusion

A close, careful, and methodologically sophisticated investigation that sought to determine whether racial or ethnic bias has infected any aspect of the operation of the D.C. Circuit courts could be valuable. This is not such an investigation. The authors have assembled some evidence of interest, but derive too many conclusions from subjective, touchy-feely material that reveals only "perceptions." Although their analysis gives lip service to the ideal of objectivity, it seems to be driven by a preconceived conviction that the judicial system is riddled with bias. The authors manage to find bias even when the relevant data do not support it. Indeed, in some cases the data suggest just the opposite of what the authors claim.

Inquiries like this are apparently under way in other federal circuits. If they are not conducted with much greater care and methodological sophistication than the one in the District of Columbia, they will waste valuable resources and unfairly sully the reputation of the judicial system. This study of the D.C. Circuit may prove useful in such efforts—as a how-not-to-do-it guide.

Editors' Note

A majority of the D.C. Circuit court of appeals has asked that a "Statement of Disassociation" be published along with the Report; Professor Thernstrom's critique has been appended to that statement. A report similar to that of the D.C. Circuit's Task Force on Gender, Race, and Ethnic Bias was issued by the Ninth Circuit in 1993; the Fourth Circuit recently rejected such a study; and the Seventh Circuit has a study under way (Chief Judge Richard Posner has appointed Judge Daniel Manion to oversee the study).

---

56. Consider the data assembled in FREDERICK R. LYNCH, INVISIBLE VICTIMS: WHITE MALES AND THE CRISIS OF AFFIRMATIVE ACTION (1989).

Making a Real Mess

THE CONFIRMATION MESS: CLEANING UP THE FEDERAL APPOINTMENTS PROCESS
by Stephen L. Carter
New York: Basic Books, 1994
252 pp., $21.00

The Confirmation Mess has ambitious aspirations. In examining the process by which Supreme Court and executive branch nominees are confirmed by the Senate, Professor Stephen L. Carter sets out to explain "what is wrong with our confirmation process, how it got this way, and what we can do to fix it" (p. 5). Professor Carter is admirably suited to accomplish this ambitious undertaking. In his previous books—*The Culture of Disbelief*, a widely praised examination of religion in America, and *Reflections of an Affirmative Action Baby*, a thoughtful and interesting discussion of racial issues—Professor Carter has exhibited the evenhandedness and careful deliberation essential to such an undertaking. It is, therefore, surprising that Professor Carter so badly misdiagnoses the ills that have afflicted the confirmation process for Supreme Court Justices that he proposes a remedy that would actually make the process even sicker. What is even more disappointing is that Professor Carter presents a badly distorted account of the very confirmation battles that he critiques.

The Confirmation Mess—which Professor Carter describes as "in the nature of an extended essay" (p. xi)—consists of seven often overlapping, loosely organized chapters. Professor Carter's opening chapter, "The Televised Backyard Fence," complains that the Senate confirmation process for Supreme Court Justices and for executive branch nominees has become a modern-day forum for gossip rather than for debate about the nominee's policies and qualifications. Professor Carter observes that, under our current approach, "we presume the nominees to be entitled to confirmation absent smoking guns, and then we look for the smoke in order to disqualify them" (p. 7). He decries the "alarming trend that turns tiny ethical molehills into vast mountains of outrage, while consigning questions of policy and ability to minor roles" (p. 8). The critical question in cleaning up this confirmation mess, he says, is understanding "why we focus so relentlessly on a nominee's *disqualifications* rather than *qualifications*" (p. 20 (his emphasis)).

To this question, Professor Carter offers a grab bag of disparate answers. The "quintessentially American puritanical streak" means that we "like to see the sinful destroyed" (p. 11). "[O]ur media culture... is notoriously weak at transmitting complicated messages but rewards those who possess a genius for reducing the messages, however inaccurately, to applause lines" (p. 15). "[O]ur well-known national rootlessness, our uncertainty as a polity about how to exercise the power of self-governance," and, most of all, "our realization that the federal government with each passing year recedes further and further from the control of the people" disable us from reaching a consensus on what sort of scrutiny of a nominee is appropriate (p. 15). At bottom, much like his presidential namesake who blamed Americans for their supposed malaise, Professor Carter sees a need to "make important changes in our national mood" (p. 22).

In his second chapter, "Of Nannies, Sound Bites, and Confirmation Nonsense," Professor Carter examines the confirmation fates of Zoë Baird and Lani Guinier, nominated by President Clinton to be, respectively, Attorney General and head of the Justice Department's Civil Rights Division. Professor Carter's judgments are blunt: Baird was "pilloried" for a relatively minor violation; Professor Guinier was "railroaded" (p. 23). In Professor Carter's view, instead of a moderate, thoughtful dialogue on the Baird and Guinier nominations, simple sound-bites prevailed.

Professor Carter's account of Professor Guinier's confirmation process (pp. 37–44) merits special scrutiny because it is the linchpin of his central complaint about "how much right and left have come to resemble each other in the gleeful and reckless distortions that characterize the efforts to defeat challenged nominations" (p. ix). Unfortunately, Professor Carter's complaint, on scrutiny, is reminiscent of that of left-wing critics of the Cold War, who argued the supposed moral equivalence of the United States and the Soviet Union by grossly exaggerating our country's flaws and covering up the heinous crimes of our enemy.

Professor Carter cannot sustain a defense of Professor Guinier even on the limited turf that he chooses. In arguing that Guinier fell "victim to a nationwide campaign resting on distorting small snippets of her scholarship" (p. 37), he identifies three positions attributed to her, none of which, he claims, was accurate. Let us examine these one by one. First, Professor Carter says, the public was falsely told that Guinier "thought minority voters should have a veto to protect their interests" (pp. 37–38). According to Professor Carter, Guinier merely suggested that "adopting a cumulative voting plan would *have the effect* of giving black voters... a veto" (p. 41 n.* (his emphasis)). This is demonstrably false. Guinier in fact specifically and expressly identified "a minority veto on critical minority issues" in a legislative body as an "alternative remedy" to cumulative voting in enforcement of Section 2 of the Voting Rights Act.[1] Strike one on Professor Carter.

Second, Professor Carter says that it is not true that Guinier thought that "a form of proportional representation (guaranteed seats, a quota) was necessary" (p. 38). But the record shows that this is not only true, but also a remarkable understatement of Guinier's views. Guinier, for example, specifically opined that "the Senate Judiciary Committee should begin evaluating federal judicial nominations with reference to specific goals for increasing non-white nominees."[2] More generally, one of her central theses was that the creation of safe majority black districts did not go far enough in that it "fail[ed] to ensure proportional legislative power"[3]—i.e., a proportionate share of legislative victories (hence her support for such procedures as "[l]egislative cumulative voting" and a minority veto[4]). Strike two.

Third, Professor Carter contends that Guinier never said that "black officials elected by white voters were not authentically black" (p. 38). Again, Guinier's own carefully written words refute Professor Carter: "Authentic leaders are those elected by black voters. In voting rights terminology, electoral ratification from majority-black, single-member districts establishes authenticity. These facts distinguish the authentic representatives from those officials who are handpicked by the 'establishment,' or who must appeal to white voters in order to get elected."[5] And:

> Identifying "black representatives" raises several questions. For example, would descriptively black representatives who were also Republicans qualify as black representatives? More generally, is it the race of the rep-

---

1. Lani Guinier, *No Two Seats: The Elusive Quest for Political Equality*, 77 VA. L. REV. 1413, 1503 (1991). *See also* Lani Guinier, *The Triumph of Tokenism: The Voting Rights Act and the Theory of Black Electoral Success*, 89 MICH. L. REV. 1077, 1140 & n.302 (1991) ("'A minority veto' for legislation of vital importance to minority interests would respond to evidence of gross 'deliberate gerrymanders.' [fn:] Alternatively, a minority veto reserved for issues of majority concern would force the majority to bargain."). Similarly, Guinier's resurrection of John Calhoun's proposal for a requirement of "concurrent legislative majorities," *see id.* at 1140, is nothing more than a minority veto combined with a majority veto.

2. Lani Guinier, *Keeping The Faith: Black Voters in the Post-Reagan Era*, 24 HARV. C.R.-C.L. L. REV. 393, 432 (1989). Guinier continued:

> The Committee could decline to consider any nominee until a sufficient number of nominations—such as twenty or thirty—were made so as to enable the Committee to consider not only the individual qualifications of each, but the impact of these twenty or thirty nominations as a totality on the composition of the federal bench.

3. Guinier, *No Two Seats*, *supra* note 1, at 1441.

4. *Id.* at 1503.

5. Guinier, *The Triumph of Tokenism*, *supra* note 1, at 1103–04.

> resentative that makes them part of the minority voting group? Although no one answer may suffice, the court should consider only a representative's status as the minority group's representative of choice. Therefore, only a representative sponsored by the black community and electorally accountable to it would count for purposes of a legislative bloc voting analysis.[6]

Strike three!

Professor Carter also oddly asserts that we must remember that "a work of scholarship . . . is not an op-ed article" (p. 38). But surely this contrast cuts against Guinier, not in her favor. Her voluminous articles set forth a carefully considered conception of how the existing civil rights laws should be enforced.[7] It is difficult to imagine a body of material that would be more probative of a nominee's qualifications to head the Civil Rights Division. In short, under the views expressed by Professor Carter in his opening chapter, Guinier's confirmation process would seem a paradigm of how a nominee should be assessed. The fact that President Clinton, on reading her writings, withdrew her nomination—Guinier herself did not withdraw, as Professor Carter misstates (p. 37)—is yet further proof that the nomination was ill-considered from the outset.

Professor Carter claims that the treatment that Professor Guinier received was on a par with that received by Judge Bork. To his credit, Professor Carter is critical of many distortions of Judge Bork's record. Yet, whereas he whitewashes Professor Guinier's record and unfairly excoriates her critics, he somehow describes Judge Bork's travesty of a confirmation hearing as a "sublime" and "famous national seminar on constitutional law" (p. 6).

Like Professor Carter, I believe that there is an apt comparison between the confirmation processes of Professor Guinier and Judge Bork. But it is very different from the comparison that he draws. In both cases, partisans of the left distorted the nominee's record—first, to Judge Bork's (and the nation's) detriment, and, now, after the fact, in the cottage industry that is rewriting Professor Guinier's record.

The core of *The Confirmation Mess* consists of the three central chapters addressing the Supreme Court confirmation process. These chapters make two fundamental assertions relevant to the confirmation process.[8]

---

6. Guinier, *No Two Seats*, *supra* note 1, at 1500 n.299.

7. *See, e.g.*, *id.* at 1509 ("the focus and basic remedial approach I propose has [sic] been mandated by *Congress*" (emphasis in original)).

8. These chapters also contain the conventional snide denigrations of Justice Thomas. To cite but one example: Professor Carter claims that Justice Thomas's "consistency in voting with Antonin Scalia is the stuff of legend" (p. 81). It is particularly odd that Professor Carter, who clerked for Justice Thurgood Marshall, would insinuate that there is anything unusual about Justice Thomas's voting patterns. For the fact of the matter is that (according to statistics compiled annually by the *Harvard Law Review*) during the 23 Terms that Jus-

First, Professor Carter dismisses the basic distinction between litmus tests on the one hand, and judicial philosophy on the other, as "a distinction that almost nobody takes seriously" (p. 57). In his view, inquiries into judicial philosophy are, and can be, nothing more than disguised attempts to determine how a potential Justice will vote on specific issues—"litmus tests." After all, Americans care about concrete results, not judicial philosophies, and the "committed activists on left and right" obviously have the same concerns (p. 57). Accordingly, a "reflective Senate... would eschew any inquiry into judicial philosophy," for such an inquiry threatens judicial independence (pp. 146–47).

The second basic assertion made by Professor Carter is that a judge's moral values are central to the judicial role. Professor Carter does not claim merely that a judge's own moral values might sometimes inadvertently color his judging. He claims, rather, that "in *every* exercise of interpretive judgment, there comes a crucial moment when the interpreter's own experience and values become *the most important data*" (p. 151 (emphasis added)). What is ultimately most important is therefore "not what sort of theory the nominee happens to indulge but what sort of person the nominee happens to be" (p. 151). Over the long run, "there should evolve a healthy convergence between the moral direction of the Justice and the fundamental moral vision of the nation the Justice serves" (p. 153). Moreover, "in the worst of times,... the morally superior individual will almost certainly be the morally superior jurist" (p. 153).

What follows from these two assertions is that the Senate should engage in a "public inquiry into the moral vision of the nominee"—which, Professor Carter assures us, "is not the same as allowing public inquiry into the nominee's likely votes" (p. 114). This inquiry should have two aspects: "First, the nominee ought to be a person for whom moral choices occasion deep and sustained reflection. Second, the nominee ought to be, in the judgment of the Senate, an individual whose personal moral decisions seem generally sound" (p. 152). Ultimately, "the political task in the real world of real interpretive problems is to people the bench not with Justices holding the

---

tice Brennan and Justice Marshall sat on the Court together, they averaged an agreement rate of 89.6%. During their last seven Terms together, their agreement rate averaged 95% and never fell below 91%, and there was even one Term in which they had a 100% agreement rate. By contrast, Justices Scalia and Thomas have had agreement rates of 85.9%, 86.0%, and 82.8%. When one factors in the remarkable indeterminacy of liberal activist judging, the much higher rate of correspondence between Justice Brennan and Justice Marshall is all the more noteworthy. In any event, the relevant inquiry should be the soundness of a Justice's reasoning, not how often he votes the same way as another Justice. Justice Thomas is performing admirably by any measure.

right constitutional theories but with Justices possessing the right moral instincts" (p. 152).

If there is a proposal that would make confirmation hearings even more of a circus than the Bork and Thomas hearings were, it is Professor Carter's. It is odd, to say the least, that Professor Carter complains in his first chapter that "the search for disqualifying factors potentially leads to a rather freewheeling investigation into the backgrounds of nominees" (p. 21), yet here recommends that the Senate undertake a "public inquiry into the moral vision of the nominee." What possible background information would *not* be relevant to such an inquiry? In a society increasingly fractured on basic moral issues—in a society, indeed, in which a portion of the elites denies the very existence of right and wrong—what moral vision should the Senate be looking for? How can Professor Carter state (correctly, in my view) that it was "ridiculous" for a reporter to publish a list of the videos rented by Judge Bork (p. 6), when such a list might well yield insights into a nominee's moral vision?

Professor Carter provides two answers to such questions. One is to leave it to the political system to sort out (p. 154). The second—even more unsatisfying—suggestion is that the privacy interests of the nominee should prevail (p. 179). Indeed, Professor Carter argues at some length that two aspects of the so-called nanny problem that felled Zoë Baird—the "requirements... that families report to the IRS what their nannies earn and that they ascertain their nannies' immigration status" (p. 182)—are unconstitutional invasions of the right of privacy! If inquiry into a nominee's moral vision is the proper focus of a confirmation hearing, it makes little sense to let the nominee's privacy interests trump the process. It is even worse that Professor Carter can salvage his bad proposal only by concocting bad constitutional law.

Professor Carter's misguided proposal is rooted in the fact that his two basic premises are unsound. It may be the case that "almost nobody" in trendy academic circles "takes seriously" the distinction between litmus tests and judicial philosophy. If so, that merely highlights a defect in academia, for the distinction is fundamental. Under the judicial philosophy of originalism (which has, until recent decades, always been the constitutional orthodoxy[9]), the Constitution is binding law—not just on the people at large, or just on the political branches, but on Supreme Court Justices as

9. This is not to say that Supreme Court decisions in the past were always genuinely faithful to the original meaning of the Constitution. But, as Justice Scalia has put it, "in the past, nonoriginalist opinions have almost always had the decency to lie, or at least to dissemble, about what they were doing." *Originalism: The Lesser Evil*, 57 U. CIN. L. REV. 849, 852 (1989). In the last 30 years or so, the constitutional heretics have become not only more numerous, but more brazen, denying and caricaturing the faith from which they stray.

well. Under this philosophy, the task of a Supreme Court Justice is to determine the meaning of a constitutional provision in accordance with the understanding of those who originally promulgated it. The Constitution is not simply putty to be molded into whatever shape suits the Justices or furthers their particular moral visions. It is true, of course, that originalism yields answers that liberal judicial activists find unwelcome on certain litmus-test issues. But this fact simply demonstrates the illegitimacy of judicial activism, not Professor Carter's purported identity between litmus tests and judicial philosophy.[10]

It follows as well, under the traditional understanding of judging, that a judge's moral values are essentially irrelevant to the decisionmaking process. Professor Carter's claim that a judge's values become "the most important data" in "every exercise of interpretive judgment" is, I am convinced, both a gross misdescription of how responsible judges operate and a frightening prescription of how judges should operate.

What Professor Carter fails to confront is that it is illegitimate judicial activism that is the source of our confirmation imbroglios. Professor Carter literally treats as a "given the awesome authority that the Justices wield in contemporary society" (p. 22). So long as judges continue to usurp power that belongs to the people to exercise through their representatives, the confirmation process for Supreme Court Justices will be a potential battlefield. In short, the solution to the confirmation mess is the very opposite of what Professor Carter advocates: we must return judges to the role of judging and not permit them (much less invite them) to act as our platonic moral guardians.

Professor Carter ends his book with "Some Modest Proposals, Reviewed," in which he addresses possible changes in Senate confirmation procedures.[11] In his closing pages, he recognizes that the real source of the Supreme Court confirmation mess is that "we rely too heavily on the Justices to correct what

10. Professor Carter's conflation of litmus tests and judicial philosophy conveniently leads to his charges that the Reagan and Bush administrations used litmus tests far more than any previous administrations (p. 71)—when they in fact did not use them at all—and pursued a "results-oriented" vision of the courts (p. 72). His charges are partisan political rhetoric, not scholarship.

11. Professor Carter's penultimate chapter, "The Disqualification Problem, Revisited," is an awkward appendage to the main body. In this chapter, Professor Carter, having earlier complained that too much attention is devoted to disqualifications, proceeds to devote too much attention to disqualifications. He divides potentially disqualifying factors into five categories, which he then ranks in order of their "relative ease of cure" (p. 178). Only the most wonkish social scientist will find any analytic value in this sterile formulization. Indeed, the fact that Professor Carter's first category of disqualifications is "lack of qualifications" serves only to call into question the distinction between disqualifications and qualifications on which his opening chapter turned.

we often view as the errors of the other branches of government" (p. 204), and he concludes that we must "surrender the bold and exciting image of the Supreme Court as national policymaker" (pp. 205–06). Given the prodigious talents that Professor Carter has displayed in his other endeavors, it is a shame that the bulk of his book is not guided by, and built on, these insights.

REVIEWED BY ORRIN G. HATCH

Who Legislates?

POWER WITHOUT RESPONSIBILITY: HOW CONGRESS ABUSES THE PEOPLE THROUGH DELEGATION
by David Schoenbrod
New Haven: Yale University Press, 1993
260 pp., $28.50

I

Delegation of legislative power by Congress is a pervasive feature of modern national governance. In the wake of the New Deal, the federal courts essentially gave up trying to enforce any serious limits on Congress's practice of granting sweeping authority to administrative agencies, and today those agencies rival or surpass Congress as the federal government's principal lawmaking organ.

The delegation phenomenon raises important questions involving such disciplines as constitutional law (what are the boundaries of permissible agency authority?), jurisprudence (are courts institutionally capable of preventing or limiting delegation?), political science (why do legislators delegate, and what effect does delegation have on governance and the electoral process?), economics (does delegation lead to more or less efficient regulation?), and normative political theory (does delegation enhance or degrade the quality of lawmaking, serve or disserve democracy, and promote or endanger liberty?). In *Power without Responsibility: How Congress Abuses the People through Delegation*, Professor David Schoenbrod of New York Law School tackles all of these questions—and more—and resolves each of them decisively against the modern practice of delegating legislative power. This slim (fewer than 200 pages of text) but comprehensive book is a manifesto aimed at keeping the power to make rules for national governance in Congress—a Congress that seemingly works overtime to find ways to avoid the responsibility and accountability that accompanies the power to govern.

Most of *Power without Responsibility* is devoted to exploring the real-world causes and consequences of legislative delegations. The author's story, developed through a generous use of anecdotes and a strong dose of public choice theory, is primarily one of legislators (and Presidents[1]) systematically trying to fool the electorate by enacting grandstanding legislation that symbolically expresses concern about great issues but avoids resolving the difficult policy questions that might antagonize interest groups. The real issues are punted to agencies, freeing the legislators to engage in Monday-morning quarterbacking and strategic casework on behalf of constituents. The story rings largely true, and the author's view of the consequences of the resulting scheme of delegation is conveyed by a representative sample of his chapter and subchapter headings: "Delegation Weakens Democracy" (p. 99), "Delegation Endangers Liberty" (p. 107), "Delegation Makes Law Less Reasonable" (p. 119), "Delegation Shifts the Focus of Lawmakers from Protecting People to Casting Blame" (p. 126), "Delegation Creates Wasteful Fantasies of Cheap, Effective Regulatory Protection" (p. 128), "Delegation Reduces the Public's Sense That Government Is Responsive" (p. 129), and "Delegation Makes Citizens Less Reasonable and More Alienated" (p. 130).

A small but important portion of Professor Schoenbrod's book argues that delegation of legislative power, whatever its practical effects may be, is *unconstitutional* and that courts can and should vigorously police this constitutional norm. Because my own expertise lies in constitutional law rather than in political science or political theory, I devote the rest of my review to addressing Professor Schoenbrod's constitutional arguments.[2] To give away the ending, Professor Schoenbrod's constitutional attack on delegation is fundamentally sound, though for somewhat different reasons than he offers.

1. Professor Schoenbrod is one of the few scholars to recognize the President's complicity in modern delegations. *See* pp. 95–96, 105. The President, no less than members of Congress, must take a stand on legislation through his constitutional obligation to sign, veto, or pocket-veto bills. *See* U.S. CONST. art. I, § 7, cl. 2. Thus, the President, no less than members of Congress, has an incentive to avoid accountability for policy choices by shunting off difficult questions to less visible agencies. Recent administrations that often professed fidelity to the constitutional separation of powers did nothing to stem the tide of delegation. *See* p. 96 (noting that the Reagan and Bush administrations did nothing to prevent delegation); Gary Lawson, *The Rise and Rise of the Administrative State*, 107 HARV. L. REV. 1231, 1241 (1994) (same).

2. Closely tied to Professor Schoenbrod's constitutional arguments are several jurisprudential claims concerning such matters as the role of precedent (pp. 158–60) and the proper exercise of remedial discretion should the courts choose to enforce the nondelegation principle (pp. 174–77). I ignore these arguments for lack of space, not for lack of interest.

II

According to Professor Schoenbrod, although the Constitution contains no express prohibition on delegation of legislative power, the available evidence of the founding generation's understanding (pp. 30–31, 155–56) demonstrates that such a prohibition is implicit in Article I's grant to Congress of "[a]ll legislative Powers herein granted...."[3] The question for Professor Schoenbrod is "not whether, but rather to what extent, Article I prohibits Congress from delegating legislative power" (p. 156). His answer is that *no* delegations of legislative power are permissible. He reasons that there are many contexts in which statutes may properly vest considerable discretion in executive and judicial actors (pp. 181–83, 186–89), but such discretion must fall within the *executive* or *judicial* powers vested in the President and federal courts by, respectively, Articles II and III of the Constitution.[4] The crucial task is therefore to determine when the statutory discretion of executive or judicial actors reflects an impermissible delegation of legislative authority or a permissible exercise of executive or interpretive authority.

Professor Schoenbrod actually says very little about that task in his book.[5] His central thesis is that "a person interested in knowing whether the statute prohibits any given conduct will, in most cases, get a clear answer from the statute that states the law, but may well get no answer, for any particular case, from a statute that delegates" (p. 183). Accordingly, when it legislates, Congress can leave room for uncertainty and interpretation, but not too much room. At a minimum, a valid statute must set forth a *rule of conduct* (p. 182) and not merely a *goal or set of goals*, and even a statute setting forth a rule of conduct can be invalid if the rule resolves an insufficient number of cases arising under it. Congress need not, however, meet this standard of specificity when its statutes merely leave executive or judicial officials with discretion within their constitutionally enumerated powers (pp. 186, 190) or when the statutes concern the management of government property (pp. 186–89).

This may not sound like much of a test for identifying unconstitutional delegations of legislative power, but it is almost entirely on the mark. The problem is not with Professor Schoenbrod's conclusions, but with the path

3. U.S. CONST. art. I, § 1.

4. *See id.* art. II, § 1 ("The executive Power shall be vested in a President..."); *id.* art. III, § 1 ("The judicial Power of the United States, shall be vested in one supreme Court, and in such inferior Courts as the Congress may from time to time ordain and establish.").

5. He said more about it in his earlier scholarship. *See* David Schoenbrod, *The Delegation Doctrine: Could the Court Give It Substance?*, 83 MICH. L. REV. 1223, 1252–58 (1985).

he follows to some of those conclusions. There is a stronger, more straightforward constitutional case against delegation than Professor Schoenbrod provides that generates a nondelegation principle very similar to Professor Schoenbrod's—complete with the seemingly odd "exception" for laws concerning the management of government property.

III

In order to understand the proper scope and limits of the nondelegation doctrine, one must understand the doctrine's constitutional *source*. Professor Schoenbrod correctly notes that the founding generation clearly contemplated some limits on legislative delegation (pp. 155–59), but because he cannot identify a specific provision in the Constitution that deals with delegation, he infers a prohibition on delegation from Article I's grant of legislative power to Congress.[6] But this search for a constitutional prohibition on delegation overlooks the first principle of American constitutionalism. The national government is entirely the creation of the Constitution. It is a government of limited and enumerated powers that can act only when and how it is authorized to do so by the Constitution. Accordingly, the first question with respect to any power claimed by the federal government is not whether the Constitution affirmatively *forbids* (either expressly or impliedly) exercise of that power, but whether the Constitution affirmatively *permits* (either expressly or impliedly) such an exercise.

All of the specific institutions of the national government—the legislative, executive, and judicial departments—are also creations of the Constitution. Thus, those institutions are departments of limited and enumerated powers; none can exercise any power that is not delegated to it by the Constitution, just as the national government as a whole is confined to its enumerated jurisdiction. Accordingly, one should approach the problem of delegation not by looking for prohibitions on delegation but by asking whether Congress has an affirmative power to delegate legislative authority and whether any other institution of the national government has the affirmative power to exercise the delegated authority.

Congress is granted no general power to delegate legislative authority. The only possible source of such a power is the "Necessary and Proper Clause"—known to the founding generation as the "Sweeping Clause"—which grants Congress power "to make all Laws which shall be necessary and proper for carrying into Execution the foregoing Powers, and all other

6. *See* p. 155 ("The Constitution does not prohibit the delegation of legislative power in so many words, but the Framers probably intended such a prohibition with Article I's opening sentence, which begins: 'All legislative Powers herein granted shall be vested in a Congress . . .'").

Powers vested by this Constitution in the Government of the United States, or in any Department or Officer thereof."[7] The Sweeping Clause, however, does not authorize Congress to delegate legislative power. As Patricia Granger and I have elsewhere demonstrated at length,[8] the requirement in the Sweeping Clause that laws be "necessary *and proper*" means that all laws enacted pursuant to this clause must be distinctively and peculiarly within the jurisdiction of the national government and cannot allow the constituent institutions of the national government to transgress their respective constitutional jurisdictions. Put more simply, a law delegating legislative power to an agency would not have been deemed a "proper" law for carrying into effect national powers by a fully informed general public in 1789 (the legislative and executive departments would not be confined to their distinctive provinces), and such a law is therefore not within the enumerated power of Congress.[9]

An example may help illustrate the way in which the Sweeping Clause enforces a nondelegation principle. Suppose that Congress passes a statute prohibiting the use or employment in interstate commerce, "in connection with the purchase or sale of any security . . . , [of] any manipulative or deceptive device or contrivance in contravention of such rules and regulations as the [Securities and Exchange] Commission may prescribe as necessary or appropriate in the public interest or for the protection of investors."[10] This statute looks like a fairly raw delegation of legislative power to the Securities and Exchange Commission: the Commission's rules, rather than the statute itself, determine the standards of conduct to which people must conform. A defender of the statute, however, might reason as follows: "Let us grant that Congress can't delegate legislative power and that no agency can constitutionally receive such a delegation. That hasn't happened here. Agencies (subject to the supervision of the President) can exercise 'executive Power.'[11] Executive power, in its most basic sense, involves implement-

7. U.S. CONST. art. I, § 8, cl. 18. Scholars sometimes point to this clause as possible constitutional authorization for Congress to grant broad authority to administrators. *See* Harold J. Krent, *Delegation and Its Discontents*, 94 COLUM. L. REV. 710, 736 (1994) (reviewing Schoenbrod's *Power Without Responsibility*); Peter M. Shane, *Conventionalism in Constitutional Interpretation and the Place of Administrative Agencies*, 36 AM. U. L. REV. 573, 592, 597–98 (1987).

8. Gary Lawson & Patricia B. Granger, *The "Proper" Scope of Federal Power: A Jurisdictional Interpretation of the Sweeping Clause*, 43 DUKE L.J. 267 (1993).

9. *See id.* at 333–34.

10. 15 U.S.C. § 78j(b) (1988).

11. The Securities and Exchange Commission has long been treated as an "independent agency" whose commissioners are not subject to at-will removal by the President. Congress frequently delegates authority to agencies that are insulated to some degree from presidential control. Under a proper interpretation of the Constitution, agencies that are not subject

ing statutes according to their terms. This statute instructs agencies to make rules concerning deceptive practices in securities trading. When the agency makes such rules, it is doing exactly what the statute instructs it to do, and it is therefore 'executing' the statute rather than making law. Congress has certainly given to the agency substantial authority, but that authority is *executive* rather than *legislative* authority, and no delegation has taken place."

The problem with this argument is that, while Congress may ordinarily entrust the executive (and the courts) with some measure of discretion in interpreting and applying laws, any such grant of discretionary power to an enforcement agent must be authorized by the Sweeping Clause and therefore must be "proper."[12] If the agency's discretion is too large, however, so that its authority partakes more of what traditionally would be viewed as legislative power rather than executive power, the law calling upon the agency to implement the statute fails to be a jurisdictionally "proper" law for carrying into execution governmental powers and is therefore outside the enumerated powers of Congress. Thus, the word "proper" in the Sweeping Clause makes enforceable against Congress certain jurisdictional constraints on the powers of executive and judicial agents to receive and exercise delegations of authority.

Identifying the word "proper" in the Sweeping Clause as the source of the nondelegation principle helps answer some of the problems with which Professor Schoenbrod valiantly struggles. How, for instance, do we tell when a statute gives the agency "too much" discretion? The answer lies, as it does for all questions of the Constitution's interpretation, in the text and its history. The "executive Power" described in Article II includes whatever powers a fully informed general public in 1789 would have understood that term to include. Accordingly, a statute unconstitutionally delegates legislative (or, perhaps, judicial) power whenever a fully informed general public in 1789 would have regarded the allocation of authority produced by the statute to be "improper."

---

to presidential control cannot even properly exercise executive power, much less legislative power, though that is a subject for another day. *See* Lawson, *supra* note 1, at 1241–45 (discussing the constitutional requirement of presidential control of agencies).

12. Congress, of course, has many enumerated powers other than the power granted by the Sweeping Clause, including the power to regulate "Commerce... among the several States," U.S. CONST. art. I, § 8, cl. 3, which might well include the power to regulate interstate securities trading. But laws empowering executive officials to apply and enforce a prohibition on deceptive trading practices, prescribing penalties for violation of such prohibitions, and so forth are not themselves laws directly regulating "Commerce... among the several States." They are quintessentially the kind of laws that the Sweeping Clause was designed to authorize: laws "for carrying into Execution" the enumerated powers of the national government. And such laws are within Congress's enumerated powers only if they are "necessary and proper."

Professor Schoenbrod's "clearly resolving most cases" (p. 183) test for unconstitutional delegations stacks up remarkably well by this standard: a statute regulating private conduct that does not resolve most cases falling under it probably would not have been regarded as "proper" in 1789. In practice, Professor Schoenbrod's test converges in large measure with the test recently put forward by Martin Redish, which requires valid statutes to evince "some meaningful level of normative political commitment by the enacting legislators, thus enabling the electorate to judge its representatives."[13] Both tests in turn essentially converge with my own (deliberately circular) formulation, which requires valid laws to make "whatever policy decisions are sufficiently important to the statutory scheme at issue so that Congress must make them."[14] One can employ any or all of these formulations so long as one understands that the inquiry must ultimately focus on the original meaning of the word "proper" and the original understandings of the legislative, executive, and judicial powers that lie behind it.

As with many constitutional questions, such an inquiry will not always be easy. Consider, for example, a statute empowering an agency to set "just and reasonable rates" for a public utility. Does the statute "clearly resolv[e] most cases" arising under it (or demonstrate a meaningful level of normative political commitment, or make the policy decisions that are sufficiently important to be made by the legislature)? The answer is "maybe." If the statute simply instructs the agency to go forth and do what it thinks is good, the statute is a raw delegation of legislative authority. But the phrase "just and reasonable rates" has a long history and can be used as a term of art with a specific meaning. The traditional understanding of rate regulation is that a regulating agency must permit a utility to earn enough revenue to cover the utility's operating costs plus a return on capital sufficient to attract investors in a competitive capital market. If the phrase "just and reasonable rates" is employed by the legislature as a term of art to describe this traditional form of ratemaking, does the statute pass muster under the nondelegation principle? Professor Schoenbrod's answer is that it depends on whether the regulatory commission "knows how to measure the capital on which the utility gets to earn a return" (p. 184). Thus, if the phrase "just and reasonable rates" is a specific enough term of art to include a method for measuring the utility's rate base, such as the amount actually spent (or perhaps prudently spent) on plant, then Professor Schoenbrod would allow the statute to stand. So would I, though the question is a close one, because even when the statute (explicitly or implicitly) specifies the form of ratemaking and the method for determining the rate base, the agency still will have considerable discretion in allocating costs across time periods, choosing dis-

13. Martin H. Redish, The Constitution as Political Structure 136 (1995).

14. Lawson, *supra* note 1, at 1239.

count rates, estimating the risk of investment in the firm, and so forth. Nonetheless, the central policy choice—to engage in cost-of-service ratemaking using historical costs (or prudent historical costs) to determine the rate base and functioning capital markets to determine the rate of return—seems to have been made by the statute. On the other hand, if the ratemaking agency can choose its own standard for the rate base (or the rate of return), Professor Schoenbrod would invalidate the statute, and so would I. There is no knockdown argument for any of these results—which proves only that hard cases are hard.[15]

Identifying the textual source of the nondelegation principle also solves some thorny problems involving the management of public property that vex proponents of a vigorous nondelegation doctrine. Must Congress make all the rules concerning the use of public lands, including setting the hours of operation, the kinds of activities allowed on each parcel during each time period, the precise fees to be charged to each user in each context, and so forth? The result seems unlikely, and Professor Schoenbrod accordingly contends that "Congress need not make rules for the management of government property, such as federal lands, monies, and corporations like the Postal Service" (p. 186). He has a difficult time, however, articulating a defense of that position. Professor Schoenbrod insists that precedent and practicality support his conclusion (pp. 187–88) and, more importantly, that "[t]he text of the Constitution permits such an interpretation" (p. 187). Congress is granted power in Article IV "to dispose of and make all needful Rules and Regulations respecting the Territory or other Property belonging to the United States,"[16] and this clause is "located outside the first three Articles of the Constitution, which focus on separation of powers" (p. 187). Nonetheless, Professor Schoenbrod admits that all of these arguments together "still leave me with doubts" (p. 188) about Congress's ability to let executive actors make the rules for management of public property, and he ultimately sides with congressional power to delegate in this context "because it can be made consistent with the safeguards of liberty in Article I" (p. 188).[17]

Professor Schoenbrod is correct to focus attention on public property management—the case for a strong nondelegation doctrine loses most of its historical and intuitive force if it requires Congress to micromanage all public assets—and his ultimate conclusion is sound. But the argument for

---

15. For a short list of some easy cases under the constitutional nondelegation principle, see *id.* at 1240.

16. U.S. CONST. art. IV, § 3, cl. 2.

17. Where exercises of proprietary power do affect liberty—for example, through conditions on grants—Professor Schoenbrod would apply his nondelegation principle. *See* pp. 188–89.

that conclusion is much stronger and more straightforward than he recognizes. As Professor Schoenbrod notes, Congress has express power in the Property Clause of Article IV to "make all needful Rules and Regulations respecting the Territory and other Property belonging to the United States." If the textual source of the nondelegation doctrine is the word "proper" in the Sweeping Clause, then the nondelegation principle does not limit Congress's property management powers because *Congress does not need to employ the Sweeping Clause to carry into effect its powers under the Property Clause.* The Property Clause is a self-contained grant of general legislative authority.[18] The only constitutional qualification on Congress's "Rules and Regulations respecting" federal property is that they be "needful," which requires only that such rules and regulations bear some purposeful relationship to the end of property management. Thus, legislation under the Property Clause does indeed stand outside the nondelegation doctrine—not because separation of powers doctrines apply only to the first three articles of the Constitution, but because the text of the Property Clause allows Congress fully to regulate the subject matter without resort to the Sweeping Clause and its requirement of propriety.[19]

IV

My focus on constitutional concerns should not mislead the reader: *Power without Responsibility* is primarily a policy-based critique of the modern practice of delegation. Even when that critique does not fully persuade, it is presented fairly and understandably. Very few books pack so much punch and information into so short a space.

Power without Responsibility is an outstanding springboard for further discussion of the many questions that Professor Schoenbrod has boldly cho-

---

18. *See* Lawson & Granger, *supra* note 8, at 310–11 (comparing and contrasting the Sweeping Clause, which reflects a principle of limited government power, and the Property Clause, which reflects—in a limited context—a principle of general government power). The *scope* of that self-contained authority is a different question. In particular, it is not clear whether Congress has the same broad power over federal property within a state's borders as it does over territory or property that is not arguably subject to a state's jurisdiction. *See* David E. Engdahl, *State and Federal Power over Federal Property*, 18 ARIZ. L. REV. 283 (1976). Whatever the scope of that power may be, however, Congress need not invoke the Sweeping Clause in order to exercise that power.

19. Similar considerations explain why Congress can create local legislatures with self-governing authority in federal territories and the District of Columbia. Territories are explicitly within the compass of the Property Clause, and Article I grants Congress general legislative power over the District of Columbia. *See* U.S. CONST. art. I, § 17 (granting Congress power "[t]o exercise exclusive Legislation in all Cases whatsoever, over such District . . . as may . . . become the Seat of the Government of the United States").

sen to face. It is not (and I do not think it was intended to be) the last word on delegation, but it is a powerful contribution to a perennial debate on fundamental issues.

REVIEWED BY GARY LAWSON*

* The author is grateful to David E. Engdahl, Patty Granger, and David Schoenbrod for their help in developing the ideas in this essay.

Grand Delusion?: Divining Constitutional Legitimacy from Legal Theory

RETHINKING CONSTITUTIONAL LAW: ORIGINALISM, INTERVENTIONISM, AND THE POLITICS OF JUDICIAL REVIEW
by Earl M. Maltz
Lawrence, Kansas: University Press of Kansas, 1994
148 pp., $27.50

The main arguments of this slim volume are presented in the four paragraphs of its "Conclusion," occupying less than one page in all. Concise exposition certainly earns a reader's gratitude: "brevity is the soul of wit" and all that. But Professor Maltz also deploys his brevity to underscore a substantive point. His arguments take aim at various constitutional theories—both originalist and nonoriginalist—which, he suggests, are all deservedly dispatched with short shrift.

Essentially, this book is a survey of the great debate over judicial review which has occupied so many able scholars over the past twenty years. It is, in many ways, a useful summary, particularly for those who have either come late to the debate or dropped out at an earlier stage. It might be called "Polemics on Constitutional Theory in a Nutshell," except that Maltz offers much more pointed commentary in his own name than one finds in the usual hornbook.

If interest in this debate has been flagging in recent years, Maltz is not at all concerned to revive it. By his own account, both sides should long since have fled the field in embarrassment, since the arguments on both sides are so easily challenged. Maltz concludes by urging all sides to move on to new arguments in "constitutional theory." But he is so impatient with the old debate that he ends up with little to say about how to improve it—beyond starting all over again.

I

Maltz begins his survey with a pointed reminder that "conservative" legal theorists are not always consistent in their doctrines. Justices Scalia and

Rehnquist, he notes, have frequently invoked "original intent" to condemn activist liberal doctrines (for instance, the Burger Court's handling of the Religion Clauses)—but then ignored evidence of original intent in their eagerness to impose their own activist doctrines. Maltz then gives as an example their eagerness to read the Fourteenth Amendment as a barrier to race-conscious affirmative action.

It must be noted at the outset that there is a problem with this particular example, because Maltz does not stop to consider whether circumstances might not justify this perceived deviation from "originalism." If, as Raoul Berger has argued,[1] the historical evidence suggests that even *Brown v. Board of Education* was a clear departure from the intent of those who framed the Fourteenth Amendment, the modern Court has no political option but to stay with *Brown* rather than with the historian's exposition of original intent. That being so, it might be quite excusable—and, in some statesmanly sense, quite "consistent"—for champions of originalism here to insist that *Brown*'s canonical status be balanced at least by a principle of race-neutrality that limits its reach.[2]

Maltz's broader point, in any event, is that any sustained effort to implement originalism will in all likelihood prove to be politically untenable. He notes, with other critics, the frequent difficulty of determining what the constitutional Framers actually did intend. He notes, with others, the difficulty of applying old doctrines to new problems, without reinterpreting old language into open-ended abstractions that would seem to justify almost anything. But his main argument is that, if originalist doctrine is invoked to justify a restricted reach for the Bill of Rights, the same doctrine demands that courts impose a restrictive reading of the enumerated powers of Congress. The implication of the "originalist approach," then, would require courts to overturn the larger part of the current U.S. Code, and this consequence, Maltz suggests, poses an insurmountable practical objection to the whole originalist strategy (p. 108):

> Although the appeal to the legitimate authority of the framers does provide the necessary rationale for judicial interventionism, the argument proves too much: the same argument that justifies interventionism in individual rights cases would also require the Court to limit sharply the power of the federal government to regulate the economy. Thus, the major difficulty with originalism is that, in practical terms, it would allow the judi-

1. Raoul Berger, Government by Judiciary: The Transformation of the Fourteenth Amendment 117–33 (1977).

2. But for a comprehensive analysis of how *Brown* might be reconcilable with a "nondiscrimination" reading of the Privileges or Immunities Clause of the Fourteenth Amendment, see John Harrison, *Reconstructing the Privileges or Immunities Clause*, 101 Yale L.J. 1385 (1992).

> ciary to intrude unduly into the functioning of government in the modern world.

Yet, even on its own terms, this latter argument will not appear quite so devastating for many readers as it seems to be for Maltz. An obvious response to this aspect of the "originalist quandary" would be to shrug off those constitutional obligations which can no longer be maintained and interpret the rest as they were intended to be interpreted—that is, in a restrictive way. One of today's leading spokesmen for originalism, Judge Robert Bork, argues for just this approach in his book, *The Tempting of America*:

> But if the judge concludes that a prior decision was wrong, he faces additional considerations. The previous decision on the subject may be clearly incorrect but nevertheless have become so embedded in the life of the nation, so accepted by the society, so fundamental to the private and public expectations of individuals and institutions, that the result should not be changed now. This is a judgment addressed to the prudence of a court, but it is not the less valid for that. Judging is not mechanical. Many rules are framed according to predictions of their likely effects, and it is entirely proper for a decision to overrule or not to overrule to be affected by a prediction of the effects likely to flow from that. Thus, it is too late to overrule not only the decision legalizing paper money but also those decisions validating certain New Deal and Great Society programs pursuant to the congressional powers over commerce, taxation, and spending. To overturn these would be to overturn most of modern government and plunge us into chaos. No judge would dream of doing it....[3]

This approach—which we might call "as much originalism as the circumstances will bear"—appeals to many conservatives for practical reasons. Most of the activist judicial decisions of recent decades do not at all require this sort of practical acquiescence, however. If they had been supported by such irresistible public demand, they would not have had to be imposed on recalcitrant legislatures by activist judges in the first place. As Judge Bork observed: "[I]t will probably never be too late to overrule the right of privacy cases, including *Roe v. Wade*, because they remain unaccepted and unacceptable to large segments of the body politic, and judicial regulation could at once be replaced by restored legislative regulation of the subject."[4] So, too, there remains overwhelming public support for school

---

3. Robert H. Bork, The Tempting of America: The Political Seduction of the Law 158 (1990).

4. *Id.* Even regarding decisions that cannot be overturned, Bork urges caution (*id.* at 159):

> To say that a decision is so thoroughly embedded in our national life that it should not be overruled, even though clearly wrong, is not necessarily to say that its principle should be followed in the future.... There are times when we cannot recover

prayer and overwhelming opposition to judicially imposed racial quotas and forced busing schemes.

Maltz, in any event, takes it for granted that originalism cannot accommodate the public without refighting ancient battles that no one wants to reopen. To put it in Burkean terms, Maltz assumes that originalism must reject prudence and prescription in the name of theoretical consistency. This may be an attractive approach for polemical attacks on originalists, but it is hard to see why conservative jurists must saddle themselves with disabling burdens contrived for them by polemicists. "As much originalism as the circumstances will bear" may not be a precise formula, but it is not inherently hypocritical, incoherent, or otherwise indefensible as a general stance.

II

Maltz is evenhanded in his polemical scorn, though. He exposes the historical fallacies in the works of Ronald Dworkin, Cass Sunstein, and others, who have sought to develop what Maltz terms "neo-originalist" defenses for contemporary judicial activism. Such theorists seek to identify the Constitution with some abstract political doctrine ("equal concern and respect" or "classical republicanism" or whatever it may be) and then extrapolate from this "Founding" doctrine to decisions which extend the logic of the doctrine in particular cases. Maltz faults this exercise (p. 73):

> The theory that interventionist judicial review should be designed to implement general political principles such as democracy, classical republicanism, or toleration does not reinforce the premises underlying the Constitution. Indeed, the theory undermines the one political premise that has been uniformly accepted by *all* supporters of the Constitution: that the framers of the Constitution had legitimate authority to make political decisions that would, at least in the absence of properly adopted constitutional amendments, bind government decisionmakers in the future. In requiring judges to act inconsistently with the compromises reached by the framers themselves, interpretive theories seeking the mandate of some broad political doctrine in essence reject the notion that the framers had such legitimate authority. Only pure originalism, which calls upon the courts to enforce those compromises, avoids this problem.

Neo-originalists present an intriguing argument. But the more one leans on it, the more one is driven back to some version of "originalism" (that is, paleo-originalism). So the argument would be more persuasive if Maltz were not, himself, so eager to discredit originalism, too.

---

the transgressions of the past, when the best we can do is say to the Court, "Go and sin no more."

Maltz is at least equally dismissive toward the apologists for "non-originalist interventionism"—those who shrug off efforts to ground activist decisions in some version of the "intended" meaning of the Constitution and appeal instead to general "functional defenses." Given his impatience with more legalistic theories, it may not be surprising that Maltz expresses initial sympathy for such pragmatic arguments: "On its simplest terms, this response to the legitimacy-based attack on non-originalist jurisprudence is entirely persuasive. Legitimacy is very much in the eye of the beholder; it is a premise rather than a matter capable of proof or disproof" (p. 74). But Maltz then proceeds to find fault with "functional" defenses on their own terms.

Perhaps our eighteenth-century Constitution, or its nineteenth-century amendments, must be read with flexibility to accommodate a changing world. But this, Maltz maintains, is not an argument for judicial activism (as many apologists would have it) but an argument for courts to eschew "interventionism" since new court doctrines can impose their own rigidities. Similarly, he argues that "expanding rights" cannot justify judicial interventionism, as other apologists argue, because rights are so often in conflict and champions of some rights may be quite opposed to others. *Dred Scott v. Sandford*, in denying the power of Congress to prohibit slavery in the western territories, was also extending "rights"—in this case, the rights of slaveholders. *Lochner v. New York*, in denying state legislatures the power to impose maximum working hours, was also extending "rights"—the right to contract for long working hours. Proponents of judicial interventionism should realize, Maltz chides, that "the impact over time of an interventionist judiciary is completely unpredictable" (p. 108).

Surely it requires a special sort of credulousness to believe that activists will find Maltz's argument here at all compelling. Should liberals of the 1960s really have worried that the Warren Court might suddenly lose its sense of direction and start enforcing the economic rights in fashion some fifty years before? Did they even need to worry that the activism of the Warren Court would justify the counteractivism of a later, conservative court? There was indeed a post-Warren Court, filled with ostensibly "conservative" appointees, and they did not dare to turn the "Constitution" of the Warren era inside out.

Maltz's point seems to be that those who applauded activism in one era will find it morally or rhetorically awkward to denounce the less favorable activism of a different era. But it is a matter of record that enthusiasts of liberal judicial activism during the sixties and seventies did not feel at all compelled to hold their tongues in shamed silence when the occasional activist decision of the Rehnquist Court cut against them (as in cases seeking to restrain racial-preference schemes). Quite the contrary, apologists for liberal activism like to criticize decisions as "activist" even when they are not, and have been among the first and the loudest in decrying the "hypocrisy" of conservative jurists. Witness the remarks of ACLU President Nadine Strossen at a recent gathering of the Federalist Society: "A court that is conservative in terms of judicial process exercises judicial restraint. It respects precedent. It does not reach sweeping issues of constitutional law unless it must. It defers to the decisions of elected branches of government. The Court has violated all these tenets of judicial restraint."[5] Such denunciations may well have an intimidating effect on some of the weaker sisters (and brothers) on the current Court.

Maltz's point makes sense only if the apologists for judicial activism are held to a high standard of consistency, one that transcends all considerations of political advantage. But if there is a reason for holding "interventionists" to this standard, it surely is not a "functional" reason. Pragmatic or functional rationales for judicial intervention are also "very much in the eye of the beholder" in the sense that they can be defined and limited to particular aims. If you believe that courts should be active on behalf of racial minorities or the poor because they are in need of special protection, you are not undermining this "function" for the courts by opposing activist interventions on behalf of whites or on behalf of the rich.

Or is it that the liberal version of this "function" cannot be sustained without opening the game to other players? In the conclusion to his book, Maltz restates the position in more general terms: "all constitutional theorists," he insists, must "disabuse themselves of the notion that an unconstrained judiciary would inevitably favor some particular political position or persuasion.... Only when this fact is fully recognized and integrated into constitutional analysis can an adequate theoretical structure be built" (p. 108). Maltz does not tell us why an "unconstrained judiciary" is the only alternative to stringent "originalism." What is even more confusing, he does not tell us what possible content there could be in a "theoretical structure" that blinds itself to substantive outcomes.

III

What we are left with, then, is a quest for some pure legal formula, not yet discovered, that is premised on the Founding Fathers' legitimate authority to adopt the Constitution and to make it binding for ages to come. At a minimum, "the legitimacy of the constitutionmaking process," while controversial, "must be the starting point for any credible justification of federal judicial review... originalist or otherwise" (p. 20). Yet Maltz remains uneasy about the legitimacy argument, observing that "questions of legit-

5. *Federalist Society Roundtable Discussion: Do We Have a Conservative Supreme Court?*, 1994 PUB. INTEREST L. REV. 125, 132.

imacy have absorbed nonoriginalists to the point that they have failed to put forth a plausible reason for the courts to adopt an interventionist approach in any but the most narrowly defined class of cases" (p. 108).

Maltz's uneasiness about "legitimacy"—and his own difficulty in shaking off its spell—reflect something inherent in the term. At least in its modern usage, it is an inherently squishy term, a fudge phrase, a stand-in for something we are no longer quite able to pronounce. The Framers of the Constitution did not talk about legitimacy. The Oxford English Dictionary records no use of the term at all before the nineteenth century. *The Federalist* does use the adjective "legitimate" but not very often; the word "just" appears more than ten times as often as "legitimate," and the term "justice" appears almost as often as "just."[6]

In its original usage, legitimacy simply referred to "legitimate birth"—the offspring of a legal marriage—and then by obvious and immediate extension to the "legitimate" claims of monarchs who inherited the throne by legitimate birth. The great Whig historian Thomas Macaulay thus derided "Legitimacy" as "the alias" under which "the doctrine of Divine Right [of kings to rule] has now come back to us."[7] But even in this usage, legitimacy had a precise meaning. Contemporary scholars invoke the term far more generally in a usage that seems to derive from the technical terminology of the German sociologist Max Weber. In Weberian terminology, legitimacy means deserving of obedience—in the eyes of the people involved. "Rational-legal authority" is one type of legitimate authority, but "charismatic" leaders have rested their legitimacy on a different basis and "traditional" regimes on yet a different basis.

The appeal of this usage is its relativistic quality. It is easy to say that absolute monarchy had "legitimacy" in the seventeenth century though it does not in our time. It is more awkward to say that slavery is now considered incompatible with "justice" but was quite compatible with justice in the seventeenth century. And a certain element of relativistic evasiveness remains part of the term's appeal even to contemporary legal scholars. To denounce certain decisions as "illegitimate" seems easier than to denounce them as "unjust." Legitimacy seems to offer a definite standard because it does not commit the user to embracing any transcendent standard. It implies, to view the issue from the other direction, that a decision may be "legitimate" because it follows logically from precedents in a system based on precedent—even if the same decision may not be entirely "just." It thus

---

6. According to *The Federalist Concordance* (Thomas Engeman et al. eds., 1980), the word "legitimate" appears only seven times in the entire text of *The Federalist*; "just" appears 77 times; "justice" appears 60 times.

7. 1 THOMAS BABINGTON MACAULAY, CRITICAL AND HISTORICAL ESSAYS 173 (1907) (from the essay "Milton," which first appeared in the August 1825 *Edinburgh Review*).

seems to offer, if not moral certainty, at least moral absolution for the successful legal advocate.

But this is delusory. Legitimate kings were overthrown to general satisfaction—as Macaulay was at pains to emphasize to romantic royalists in his own day. The conflict between legitimacy (in this narrow sense) and other claims to rule (like kingly virtues) is the stuff of Shakespearean drama, in such plays as *Richard II* and *Henry IV*. They are dramas precisely because the conflict is evenly matched. Even in our republic, great constitutional acts that violated clear rules of "legitimate" action have nonetheless acquired retroactive "legitimacy." Maltz himself notes that the Fourteenth Amendment was adopted by coercion of southern states to an extent that would be hard to accept as legitimate—were the outcome not by now so thoroughly accepted. West Virginia is taken to be a fully legitimate state of the union, though it was created when Virginia had withdrawn from the union and could not provide legitimate consent to this division of its territory. So it is with *Brown v. Board of Education*: whatever its defects as legal reasoning, it has acquired unshakable legitimacy because any other result seems morally indefensible.

The real challenge to legitimacy does not come from individual exceptions. Hereditary monarchy could survive some awkward displacements from the legitimate line of succession. Constitutional republics can survive occasional deviations from strict legal propriety. Legitimacy is threatened by a *pattern* of intolerable actions or inexcusable failings. Beyond a certain point, the pattern will shake people's confidence in whatever principle of legitimacy was supposed to justify the particular actions or failings. Beyond a certain point, people will doubt the principle itself rather than continuing to doubt their own assessment of the results it sanctions.

Because it is the pattern that counts, it is delusory to think that controversial court decisions—or an overreaching approach to judicial review—can retain legitimacy in isolation from the wider pattern of political practices they help to sustain. If the liberal jurisprudence of recent decades is now suffering a crisis of legitimacy, this is not owing to technical defects in the academic theories purporting to justify the work of activist courts. It is, of course, because people have lost confidence in the whole liberal vision—of an all-powerful central government, continually taxing, spending, fussing, and fixing and continually inventing new "rights" to the detriment of family, religion, and local authority.

IV

For similar reasons, even the purest version of "originalism," to the extent that it presents itself as a nonpolitical formula for judicial decisions, also remains in some fundamental way a delusion. Beyond all the technical disputes over interpretative methodology and historiographic authority, originalism is, at bottom, an appeal to continuity. That is often a very powerful appeal. But it is by no means an irresistible or unanswerable appeal in a diverse nation where large parts of the electorate view large parts of the national past with resentment or disdain. The appeal of "originalism" is not separable from a conservative appeal for continuity with the past—and a conservative affirmation that our national past is, at least in its main elements, worth preserving. If most people do not believe this, then the technical arguments for originalism will never withstand the demands for constitutional innovation.

To be sure, doubts about "legitimacy"—precisely because they are entangled with larger tides of opinion—are rarely all-or-nothing. Even revolutions leave many institutions untouched. A judiciary which stands removed from the most contentious issues may be better able to survive political upheavals. But, as Maltz notes, a noninterventionist judiciary is not the same as an originalist one. A court that holds itself (and its version of the Constitution) altogether aloof from contentious issues also may imperil national continuity on all but inessentials. It is not easy to say how obdurate or aggressive a court should be in insisting on its own vision of the Constitution—even if it is an originalist vision, with the pedigree of the Framers' intent. And it is delusory to think that this can be determined by a theoretical formula.

As Maltz notes, some scholars have sought to build a new legal theory on this inescapable political dimension of judging. Most notably, Bruce Ackerman has argued that the Constitution has been amended by "irregular" but still authoritative expressions of the popular will, as in the national elections of 1936 providing popular endorsement for the New Deal.[8] As Maltz says, this is a very dubious interpretation of what the amending provisions in Article V allow or of what *The Federalist* endorsed. What Maltz should have added is that this approach seeks to retain the cake of constitutional authority even while allowing elections to devour it: Ackerman wants courts to stand on the New Deal political coalition as if it could supply the same prestige as the original Founding, just because of elections. It is another delusion. There is no escape from a continual weighing of the political dimension to jurisprudence. Legitimacy must be earned continuously, not just assumed by electoral mandates dressed up as legal formulas.

Liberal activism has long since overdrawn its reserves of popular patience. The 1994 elections punctuate the point. If a new Congress challenges the Court's recent constitutional ventures, the Court will not likely be able to

---

8. Bruce Ackerman, We the People (1991).

summon much popular allegiance or political deference to its own pronouncements. Controversial Court rulings no longer command acceptance simply because they are rulings of the Court. That is the risk of taking legitimacy for granted or thinking that it can be supplied by clever law professors when no longer sustained by winning politicians.

It is understandable that sharp-eyed observers—and Earl Maltz certainly belongs in that category—have grown weary and impatient with the unresolved academic debate about "judicial legitimacy." It is harder to see the logic in his invitation to press forward with the construction of a "constitutional theory" unrelated to larger political currents. In the broader political battles that finally determine legitimacy even in the realm of constitutional doctrine, law professors may not play a very large role. But the greatest delusion of all is to think that a constitutional republic can be maintained by technical experts, operating at a far remove from the general citizenry. For better or worse, we are *all* in it together.

Legal theorists should therefore learn modesty—and patience, a virtue Professor Maltz does not display to excess in this volume. He may be consoled by the discovery that we now have a lot more things to talk about. A new politics will demand much new constitutional doctrine—or the rediscovery of much older doctrine, previously given up for lost.

REVIEWED BY JEREMY RABKIN

Justice Breyer's Case for Centralized Executive Government

BREAKING THE VICIOUS CIRCLE: TOWARD EFFECTIVE RISK REGULATION
by Stephen Breyer
Cambridge, Massachusetts: Harvard University Press, 1993
127 pp., $22.95

The conventional wisdom among conservatives is that Stephen Breyer's appointment to the United States Supreme Court is about as good as could have been expected from President Clinton. While Breyer is thought likely to vote with the liberals on civil liberties questions, it is anticipated by many that his demonstrated understanding of economics and of administrative law will lead him to side with the conservatives on at least some challenges to the ever expanding regulatory state.

The first two chapters of his book *Breaking the Vicious Circle: Toward Effective Risk Regulation* will sustain conservative optimism, but the third and concluding chapter should convince readers that Justice Breyer, at least when wearing his policy hat, is optimistic about the possibilities of the regulatory state. The first two chapters confirm that the regulatory state has not been working very well. The final chapter is, as the book's subtitle forewarns, Breyer's prescription for how to make it work better.

In the first chapter Justice Breyer does a superb job, with the assistance of several excellent charts and graphs, of demonstrating the complexity of risk regulation and the irrationality of many existing regulations. He focuses on regulations designed to reduce the risks of cancer, but he believes that the lessons he draws have relevance to other regulatory challenges.[1] Breyer reports that we use no fewer that twenty-six statutes administered by no fewer than eight agencies to regulate somewhere between two and ten percent of human exposure to life-threatening carcinogens. Our objec-

1. In his conclusion, Justice Breyer draws general conclusions in an effort "to satisfy Oliver Wendell Holmes' admonition to find general lessons in...[the] particular" (p. 80).

tive in this regulatory broadside, says Breyer, is to reduce the risk of "extra deaths" from cancer to less than one in a million.[2]

In pursuit of this objective, says Justice Breyer, we engage in risk assessment and risk management. The former is the business of science, the latter of policy. As we see in chapter three, Justice Breyer believes that risk-management policy can be separated from risk-management politics. The key to this bifurcation, says Breyer, is in the design of institutions which will enable the good and well-motivated people of the federal bureaucracy to avoid the counterproductive results which they have produced heretofore.

Justice Breyer identifies three specific problems which evidence institutional failure. First, regulatory agencies suffer from "tunnel vision" or "the last 10 percent problem" (p. 11). Because their regulatory missions are narrowly defined, agencies fail to consider the opportunity costs of seeking to eliminate all exposure to the particular risk in question. They have no incentive, says Breyer, to optimize risk-avoidance expenditures.[3] Thus, because of the uncertainties inherent in risk regulation, agencies choose to err on the "safe" side without regard for the relative costs of avoiding other risks. Second, agencies suffer from "random agenda selection" (p. 19) because public perceptions of risk have little relation to real risks. Congress, and in turn agencies, regulate the risk of the day, whether or not it is significant in relation to other risks and whether or not its regulation creates other risks which are even greater. Third, the independent regulation of discrete risks leads to an inconsistency among agency regulations insofar as we have regulations which impose costs per life saved of anywhere between $100,000 and $125 million (p. 22).[4]

The second chapter of the book explains the institutional problem—the "vicious circle"—which leads to the regulatory failures described in the first chapter. Justice Breyer contends that public perceptions of risk, congressional response to those perceptions, and our approach to risk regulation combine to "create a vicious circle, diminishing public trust in regulatory institutions and thereby inhibiting more rational regulation" (p. 33).

Public perceptions of risk vary markedly from expert assessments of risk.

2. While he points out that the one in a million standard has little meaning to the general public, he fails to point out that reliance on the concept of "extra deaths" is an invitation to what he describes as a general tendency of the public to overestimate the magnitude of the risks he is examining. What Justice Breyer and the risk regulators call "extra deaths" are in fact deaths that occur anywhere from a few days to many years earlier than they otherwise would have. Thus, not every so-called extra death is equal.

3. The failure to optimize is not only an institutional problem. Risk regulators are lobbied by a significant environmentalist constituency which continues to believe that the only acceptable pollution is zero pollution.

4. These figures are from a 1992 OMB study. Breyer cites another OMB study which concluded that one regulation cost $5.7 *trillion* per life saved.

For example, Justice Breyer reports that members of the League of Women Voters and college students both rank nuclear power as posing the greatest risk among a list of thirty activities and technologies. Experts rank nuclear power twentieth on that same list. Breyer attributes this disparity to several factors and concludes that changing public perception to conform better to actual risks depends either on "widespread public education in risk analysis" or on instilling "greater public trust in... experts" (p. 39). The solution he proposes in chapter three reflects his conclusion that "the first alternative seems unlikely [to succeed]" (p. 39).

Congress responds to these public perceptions of risk "as it ought to" (p. 42) by enacting "detailed statutory instructions" for agencies to follow in regulating risky activities (p. 39). Justice Breyer's point is that we should not expect Congress to pay attention to the experts when the voters disagree. Voters, not risk experts, elect the Congress. If the public misperceives relative risks, we should not be surprised that Congress's regulations reflect those misperceptions.

Regulatory agencies are thus faced with implementing the statutes which Congress adopts, whether or not those statutes make any sense in terms of optimizing benefits to human health and safety. Because agencies tend to have risk-specific mandates and because the business of risk assessment is uncertain at best, concludes Justice Breyer, it is "difficult for agencies to resist Congressional or public efforts to set agendas and to manage particular results" (p. 50). The consequence is a risk-regulation system which persistently overregulates many small risks while investing little in mitigation of more serious risks.

The question which Justice Breyer sets for himself in the third chapter is how to break out of this "vicious circle." It is here that Breyer makes clear his commitment to government regulation as the solution to the problem he has described in the first two chapters. He proposes "to attack the vicious circle at its weakest point," which he asserts is "the regulatory link" (p. 55). Having concluded in chapter two that public education is not an answer, he prefaces his proposal with other conclusions about what will not work.

Justice Breyer dismisses deregulation because "some substances involve serious risks that must be regulated," and because it "does not address the failures of agencies to pursue... more serious environmental problems, or to examine... unexamined risks" (p. 56). Neither reason is persuasive. It is circular to assert that deregulation will not work because regulation is necessary. Indeed, the assumption that regulation is necessary underlies most of the regulations which Breyer says have failed. Breyer's second reason for dismissing deregulation is rooted in the same circular reasoning. There is no reason to assume that the regulatory approach will work better if somehow made to focus on more serious environmental risks. The regulation of the wrong risks is not the only failing of the regulatory process.

One deregulatory approach which Justice Breyer specifically rejects is the tort system because of its "random, lottery-like results" and its "high transaction costs" (p. 59). He offers no evidence on either of these empirical claims, nor does he compare the tort system to regulation in terms of results or transaction costs. He also does not discuss possible reforms to mitigate these (relatively new) abuses of tort litigation. And, as with all of his discussion of deregulation, he seems to view the tort system and other non-regulatory approaches as all or nothing solutions. Of course they are not.

But putting aside the circularity of his reasons for dismissing deregulation, Justice Breyer would remain intent on regulation because "public demand for regulation is likely to continue, a demand that governments should not, and will not ignore" (p. 56). Perhaps Breyer would have been less confident in the public demand for regulation had he written the book after the 1994 elections. He seems to be coming down on the side of popular sovereignty, which would not be surprising but is inconsistent with the centralist and bureaucratic solution he proposes.

Justice Breyer concludes that Congress will be of little help due to various political and institutional limits. He also believes that the "federal courts cannot do much better" because their slavish enforcement of congressionally mandated deadlines "can distort agency agendas" (p. 57). His observations about Congress and the federal courts are surprising for a man who now sits on the highest court of a constitutional democracy. One might fairly ask how reform is to happen, consistent with the constitutional separation of powers, without help from Congress. And one might ask further what the federal courts are supposed to do when faced with a claim that an agency has not complied with a congressional mandate.

Since deregulation is not an acceptable solution, it seems that to Justice Breyer the problems identified in his first two chapters are in significant part a product of the constitutional allocation of limited powers to the executive branch. The situation Breyer has described is this: Popular perceptions of risk, which are different from expert perceptions, lead the people's representatives in Congress to enact laws which reflect these popular perceptions. The federal courts then require the executive to comply with those laws rather than pursue the agendas which their expert risk assessments would suggest. Breyer's solution would shift more power to the executive, but apparently without any concern for the limiting constitutional provisions or for Congress's responsibility to delegate power to the executive.

Justice Breyer's prescription is vague, but the basic idea is for the executive branch to create "a small, centralized administrative group, charged with a rationalizing mission" and staffed by civil servants who have pursued "a new career path that would provide... experience in health and environmental agencies, Congress, and OMB" (p. 59). This group would have five essential features: (1) "a specified risk-related *mission*," (2) "*inter-*

agency jurisdiction," (3) "a degree of *political insulation*," (4) "*prestige*," and (5) "*authority*" (pp. 60–61). In Breyer's judgment, most of these attributes will evolve naturally from the "virtues of bureaucracy" (p. 61). He is optimistic of success because "one can fairly easily draft a specific agenda that would take advantage of these inherent bureaucratic virtues" (p. 64).

In support of his assertion that the new centralized administrative group will succeed where existing agencies have failed, Justice Breyer suggests various examples of comparable, existing entities which, in his judgment, have worked, including the EPA Science Advisor, OMB and its Office of Information and Regulatory Affairs (OIRA), and the French Conseil d'Etat. In perhaps the understatement of the book, Breyer acknowledges that "America is not France" (p. 71). Indeed the United States is not France. The French constitution provides for a highly centralized and heavily administrative government. A core objective of the United States Constitution is to limit the power of the federal government, including its executive.

Ironically, Justice Breyer seems to have succumbed to the very problem which has plagued risk regulation. He has focused his attention on a particular problem and proposed a governmental solution which takes no account of *other* problems associated with government action. The United States Constitution is republican and federal. The powers of the national government are limited by enumeration, by the Bill of Rights, and by the separation of powers. Justice Breyer's proposal, vague as it is, evidences no concern about these constitutional concepts nor about the values of liberty and limited government which they are meant to serve. Of his catalogue of anticipated objections—"undemocratic, elitist, ineffective, politically unfeasible, and without practical means of implementation" (p. 60)—only the first gives any hint that he is concerned about the constitutionality of what he proposes.

Justice Breyer does not propose that Congress be called upon to create the kind of administrative group he has proposed. Rather he suggests that the executive simply undertake to make it happen. Breyer speculates that "[t]he immediate source of this group's power might lie in its assumption of OIRA's present mandate . . . , augmented by its missions to rationalize risk regulation and seek tradeoffs" (p. 72). Once a modified OIRA has had some successes, Breyer imagines that additional powers "might naturally gravitate toward such a group" (p. 72). It is, to say the least, an interesting approach to centralizing power in a constitutional democracy.

Justice Breyer argues that his analysis "offers an important substantive argument against a 'Balkanized' Executive Branch and suggests a need, extending beyond the subject itself, for more centralized coordination" (p. 80). A unified executive is consistent with—indeed required by—the Constitution, but that is apparently not the reason Breyer wants it. He has, instead, a Hayekian fatal conceit about the ability of central planners to improve the market. His preference for a regulatory bureaucracy that works wisely is, to borrow a phrase from Milton Friedman, a preference for (nonexistent) "barking cats." The fact that Breyer's analysis of a major governmental failure in the area of risk regulation leads him to dismiss private solutions—and to propose greater centralization of federal power in areas beyond risk regulation—should worry those who understand our Constitution as rooted in liberty, limited government, and federalism.

REVIEWED BY JAMES L. HUFFMAN

The Once and Future of the Legal Profession

A NATION UNDER LAWYERS: HOW THE CRISIS IN THE LEGAL PROFESSION IS TRANSFORMING AMERICAN SOCIETY
by Mary Ann Glendon
New York: Farrar, Straus and Giroux, 1994
331 pp., $24.00

THE LOST LAWYER: FAILING IDEALS OF THE LEGAL PROFESSION
by Anthony T. Kronman
Cambridge: The Belknap Press of Harvard, 1993
422 pp., $35.00

All is not well in the state of American lawyering. Hardly a month passes without a book, report, or major speech dissecting this or that organ of the legal profession as if it belonged to a decaying body. Today it might be the worship of the billable hour or the continuing crisis in the tort system; yesterday it may have been the ideologization of law schools or the unreadable banality of law reviews; tomorrow it will be (yet again) a disturbing analysis of overcrowded court dockets or more tales from the crypt of judicial excess. Any such list of woes would of course differ from critic to critic, but one thing seems certain: the good news would be hard to find.

Whether this condition represents a passing bout of dyspepsia or something more permanently debilitating, we do not know. We do know that the American bar has suffered through periods of self-critical ferment in the past yet lived to tell the tale, most notably in the closing decades of the nineteenth century when many of the bar associations prominent today first came into existence. Then, the rallying cry was for higher professional standards. Today, the rallying cry is for... well, what? More rigorous professional standards, surely, but is that what the fuss is all about?

Not if you ask Mary Ann Glendon, Professor of Law at Harvard, or Anthony Kronman, recently appointed Dean at the Yale Law School. Each has written a formidable critique of the legal profession, covering everything from law school curricula to the private bar and the judiciary. Each comes to the task with distinctive complementary virtues: Glendon is a realist tempered by philosophical reflection, Kronman a philosopher tempered by practicality. Glendon, who practiced law for some years and knows her way around commercial subjects, has a lively, conversational style. She is perfectly comfortable with the world of ideas, but her feet remain at all times earthbound. Kronman, who trained in philosophy before taking up law, is more overtly abstract and scholarly. His first home is the world of ideas, but he is no stranger to the everyday life of lawyers.

Despite these differences in temperament and perspective, both authors come to a substantially similar (and substantially pessimistic) conclusion: the profession is now at sea without rudder or compass. Its myths have lost the capacity to nourish, its heroes are hard to find and rarely celebrated, its goals can no longer be easily stated. Its training schools seem to teach cynicism and self-interest more effectively than they do prudence or professionalism; its judges are increasingly mired in their own bureaucracies (Kronman) or prone to second-guess the political branches (Glendon); its private practitioners seem preoccupied with material rewards, celebrity, and the trappings of power. What is worse, neither Glendon nor Kronman thinks much of this will change anytime soon, nor does either have a handy kit bag of remedies. You will not find in these pages, for example, the tired reformist prescriptions so often trotted out as a cure for the ills of the bar, such as increasing pro bono hours or the budget of the Legal Services Corporation. The size of both could be doubled overnight and still not address what most bothers Kronman and Glendon, namely the state of the American lawyer's soul and how it got that way.

I

Mary Ann Glendon's *A Nation Under Lawyers: How the Crisis in the Legal Profession Is Transforming American Society* is an eloquent and spirited tribute to the craftsmanship of the common-law tradition, a lament for its passing, and a plea for its restoration. Along the way, Professor Glendon writes love letters to Holmes and Cardozo and the Hands, and to the now all-but-forgotten Karl Llewellyn (whose virtues feature prominently in the Kronman book as well). She also proffers trenchant observations on tendentious academic scriveners, the inanity of much that is published in law reviews, the personal and constitutional vanity of overreaching judges, and the maniacal pursuit of the billable hour by modern-day lawyers. This is a tough-minded, practical, and comprehensive assessment of contemporary lawyering, written by one familiar with the foibles she surveys. In less competent hands, so broad an indictment might mark its author as a carping critic, but Glendon is anything but a scold. Her concern for the profession she entered a generation ago is apparent on every page. So is her love of craft—and her impatience with shoddy work, humbug, and vainglory.

Professor Glendon knows exactly what Burke meant when he said that the study of law broadens the mind by narrowing it. She also knows that law is a trade, albeit a trade affected with a public interest. Lawyers would be a lot happier (and society much better off), she implies, if they dropped some of their highfalutin pretensions—whether for moneymaking, fame, or power—and instead took greater pride in delivering useful services for their clients. As things stand today, Glendon suggests, lawyers tend to feel dissatisfied unless they're making a million bucks, acquiring reputations as courtroom killers, or reconstructing society to accord with some textbook formula. Too many movies taken too much to heart, perhaps. A more likely suspect, Glendon says, are the faculties of many law schools, which breed cynicism about the rule of law while denigrating the virtues of private practice.

Glendon's critique of the legal profession is in some respects a continuation of themes she broached in her widely praised 1991 book, *Rights Talk: The Impoverishment of Political Discourse*. There, she lamented our diminished sense of political community and the degeneration of constitutional debate into a feckless logomachy about whose rights trump whose. Although the narrow focus of her new book is what lawyers think about themselves and their chosen occupation, its broad theme is the self-denigration of the legal profession and what that means to a nation whose roots are uniquely intertwined with the rule of law. Appropriately enough, Professor Glendon begins with Tocqueville's praise of lawyers and lawyering in the early Republic. Lawyers were, he said, the closest thing to an aristocratic class that he had observed in America. They brought continuity and stability to a society whose tendencies were otherwise turbulent and centrifugal. Tocqueville was acutely aware—in ways that we are not—of the ancient skepticism concerning democracy. According to this view, democratic regimes were preoccupied with short-term, venal interests and inclined to volatility and envy. For these reasons, they tended to be weak and often short-lived: if they did not crumple from within, they were apt to be overrun from without. When the Framers undertook to create, in James Madison's words, "a republican remedy for the diseases most incident to republican government,"[1] they believed that the rule of law as solemnly embodied in the Constitution could overcome the ancient prejudice against the deficiencies of popular government. As Martin Diamond once put it, they believed that a properly constituted government could make democracy safe for the world.

This emphatic reliance on the rule of law in the American regime necessarily enhanced the social and political dignity of the lawyer, which is one

1. THE FEDERALIST, No. 10, at 84 (James Madison) (Clinton Rossiter ed., 1961).

reason why Tocqueville hoped that lawyers would act as ballast for the democratic ship of state. For the better part of our history, Glendon argues, the best lawyers were esteemed not merely because they were clever rhetoricians or wealthy pillars of the community, but because they exercised a conspicuously important public trust as stewards of the rule of law. To be sure, not all lawyers thought or acted in such high-minded terms, but the ideal was proclaimed by school and bench and bar alike. There were scalawags aplenty, but they wouldn't have dreamed of defending their behavior in public, nor would their cunning have been acclaimed in the popular media. This older dispensation, however, appears to have gone the way of parchment and quill. The new order, says Glendon, is represented by a series of propositions utterly inconsistent with the earlier tradition (p. 6):

> that we live under a rule of men, not law; that the Constitution is just an old text that means whatever the current crop of judges says it does; that all rules (including the rules of professional ethics) are infinitely manipulable; that law is a business like any other; and that business is just the unrestrained pursuit of self-interest.

The remarkable thing, says Glendon, is not that these opinions are new (they are not), but that they now have a sizable following and are openly advanced and defended by many leading lights of the law.

The world of private practice has absorbed the new doctrine all too well. Professor Glendon, who practiced in Chicago for some years before turning to teaching, has a good feel for life in the modern firm and how it has changed over the past generation. She eschews the overworked distinction between "trade" and "profession" which has dominated public discussion of late and relies instead on Jane Jacobs' distinction between "raider" ethics (which prize combative strength and cunning) and "trader" ethics (which prize conciliation and reasoned discourse). Acknowledging that the law has always had its share of both types, Glendon worries that the raider mentality now exercises a talismanic hold on today's practitioners. The result has been in many cases "a mutually destructive war of all against all" (p. 286). She notes the moral ambivalence that so often attends discussions of professional ethics today, throwing the lawyer back upon his own instinct, which in turn seldom moves beyond an unreflective calculation of his own self-interest. But where self-interest reigns supreme, in what is a lawyer to vest personal pride? Alas, it seems to be litigation, the pursuit of billable hours, and the celebration of politically fashionable causes. These goals have been achieved, she says, "at the expense of the useful services that have always given lawyers in the aggregate their best chance to achieve personal satisfaction while contributing to the well-being of their fellow citizens" (p. 108).

Professor Glendon next turns her attention to the judiciary, and in three short essays that make one yearn for more, she excoriates those latter-day solons whose personal vanity is exceeded only by their sense of constitutional plasticity: nary a social problem in sight, they presume, that can't be cured by a nattily inventive judicial decree. By way of contrast, Glendon offers the models of Holmes, Cardozo, and Learned Hand who, for all their genius, practiced a kind of professional humility that is in short supply among judges today. She has much to say about the presumption and immoderation of judicial excess today, and she says it with commendable brevity. Justices Kennedy and Brennan here meet a stiletto that is wielded with devastating effect.

Having analyzed the bench and the bar, Professor Glendon turns a gimlet eye upon the academy. Here she laments the declining prestige of the legal treatise (once the most honored product of faculties and the staple of law reviews) and the rise of "one-sided advocacy in the guise of scholarship" (p. 208). She traces the origins of this new "scholarship" to its relativist roots (p. 209):

> Many legal academics still share with their colleagues in other disciplines the scholar's commitment to pursue knowledge wherever it leads and whatever its unpopularity. But for a growing coterie of professors in the human sciences, including law, that ideal is simply meaningless. In some quarters, notions of knowledge, objectivity, and truth have come under heavy attack. If truth is whatever you want it to be, or the will of the stronger, the distinction between scholarship and advocacy collapses. If all law is radically indeterminate, then all legal scholarship becomes a form of advocacy.

Over time, teaching based on such beliefs breeds cynicism about the rule of law and therefore indifference to its defense. It also tends to undermine that indispensable sense of craftsmanship which makes the pursuit of law both dignified and pleasurable. So long as such doctrines reign in our schools of law, Glendon argues, we cannot hope to cure the ills of the bar. In the end, what lawyers *think* about themselves and their profession turns out to be decisively important in determining what they *do*. And if they think the rule of law is but a fiction, ultimately indistinguishable from the caprice of men, their actions will follow suit. In a society uniquely dedicated to and dependent upon the rule of law, such a change is not only sad, it is dangerous.

II

Yale Dean Anthony Kronman would not disagree. His is not a happy tale, as the title of his book suggests: *The Lost Lawyer: Failing Ideals of the*

Legal Profession. Kronman believes that the profession has lost any coherent understanding of what it once was or could be, other than a trade organized for profit. The profession, he says, "now stands in danger of losing its soul" (p. 1). For the better part of two centuries, he argues, that soul had been decisively formed by a particular set of aspirations and values. Chief among these was the belief (pp. 2–3)

> that the outstanding lawyer—the one who serves as a model for the rest —is not simply an accomplished technician but a person of prudence or practical wisdom as well.... To those who shared this view it seemed obvious that a lawyer's life could be deeply fulfilling. For the character-virtue of practical wisdom is a central human excellence that has an intrinsic value of its own. So long as the cultivation and exercise of this virtue remained an important professional ideal, lawyers could therefore be confident that their work had intrinsic value too. But in the last generation this ideal has collapsed, and with it the professional self-confidence it once sustained.

The old dispensation expressed itself most emphatically, says Kronman, in the ideal of the "lawyer-statesman," the practitioner who was at once a skilled technician, a public-spirited citizen and, above all, a paragon of practical wisdom. *The Lost Lawyer* recounts how that old ideal got itself transmogrified on its way through nineteenth-century America and, from there, fell into desuetude almost altogether in our own time. The lawyer-statesman was distinguishable by two traits above all: his love of the common good and his prudence. His civic-mindedness, Kronman says, grew out of a social order that understood the defense of the common good to be a higher calling than pursuit of private gain. Practical wisdom, in turn, was understood to be not merely a skill (like cleverness) but a trait suggesting moral character as well.

Kronman points out how modern philosophy has devastated the rationale underlying the lawyer-statesman ideal. The greater part of *The Lost Lawyer* is devoted to the reestablishment of that ideal on what Kronman considers to be philosophically defensible grounds. Readers will differ on whether he is successful, but it is remarkable that the dean of a major law school should be cognizant of such matters at all; it is even more remarkable that he tries to do something about it. The essence of his argument is that the good lawyer must, in some significant sense, also be a good man or woman. This understanding, Kronman says, was once widely accepted implicitly if not explicitly, but is now under attack almost everywhere. Such an argument would be greeted by hoots of derision in most law schools and law firms today, and anyone advocating such an opinion would be thought at best quaintly romantic if not hopelessly delusional. Even so, Kronman is certainly correct in suggesting that a legal profession severed from the idea of moral character will have a hard time distinguishing itself from those who practice, say, money-laundering, plumbing or, for that matter these days, baseball. Nor will such a profession have much to say about why the rule of law is important or worth defending.

Of the law schools, Kronman observes that they have long since abandoned the effort to inculcate practical wisdom in their students. If anything, faculties tend to be downright hostile to the idea, if they understand its importance at all. Kronman lays almost equal blame at the door of two seemingly disparate trends in modern law curricula: the law and economics movement and the critical legal studies movement. Despite their ideological differences, both schools share the belief that law is essentially a subsidiary or derivative form of knowledge. In order to give an adequate account of themselves, they refer to a higher, architectonic body of knowledge so as to explain and justify their existence. In the one case, that higher science or understanding will be found in economics; and in the other, in the gender, psychological, race, or class preferences that are said to constitute the "real" basis of law. Both schools are seen by Kronman as latter-day extensions of the effort, begun in the nineteenth century, to establish a foundation for law akin to that which underlay the natural sciences.

Here Kronman is at his best. His description of how the case method came to be the more or less exclusive model for law instruction is masterful, as is his discussion of the legal realists and their various progeny. The reader will not find anywhere a more lucid or fair-minded discussion of either topic or of how the modern law curriculum came to be what it is. Ultimately, Kronman traces the intellectual fashions of modern law back to a common ancestor, the seventeenth-century *more geometrico* of Thomas Hobbes and, in particular, his *Dialogue between a Philosopher and a Student of the Common Laws of England*. There Kronman finds the intellectual wellspring of the effort to replace the common-law method of reasoning (which relies inter alia on custom, instinct, precedent, and prudence) with a more "scientific" understanding. Kronman is precisely on target here. His discussion of the process by which Hobbes's argument later informs the jurisprudence of Bentham, Austin and, in turn, Langdell, the realists, and their latter-day descendants is a rich and subtle argument that will repay close reading.

Like Glendon, Kronman is worried about the curious detachment of law schools from the everyday experience of practicing lawyers. The tension between theory and practice has always marked the boundary between school and what came after, but never has it been so sharp. Many professors today are almost openly disdainful of the life lived by most practicing lawyers. One suspects that most practitioners would return the favor if they stopped to think about it, but the larger truth is that most practitioners think the professoriate is simply irrelevant. It takes a hardy soul these days to read the law reviews: never has so much been written by so many for so few about so little.

On the subject of private law practice, Kronman, like Glendon, focuses primarily on life in the large corporate firm. Both recognize the limitations presented by examining so small a group, but it is true that large firms exercise disproportionate influence both inside and outside the profession. It is also the case that much more is known about their mores than about the rest of the bar. In any event, Kronman's simple and compelling point is that even as the law schools have moved toward ever more obscurantist academic doctrinalism, so the large firms have undergone a structural revolution of their own. The result in both cases is the same: neither seems to have much room for the ideals represented by the lawyer-statesman. No one who has been at the bar for a dozen years or more could doubt this. A large-firm lawyer up until 1980 or so would have had much in common with his predecessors of one, two, or perhaps even five decades ago. The changes would have been dramatic in many aspects of his practice, from billing arrangements to the status and role of associates, but an enduring substance beneath the change would have been recognizable across the decades.

The pace and character of change in recent years, however, have no analogue in this century. Among the innovations noted by Kronman as having great impact are the dramatic increase in firm size and in the number of multiple-office firms; the gradual disappearance of the generalist and his replacement by specialists of increasingly narrow perspective; a remarkable shift in the character of firm-client relationships (away from long-term and toward transactional engagements); and a generic weakening of the ties that once bound an attorney to his firm and the firm to him. Taken together, these and other changes over the past generation constitute a revolution in the world of private practice. Kronman's discussion of this sea change, although rhetorically judicious, paints an alarming picture of life in the large corporate firm. It not only casts doubt on the survivability of the lawyer-statesman ideal, but questions whether (if trends continue) large-firm practice will be distinguishable from a hundred other activities whose primary purpose is to make money. Proprietors of large firms will not like his message, but no one who has spent even a few hours perusing random issues of *The American Lawyer* could doubt the general thrust of his argument.

In the final section of its critique, *The Lost Lawyer* turns to the courts. The dramatic increase in caseload in recent years, Kronman says, has reoriented "the entire professional culture in which judges work," leading to "a depreciation of the lawyer-statesman ideal similar to the one that has taken place in... teaching and practice" (p. 320). The consequence is not only a heavily bureaucratized judiciary, but judges who willy-nilly start to think in terms of efficiency rather than of wisdom. Kronman is no enemy of efficiency, to be sure, but he does worry that something vital to the rule of law dies when efficiency becomes the *summum bonum*. That vital something is what he calls "deliberative imagination" (p. 325), the ability of the judge to entertain a point of view different from his own without actually embracing it. This virtue, which he earlier described as also the distinguishing feature of the prudent practitioner, constitutes the essential ingredient of good judging as well.

Kronman also laments the decline in collegiality among judges, especially at the appellate level, and the increasing tendency to file separate concurrences and dissents. He zeroes in on "the culture of the clerks," whom he rightly blames for "the increasing length of opinions," "obsessive footnoting and heavy use of legal jargon," "the growing use of carefully structured multipart tests," and the "increasing reliance on the rhetoric of balancing" (p. 348). All of these features, he argues, are the products of excessive zeal or timidity born of inexperience. Once upon a time, Kronman says, these understandable vices of youth could be monitored and corrected by gray-haired tutors. But we no longer have the assurance that the appropriate instruction will take place (p. 352):

> Contemporary legal theory has a strong anti-prudentialist bias that has begun to seep into the classroom too. So long as law students continued to read cases written by older judges who understood the importance of prudence in their work, this bias was counterbalanced or offset. But that counterbalance no longer exists. Indeed, in the opinions they study today, law students are more likely to find the outlook of their teachers confirmed and strengthened rather than opposed.

These opinions, Kronman goes on to say, are characterized by the same analytical spirit that informs the work of many academic lawyers. It is a vicious cycle. "In this sense one might say that in America today the normal process of legal education—of the old teaching the young—has been interrupted, or more precisely, that it never even begins" (p. 352).

Despite his sharp and useful criticisms of the present-day judiciary, Kronman nevertheless shies away from the implications of his own argument. He seems oblivious, for example, to the possibility that judges gratuitously involve themselves in far more business than the judiciary can intelligently handle. For a work that is otherwise meticulous in its scrutiny of judicial shortcomings, Kronman's book is strangely silent on the growth of judicial power in our time and the ways in which that growth diminishes the idea of limited government and thereby the rule of law. (Glendon's discussion of related issues, by contrast, reveals a keener grasp. To pick but one revealing example: while Glendon sees the majority opinion in *Casey v. Planned Parenthood*[2] as an extraordinary if not unconscionable display

2. 112 S. Ct. 2791 (1992).

of judicial presumption, Kronman sees it as a gesture of prudential wisdom consistent with the highest ideals of American law. This judgment casts doubt on the sufficiency of his understanding of the lawyer-statesman.)

III

In broad theme, Glendon and Kronman weave a credible if depressing tale and for the most part sustain it with apt and thoughtful evidence. Given the comprehensive quality of their assessment, it is somewhat surprising that neither really addresses head-on the issue that is otherwise present (for the most part silently) on almost every page of both books. I refer to the deluge of law in the past thirty to forty years. There is no better word to describe what has happened in every field of law, public and private, and at every level of government. We are positively drowning in the stuff, which is not quite the metaphor the poets have in mind when they sing praises to the rule of law.

These days, federal and state judicial opinions overwhelm library shelves, as do the reports of countless administrative bodies. The Federal Register spews out multiple tens of thousands of pages annually, echoed by relevant analogues at the state, county, and municipal levels. Legislators vote for bills with only limited knowledge of their content, devolving responsibility for their interpretation to judicial or administrative tribunals remote from the people.

Such are, it will be argued, the inevitable consequences of the modern administrative state. This is only partly true. Is it really necessary, for example, to produce (as OSHA apparently did) some twenty-odd pages of specifications defining the proper form of a ladder? In this (and one could adduce countless other examples), the modern state resembles nothing so much as the legendary regimes of the Medes and the Persians, known throughout antiquity as the model of tyrannical caprice. Any resemblance between these bureaucratic concoctions of the welfare state and the rule of law celebrated by Glendon and Kronman is at best coincidental. When they sing the praises of common-law reasoning (and they do so eloquently), they note its respect for precedent, its capacity to accommodate change, its civilizing effect upon those over whom the rules operate, its instructive discipline upon practitioners, and in general its appeal to the rational faculties.

Such virtues are not easily detected, however, in the commands of behemoth government, which even when it happens to be right cannot help behaving clumsily or arbitrarily. That, in turn, may explain in part why modern-day practitioners tend to be ignorant of or indifferent to those habits of mind and heart extolled by Glendon and Kronman. The flood of law also helps to explain the disappearance of the prudent generalist, who is prized for judgment, and the rise of narrow specialists, who are prized for technique. Besides, there is only so much intellectual rigor and moral satisfaction to be found in parsing the turgid and often arbitrary regulatory excrescence of the contemporary administrative state.

In short, the rediscovery of the deliberative qualities extolled by Glendon and Kronman may require that we first reduce the size of government.[3]

One last word. As with any general treatment of so large a subject, one might take issue with the authors' handling of particular subthemes: Kronman, for example, is splendid in describing the bureaucratization of the courts, but oblivious to the dangers presented by judicial overreaching; Glendon is at times unrealistically wistful in her evocation of the virtues of law practice; both overstate the actual influence of the lawyer-statesmen in the past. But these and similar minor defects do not detract from the authors' larger and more important point, which is that the American bar today is almost entirely bereft of a sustaining credo through which it can understand and justify itself. On that score, Glendon and Kronman have delivered a valuable and long overdue message. Let us hope someone is listening.

REVIEWED BY MICHAEL M. UHLMANN

3. Now *there's* a task for deans who worry about how to keep their 3L's motivated—and focused on something other than the prospect of the almighty dollar. Consider the possibilities presented by an imaginary course like this:

> *Law 317, The Restoration of the Rule of Law.* The course will analyze the exponential growth of government in the United States, with emphasis on inefficiency and injustice as well as adverse consequences for the Constitution and individual liberty. Particular attention will be paid to the law of unintended consequences and the fallacy of good intentions. Students will be required to prepare a comprehensive "Brandeis brief" justifying the reduction or elimination of selected government programs and agencies.

Farewell *Miranda*?

CONFESSIONS, TRUTH, AND THE LAW
by Joseph D. Grano
Ann Arbor: University of Michigan Press, 1993
303 pp., $42.50

In *Confessions, Truth, and the Law*, Wayne State University law professor Joseph D. Grano exhaustively reviews the law of confessions in order to make the case for overruling *Miranda v. Arizona*[1] and reinstating the "voluntariness" test as the sole standard for determining the constitutional validity of a confession made during police interrogation. Whatever one thinks about Grano's overall conclusions—which Grano himself acknowledges are "politically incorrect, at least in academic circles" (p. vii)—it cannot be denied that he has written an important work. The book's comprehensive analysis of the academic literature and its thorough review of the principal disputed issues in the field ensures that, for some time to come, any serious scholarly writing on the topic of confessions will have to confront and address Grano's arguments.

The book, however, is not without flaws. Chief among them is an occasional tendency to fall back too quickly to "second best" theories—arguments whose underlying premises one suspects (or at least hopes) that Grano himself might question but for the fact that those premises are so widely accepted in the legal community. Although Grano makes such arguments in the seeming hope of persuading a wider audience that *Miranda* should be jettisoned, these sorts of pragmatic accommodations to conventional wisdom have a way of being self-fulfilling: questionable assumptions become settled precisely because no one is willing to challenge them. Having already taken on quite a lot in challenging *Miranda*, Grano perhaps did not want to bite off more than he could chew, but one wonders whether the overall

1. 384 U.S. 436 (1966). *Miranda* held that, in order to "secure the privilege against self-incrimination," statements obtained during custodial interrogations by police may not be affirmatively introduced by the prosecution at trial unless a series of warnings had been provided to the suspect. *Id.* at 444–45.

argument is aided by relying on popular, but often erroneous, intermediate premises.

The second major flaw of the book is that it belabors, occasionally at some length, points that seem painfully obvious. The cause of this problem is readily apparent: Grano spends pages discussing and refuting articles by other law professors containing arguments so obviously mistaken that only an academic could have made them. Grano's tendency to overargue some points also reinforces the impression that the book is largely written for a narrow audience consisting of other law professors; the reader sometimes has the sense of having accidentally wandered into the faculty lounge. The focus of the book, as well as its readability and accessibility to a wider audience, could have been enhanced by slighting a few of the professors whose articles did not merit such lengthy responses.

Most importantly, Grano's reformulation of the voluntariness standard, which he would leave in place of *Miranda*, seems in significant respects wrong, overbroad, and dangerously susceptible to manipulation. If the price of correcting *Miranda*'s error is accepting an even greater and more harmful one, then that price is too high.

Overall, however, the positives of this book substantially outweigh its negatives. Grano has accomplished something that is no mean feat: presenting a forceful, cogent, and ultimately persuasive argument for overturning one of the best-known and most well-established legal decisions of our time. He does so by considering, and rejecting, each of the various grounds for defending *Miranda*: policy considerations, general conceptions of voluntariness, the *due process* voluntariness doctrine, the Fifth Amendment, the Sixth Amendment, and stare decisis.

I

The first portion of Grano's book addresses "Policy Considerations," while the second half deals with "Constitutional Considerations" (pp. 1, 85). Grano's stated purpose for using this format is his belief that, "to achieve perspective, it helps to put aside the Constitution, if only temporarily, to consider how we might choose to structure the criminal justice system were we permitted to build our own foundation" (p. 5). This approach, however, both reflects and exacerbates the book's most serious weaknesses.

On a stylistic level, Grano's approach occasionally causes the first part of the book to be abstract to the point of tedium. The entire first chapter, for example, is devoted to establishing the utterly trivial proposition that "the tension between truth discovery and other goals [in the criminal justice system] should be resolved in a way that leaves truth a dominant goal of the procedural system" (p. 24). Because Grano himself is unwilling to say that truth should be "*the* dominant goal" (p. 6, emphasis in original), he has sought to demonstrate only the more limited proposition that the goal of pursuing truth in the criminal justice system should not be sacrificed except for a very good reason. But who could seriously dispute that? The reader is left wondering why it was necessary to take such a lengthy detour—including an overview of various abstract models of criminal procedure—only to return to the main path and realize that one has advanced hardly a step down that road.

Moreover, by devoting the second chapter to a policy critique of the various objections that have been put forth to police interrogation, Grano has arranged his argument exactly backwards. The declared purpose of the second chapter is to "demonstrate that even under... an unrestrained approach to constitutional interpretation"—which Grano characterizes as one that "endorse[s] judicial imposition of value choices on the nation"—there is no good reason for "curtailing the effectiveness of police interrogation" (p. 27). But if the point of the book is to show that a particular set of judicial decisions is wrong and should be overturned, it would seem more appropriate to begin with a discussion of the relevant authoritative principles that bind judges (that is, the relevant constitutional provisions and their correct interpretation) and show that those decisions cannot be justified under those principles. Only then (if at all) should it be necessary to make the collateral and incidental argument that, even assuming that judges are not bound by anything other than their own predilections, they ought not want to maintain such ill-advised decisions. By opening with free-wheeling policy discussions, the book inadvertently gives obeisance to what might be called the prevailing legal culture's jurisprudential "atheism" (there are no authoritative principles), "agnosticism" (no one can seem to figure out what principles are authoritative anyway), and "idolatry" (*my* principles are authoritative). Although it is understandable that, given the book's aim of being comprehensive, Grano wants to persuade even those who believe that policy is everything, that effort should have been a brief epilogue rather than a lengthy prolegomenon.

On the merits, Grano is generally persuasive in arguing that, as a matter of policy, the degree of pressure inherent in custodial interrogation is insufficient to warrant *Miranda*'s restrictions. Grano groups the policy objections to police interrogation into four main categories: arguments based on (1) giving the defendant a "fair chance"; (2) equality; (3) the accusatorial nature of our criminal justice system; and (4) human dignity. As examples of the "fair chance" argument, Grano cites the Court's embarrassing opinion in *Escobedo v. Illinois*[2] as well as the writings of various academ-

2. 378 U.S. 478 (1964).

ic commentators, all of which express the view that police interrogation is undesirable because it will render the subsequent trial a "meaningless exercise" (p. 29).[3] Borrowing a phrase from Bentham, Grano rightly derides such reasoning as a "fox-hunter's argument" ("'[t]he fox is to have a fair chance for his life'")[4] and notes that, "outside the realm of confessions, one does not encounter the view that certain techniques of law enforcement should be abandoned or curtailed simply because they are too successful in convicting guilty defendants" (p. 31).

Grano also effectively addresses and refutes two objections based on "equality." The first, which has been reflected in academic commentary as well as (to some degree) in *Miranda* itself, is that something had to be done to balance the "perceived inequality between the interrogating officers and the hapless defendant" (p. 32). But, as Grano notes, in virtually every other context the fact that the police are able to uncover the truth by taking advantage of a criminal's stupidity is a cause for celebration, not consternation (p. 36). And to the extent that the inequality between defendants and the police leads either to coercion or false confessions, such cases can be identified and addressed "by less drastic means" than those used in *Miranda* (p. 34). The second equality argument—that it is unfair to deny the impoverished defendant a lawyer when the wealthy can bring one to the police station—is, in Grano's view, circular: "[I]t begs the question to begin with a preexisting right to counsel *for anyone* in the police station" (p. 37, emphasis added).

In addressing the argument that restrictions on police interrogation are necessary because "'ours is an accusatorial and not an inquisitorial system,'"[5] Grano maintains that the use of such language reflects rhetoric rather than reasoned argument. "[U]nless one can identify the essential attributes and institutional arrangements of the competing systems, the analysis of concrete issues cannot be facilitated by positing that a given system or a particular practice is accusatorial rather than inquisitorial" (pp. 47–48). Moreover, Grano observes that there are numerous inquisitorial features to American criminal procedure, and that these features are generally thought acceptable "because the Constitution permits them" (p. 52). And that makes the whole inquisitorial/accusatorial argument hopelessly circular: one cannot both try to "define the Constitution by reference to our accusatorial sys-

3. Grano notes that *Escobedo* goes so far as to say that a police interview without a lawyer present would reduce the trial to "'no more than an appeal from the interrogation'" (p. 28 (quoting 378 U.S. at 487–88)).

4. P. 29 (quoting 5 JEREMY BENTHAM, RATIONALE OF JUDICIAL EVIDENCE, bk. 9, pt. 4, ch. 3, at 238–29 (1827)).

5. Moran v. Burbine, 475 U.S. 412, 434 (1986) (Stevens, J., dissenting) (quoting Miller v. Fenton, 474 U.S. 104, 110 (1985)).

tem and to define our accusatorial system by reference to the Constitution" (p. 52).

It is in responding to the "human dignity" argument that Grano runs into trouble. The primary difficulty is that one of his premises is both wrong and inconsistent with the Fifth Amendment.[6] Grano's principal argument that it is not cruel to *ask* questions for the purpose of obtaining incriminating answers is as follows: (1) "an individual has a moral obligation at least in some circumstances to confess wrongdoing"; (2) "an individual, at least in a just society, has a general obligation to obey society's valid [i.e., justifiable, not cruel] laws"; (3) "a societal requirement of truthful answers would not be cruel, inhumane, or a violation of human dignity at least in those cases (few or great in number...) in which the requirement coincides with the individual's moral obligation to tell the truth"; and (4) "if requiring truthful but self-incriminating responses is not cruel, then interrogation as such cannot be cruel either" (pp. 38, 42).[7]

The problem with this argument is the third premise. It is simply not true that a law which merely compels an individual to do what he or she is morally obligated to do can never be "cruel, inhumane, or a violation of human dignity." You may, for example, have a moral obligation to buy your spouse an anniversary gift, but that does not mean that a law requiring you to do so would not be a violation of "human dignity." And even though you may be morally obligated to pay tithes to your church or to do volunteer work in your community, it would be unjust for the state to require you to do so. In short, the mere existence of a moral obligation to do an act is insufficient to establish the quite different proposition that it is proper for the state to enjoin you to do that act; rather, the propriety of any state command must be independently justified.

It is debatable whether any such justification can be given that is consistent with the theory of the Fifth Amendment that it *is* wrong to require a criminal defendant to disclose those facts contained in his mind and memory that establish his guilt. Grano, however, maintains that requiring truthful incriminating answers is less cruel than intrusive (and possibly destructive) physical searches and that requiring such answers is not much different from requiring an individual "not to escape or commit perjury" (p. 42). Both claims are wrong. The Framers reasonably (and correctly) concluded that the state's forcible extraction of facts from the minds of those whom it

6. I recognize that, as Grano notes later in his book (pp. 123–31), *Miranda*'s application of the Fifth Amendment to custodial questioning is itself controversial. But Grano concedes that the due process voluntariness principle (which concededly does apply to jailhouse interrogation) would forbid state compulsion of incriminating answers (pp. 107, 114, 135).

7. Grano actually presents what I have listed as the first three steps of his argument as a more detailed five-step syllogism, but the main premises are the ones that I have summarized.

seeks to incarcerate is more troubling than even a search of one's home. And it seems clear that permitting an individual to stand silent is different in kind from requiring him not to engage in further affirmative acts of wrongdoing; the distinction between nonfeasance and malfeasance is well-established and not hard to draw.

Grano's argument on this score is unfortunate in an additional respect. By tying his argument to a premise that is at war with the Fifth Amendment, Grano risks discrediting his whole enterprise, which is, after all, to demonstrate that *Miranda* is a wrong legal decision. It seems clear that, to have any hope of persuasiveness, no portion of that overall argument can be premised, even implicitly, on the assumption that the value judgment reflected in the Fifth Amendment is invalid.

Fortunately, Grano does make an alternative argument concerning the alleged "cruelty" of police questioning that is not based on such a flawed premise. Grano notes that, although particular police practices might be deemed troubling, merely encouraging (rather than compelling) suspects to tell the truth about their crimes should not be deemed "cruel" (pp. 44–45). Although it might be argued that "it is cruel to influence a suspect to act against the suspect's best interests," that view "limits its focus to the suspect's material as opposed to moral interests" (p. 45).[8] That is, it cannot be cruel merely to encourage a suspect—who remains free to refuse all entreaties—to do the right thing by telling the truth. Where the police have not coerced the suspect, there is no apparent reason why truth should be sacrificed for the sole purpose of advancing the material interest of the suspect in beating the rap.

II

Having addressed the various policy objections to police interrogation, Grano then launches, in chapter 3, into an abstract analysis of what he views as the principal legitimate restriction on police interrogation, namely the concept of "voluntariness." The aim of this discussion is to establish the proposition that "the issue of voluntariness, in all its component parts, requires normative rather than empirical judgments" (p. 60)—that is, that it inevitably requires value judgments rather than factual determinations. This chapter, which is something of an excursus that is not particularly well

8. Prompt confession may also often be in the defendant's material interests. For example, a drug courier intercepted by police can help himself ultimately to obtain a lower sentence by confessing, cooperating with the police, and completing the drug transaction in order to capture the intended recipients. If the courier refuses to speak until he has consulted with counsel, it will be too late for him to cooperate in that fashion; the recipients will by then have realized that the defendant was caught.

integrated into the overall argument, is perhaps the most disappointing in the entire book.

Grano begins by criticizing the courts' frequent pronouncement that a statement is involuntary if the suspect's "'will has been overborne.'"[9] He asserts that such terminology is confusing because there are circumstances in which a person's actions will undoubtedly be deemed involuntary "even though the actors clearly had the ability to resist the pressures to which they responded" (p. 62). Grano argues, for example, that the "overborne wills" approach, taken literally, would lead to the conclusion that "a person acts voluntarily by acceding to a terrorist's command to commit a crime or face the death of family members, for such a command requires the person to choose between competing alternatives" (p. 61).[10] Grano then rejects the "polar opposite approach" under which a confession will be regarded as involuntary "whenever the police increase, however slightly, the defendant's psychic strain" (p. 64). Like Goldilocks, he then finds the middle ground to be just right:

> With these extreme positions eliminated, the only remaining possibility is that the voluntariness doctrine in the law of confessions, at least to the extent that it addresses volitional freedom, must be concerned with the kind and degree of volitional impairment that should relieve defendants from being held accountable for their statements. That is, the relevant inquiry, in Justice Harlan's words, must be "*how much* pressure on the suspect [will be] permissible," or, from the other direction, how much will be "undue." Whether pressure is too much or undue obviously requires a normative judgment.[11]

Because it merely eliminates two positions that he has made into straw men, however, Grano's argument thus far establishes almost nothing. No one could seriously deny that the question whether someone should be held "accountable for [his] statements" is a normative inquiry; the key issue in dispute is whether the concept of voluntariness has sufficient determinate content that it can provide that norm. Grano concludes that it does not. To say that something is involuntary, in Grano's view, merely means that two things have been established: (1) the police have used pressure that left the suspect "no reasonable choice" or "no acceptable alternative" but to con-

9. Pp. 59–60 (quoting Columbe v. Connecticut, 367 U.S. 568, 602 (1961) (opinion of Frankfurter, J.)).

10. Grano uses this example to illustrate Aristotle's narrow definition of involuntary and then states that "[w]ere we to take it literally, the overborne will language would seem to correspond with Aristotle's definition of involuntary action" (p. 61).

11. P. 64 (quoting *Miranda*, 384 U.S. at 507 (Harlan, J., dissenting) (emphasis in original)).

fess and (2) the pressure applied was "wrongful."[12] Because, Grano argues, a definitional approach to voluntariness yields nothing more than those two propositions (and the third requirement that there be a sufficient causal link between the wrongful pressure and the confession) (pp. 73–79), and since each of these propositions requires a further normative judgment, the concept of voluntariness does not have much content (pp. 67–68):

> [W]e remain free to decide both what conduct should be regarded as wrongful and what alternatives available to the actor should be regarded as reasonable. Those who are hostile to police interrogation remain free to argue that even the slightest pressure is "wrongful" and that such pressure confronts the defendant with "unacceptable" alternatives.

These conclusions seem doubtful. Although Grano is probably correct that the concept of "voluntariness" is not alone sufficient to provide a complete code for the admissibility of confessions, it is not as empty of content as he claims. In common parlance—even in the eighteenth century—the term "involuntary" means "dictated by authority or circumstance"[13] or "[n]ot chosen; not done willingly."[14] The term used in the Fifth Amendment—"compelled"—is a form of "compel," which means "to obtain [responses] by force, violence, or coercion"[15] or "[t]o force to some act; to oblige."[16] It stretches the meaning of these terms beyond recognition to claim, as Grano does, that it can cover an act done in response to "even the slightest pressure." Prodding, goading, or cajoling someone to do something is simply not the same as compelling him to do it. Grano's definition of "involuntary" is thus substantially overbroad, and he thereby too quickly concludes that it has no real content.

For similar reasons, Grano too hastily dismisses "overborne wills" language as having no utility. The reason why such language has repeatedly found its way into judicial opinions is not hard to figure out; as the definitions cited above indicate, the terms "involuntary" and "compelled" both

---

12. P. 67 (citing ALAN WERTHEIMER, COERCION (1987)). In a footnote (p. 246 n.65), Grano suggests that a better formulation of the first prong might be "not whether the threat left the actor with no reasonable choice but rather whether the actor's choice in response to the threat was reasonable." This latter formulation would significantly expand the scope of the "involuntary" category.

13. WEBSTER'S THIRD NEW INTERNATIONAL DICTIONARY 1191 (1966) [hereinafter WEBSTER'S THIRD].

14. SAMUEL JOHNSON, A DICTIONARY OF THE ENGLISH LANGUAGE 406 (H.J. Todd ed., 1843) (originally published in 1756).

15. WEBSTER'S THIRD, *supra* note 13, at 463.

16. JOHNSON, *supra* note 14, at 133.

seem to suggest that the suspect has been the object of an overpowering force.[17] The flavor of this notion, which is captured by the phrase "overborne will," is absent from Grano's broader definition.

As noted earlier, Grano rejects the use of the phrase "overborne will" only because he concludes that it cannot be applied literally in the context of a person who retains some residual power to resist. That conclusion, however, is not at all obvious. In most situations where voluntariness is disputed, the suspect initially expresses reluctance to admit guilt but ultimately confesses during the course of his conversation with the police; it makes sense in such cases to focus the inquiry on whether the suspect's will was diverted from one object to another through force or intimidation (as opposed to moral suasion, a persuasive analysis of defendant's legal predicament, cajoling through offers of leniency, or even trickery)—in short, whether the suspect's will was overborne.[18]

Grano's rejection of "overborne wills" language also may have very undesirable consequences: by liberating the concept of voluntariness from the demanding strictures of that phrase, and instead rendering voluntariness wholly normative "in all its component parts," Grano eliminates any possibility that "voluntariness" has *independent* doctrinal content that will constrain judges.[19] That is, if Grano is correct that the concept of "voluntariness" merely directs one to make normative judgments on the basis of criteria that are not in any way provided by that concept itself, then the grounds of the debate necessarily shift to a determination of where those criteria might come from. This strikes me as somewhat akin to abandoning a well-secured fortress in order to confront the opponent instead in the

17. Indeed, in his discussion of the issue of causation between the wrongful police pressure and the decision to confess—an inquiry that Grano again deems to be wholly normative—he acknowledges that "[t]he concept of coercion ordinarily conveys some sense of force or of 'overpowering' pressure" (p. 77). In a footnote, Grano hastens to explain that the quotation marks around "overpowering" are needed "because, as already discussed, the concept of overpowering cannot be taken literally" (p. 252 n.134).

18. Force or intimidation, of course, may take many forms. For example, it may include, depending on all of the circumstances, keeping someone awake for hours on end; persisting in questioning someone who is drunk, withdrawing from medication, or in pain; or withholding something to which the defendant is legally entitled.

19. The phrase "overborne wills" is useful in emphasizing the demanding nature of the involuntariness standard and thereby discouraging the use of the voluntariness doctrine as a vehicle for activist innovations in the law; for example, a claim that "even the slightest pressure" constitutes an overbearing application of force would be greeted with giggles. There are, in other words, arguments that would be plausible under Grano's approach that cannot plausibly be made under the rubric of overborne wills. Indeed, it has been my experience as a prosecutor that a judicial finding of involuntariness under the prevailing "overborne wills" standard is very rare.

open field. In chapter 4, Grano argues for a narrow, Harlanesque view of the relevant normative criteria, thereby ultimately constraining the operation of the voluntariness concept as a *constitutional* doctrine.[20] But those whose approach to interpreting the normative commands of the Constitution is much more flexible will reject this second step of the argument, while gratefully embracing the first. That is, those who believe that constitutional directives to make normative judgments permit them to apply "evolving" or "contemporary"—or, worse yet, their own—standards of "justice" will take heart from Grano's conclusion that the concept of voluntariness is merely another call for such judgments. The voluntariness doctrine, which had seemed so narrow and unpromising an area for doctrinal innovation, is under this view quite the opposite.

In discussing the voluntariness concept, Grano also too quickly rejects the usefulness of the distinction between threats and offers (pp. 69–73). Grano notes that several commentators have taken the position that offers cannot coerce, but Grano rejects this position, concluding that it does not yield satisfactory answers to certain hypotheticals and that no American court would seriously accept it in the context of police interrogation (pp. 69–71). The principal hypothetical that Grano uses is one in which a millionaire offers to provide a woman the funds needed to pay for her daughter's surgery on the condition that the woman become his mistress (p. 70). Without further argument, Grano simply declares that "it seems virtually certain that an offer by interrogating officers along the lines of the millionaire's proposal would prompt courts to find the resulting confession involuntary because of coercion" (pp. 70–71). It seems a curious line of reasoning, in a book whose aim is to critique almost thirty years of settled judicial decisions, to reject an argument on the ground that courts would not accept it. It seems clear, moreover, that Grano himself thinks that the millionaire's offer is coercive, yet he does not fully articulate why. Rather, he states that the coerciveness of offers probably depends upon "the propriety of conditioning the proposal on the recipient's performance of the desired action," but that "[t]his book is not the place to develop such a theory" (p. 71).

Grano provides little additional elaboration when he again picks up on the theme of improper conditional offers in discussing *Lynumn v. Illi-*

20. In chapter 3, Grano acknowledges that the constraints that he will impose on the constitutional doctrine of voluntariness arise, not from his views about what it means for something to be voluntary, but rather from his view of what norms may properly be constitutionalized (p. 65): "[T]he constitutional inquiry regarding voluntariness, as the next chapter will develop, may be less indeterminate or relativistic than the inquiry made solely from a normative perspective."

nois.[21] In *Lynumn*, the interrogating officers told the suspect that she faced ten years in prison, that her welfare benefits might be cut off, that she might lose custody of her two children, and that "if she cooperated, it would go light on her."[22] Although Grano hints that he believes *Lynumn* was wrongly decided in the defendant's favor,[23] he states, again without elaborated argument, that a critique of *Lynumn* "based entirely on the offer-threat distinction rings rather hollow" (p. 71).

Grano's failure to articulate more fully his views on the offer/threat distinction is unfortunate, since his conclusions seem open to question. It is not a sufficient defense of *Lynumn* to state that a police offer of leniency in exchange for cooperation, coupled with a truthful description of the consequences of a conviction without such leniency,[24] is coercive because it is improper to put a parent to "the wrenching choice of self-destruction or loss of her children" (p. 106). This sort of lapse into rhetoric might be enough to pass for reasoning in a judicial opinion, but it is inadequate for a serious analysis. What the police did in *Lynumn* was instead to present the defendant with the option of avoiding *what she already faced*, which was *both* "self-destruction" *and* the "loss of her children." It takes more than a rhetorical flourish to show that a police offer to alleviate Lynumn's plight in exchange for her cooperation is coercive.

Similarly, there is good reason to question whether the millionaire hypothetical implicates a concern about coercion. If, for example, the millionaire's condition were, not that the woman become his mistress, but instead that she agree to volunteer a few hours a week at the local children's hospital, would anyone think that was coercive? This suggests that the real basis of one's gut reaction to the millionaire hypothetical is not the coerciveness of the offer, but rather its immorality. Similarly, it is not obvious that coercion is the problem with "too-attractive" offers during police interrogation; rather, the real concern is that, when presented with such an enticing option, a suspect will choose—freely and voluntarily—to provide false statements in order to secure a benefit that is worth more to the suspect than avoiding a criminal conviction. That is, the problem in such cases may not be *invol-*

---

21. 372 U.S. 528 (1963).

22. *Id.* at 533.

23. P. 71 ("Of course, we might want to conclude on careful consideration that the Court decided *Lynumn* incorrectly..."); p. 72 (noting that it is unclear "why we should want to regard the police conduct at issue in *Lynumn* as improper"). It seems difficult, however, to criticize the Court's decision in *Lynumn* in view of the fact that the State conceded, for purposes of argument, that Lynumn's confession was coerced and sought to defend the judgment only on other grounds. 372 U.S. at 534–35.

24. As Grano notes, the Court in *Lynumn* did not question the truthfulness of the information described by the police to the suspect (pp. 71 & 250 n.99).

untary confessions, but *unreliable* ones. Indeed, Grano himself expressly suggests that it "is possible that *Lynumn* really reflects a concern about the trustworthiness of confessions made under such circumstances" (pp. 250–51 n.104). If that is correct, then the relevant question in such contexts should be whether the Constitution bars the introduction at trial of voluntary confessions that nonetheless lack sufficient indicia of reliability.[25] By more explicitly addressing the offer/threat issue, Grano might have strengthened his argument (the correctness of which is not self-evident) that reliability is not an independent concern apart from voluntariness, and he might have alleviated the concern that he is trying to make the voluntariness concept carry more weight than it can bear.[26]

III

After analyzing the voluntariness concept in the abstract, Grano next attempts to define more narrowly the *constitutional* concept of voluntariness. The primary means by which Grano limits (in chapter 4) what he labored to show (in chapter 3) is a very open-ended concept of voluntariness is by adopting a Harlanesque approach to the meaning of the Due Process Clause. In doing so, however, Grano once again reaches a debatable conclusion by using a thoroughly unsatisfying "Goldilocks" argument.

On the one hand, Grano rejects a strict "textualist or originalist" position—which Grano assumes would eliminate entirely a due process voluntariness requirement—because such a position "would not be taken seriously at this late date" (p. 94). He also rejects the "extreme opposite position" that "the due process clauses should be read as inviting judges simply to write their own moral preferences into the Constitution" because, as Professor Ely has pointed out, this theory is difficult to reconcile with our democratic theory of government.[27] Grano then concludes that the "only remain-

25. The Court appears to have answered this question in the negative:

> We think the Constitution rightly leaves this sort of inquiry to be resolved by state laws governing the admission of evidence and erects no standard of its own in this area. A statement rendered by one in the condition of respondent [a chronic schizophrenic] might be proved to be quite unreliable, but this is a matter to be governed by the evidentiary laws of the forum, see, *e.g.*, Fed. Rule Evid. 601, and not by the Due Process Clause of the Fourteenth Amendment.

Colorado v. Connelly, 479 U.S. 157, 167 (1986).

26. I hasten to add that Grano may well be correct in his conclusion that offers can be coercive; my point is not to disprove it, but merely to raise enough doubts to suggest that further supporting argument is needed than Grano has given.

27. P. 95 (citing JOHN ELY, DEMOCRACY AND DISTRUST 45 (1980)).

ing course" is to "attempt to steer between the two unacceptable interpretational poles" and adopt the approach taken in the Court's early due process decisions, namely that the voluntariness doctrine "should be premised on notions of fundamental fairness that are rooted in some 'objective' source, such as tradition or the concepts of ordered liberty and justice" (p. 95). In short, Grano concludes that "the moderate judicial philosophy of Justices Frankfurter and Harlan may provide the second best solution for those who want the Constitution's text to remain substantially relevant to constitutional law" (p. 97).

Grano's Goldilocks argument, however, rests on a dubious taxonomy. It is a caricature of the originalist position to suggest that one may never consider sources outside the text in interpreting the language of the text; what an originalist does is to attempt to ascertain the meaning of the text in light of the understanding that would have been attached to the language at the time it was adopted, an enterprise that requires some knowledge of contemporaneous legal principles and the traditional understanding attached to legal phrases. Grano appears to classify this (originalist) position as a variant of Harlanism, but it is not. Harlan's approach to constitutional interpretation permitted judges to consider, not just the traditional meaning of legal phrases, but also such amorphous concepts as the "basic values that underlie our society."[28] There is a vast difference between stating that a judge may give effect to the contemporaneous and traditional understandings of legal language and stating that he may enforce any principle he deems to be rooted in tradition;[29] it is even more problematic to state that he may enforce any values he believes "are basic to the American system of justice" (p. 97).

Grano does not consider whether an originalist position of the sort described above—that is, one that is not a straw man—would require the elimination of the voluntariness concept as a constitutional principle. The answer is far from obvious, despite the fact that originalism seems to have acquired the reputation of permitting the government to do anything it wants. Using an originalist approach, the Court, speaking through Justice Thomas, recently concluded that the Fourth Amendment generally requires officers executing a warrant at a home to knock and announce their presence before entering by force (a conclusion that is certainly not obvious if

28. Griswold v. Connecticut, 381 U.S. 479, 501 (1965) (Harlan, J., concurring in the judgment).

29. Professor Ely sarcastically criticized the latter position by quoting Garry Wills's comment that "'[r]unning men out of town on a rail is at least as much an American tradition as declaring unalienable rights.'" ELY, *supra* note 27, at 60 (quoting GARRY WILLS, INVENTING AMERICA xiii (1978)).

one reads the text in isolation).[30] Similarly, Justice Thomas has suggested that a tradition-based approach to interpreting the guarantee of due process would preclude trying a criminal defendant who is subject to state-imposed physical restraints that "diminish substantially the defendant's mental faculties during the trial."[31] In view of the fact that, as Grano notes, "English and American cases during the eighteenth century consistently enforced a voluntariness requirement for confessions" (p. 101), it is at least plausible that an originalist approach may retain such a requirement. Since Grano's sole argument for rejecting an originalist approach is the observation that "the Court, regardless of its makeup, is not going to abrogate the voluntariness doctrine" (p. 95), he has failed to make the argument against an originalist approach to this area of the law.

To Grano's assertion that Harlanism represents the "second best solution" for those "who want the Constitution's text to remain substantially relevant to constitutional law"—that is, those who still hope that constitutional law will have something to do with the Constitution—one can only answer with an emphatic "No!" At bottom, Harlanism is different in degree, but not in kind, from the values-importing approach to constitutional interpretation that Grano properly rejects. This is most painfully illustrated by Grano's use of the "shocks the conscience" test to illustrate the supposedly restrained approach he is advocating. Grano states that "the notion that judicial intervention requires a shocked judicial conscience conveys a message of judicial restraint, one instructing judges to refrain from relying on their private notions of fairness or right and wrong" (pp. 97–98). The concept is "useful not as a black-letter test, which it cannot be," but as a "symbolic reminder" that "suggests that federal judges must always strive to distinguish broadly contestable, moral judgments . . . and society's bedrock moral or political principles" (p. 98). I would prefer more than a "symbolic reminder" to judges that they are not free to constitutionalize their own values; I would prefer a doctrinal approach that will make it very difficult for them to do so. Anyone who thinks that judges will be able to resist the temptation to conclude that their strongly held beliefs reflect "society's bedrock moral or political principles" is either willfully blind or hopelessly naive. Harlan's approach—which, in practice, readily allows judges to do what they want while pretending merely to follow the law[32]—is hardly

30. Wilson v. Arkansas, 115 S. Ct. 1914, 1916–18 (1995).

31. Riggins v. Nevada, 504 U.S. 127, 154 n.4 (1992) (Thomas, J., dissenting) (emphasis omitted).

32. *See, e.g.*, Planned Parenthood v. Casey, 112 S. Ct. 2791, 2805–06 (1992) (opinion of O'Connor, Kennedy, & Souter, JJ.) (relying upon Harlan and Frankfurter in order to create a constitutional right to abortion). Grano notes that he himself has previously criticized Harlanesque approaches as "hopelessly subjective" (p. 261 n.74 (citing Grano, *Judicial Review*

second best. On the contrary, it is the worst of both worlds. If we are to have a judicial tyranny, at least let us have it without the "base alloy of hypocrisy."[33]

The concerns over a Harlanesque approach to voluntariness are borne out in Grano's subsequent discussion. Grano canvasses a number of the Court's voluntariness cases, as well as several hypotheticals, to illustrate how his approach would work (pp. 102–14). Grano readily concludes that the "normative concerns so apparent in *Miranda*" do not have the requisite "universality or moral hold" to warrant incorporating them into the Due Process Clause and that, for the same reason, police trickery in custodial interrogation generally cannot be deemed unconstitutional (pp. 102, 112–14). On other occasions, however, Grano stretches his theory to reach some highly doubtful conclusions. As noted earlier, in order to defend the Court's finding of involuntariness in *Lynumn*, Grano is forced to conclude that "it violates a fundamental precept of American justice for the police to put a parent to the wrenching choice of self-destruction or loss of her children" (p. 106). Similarly, in order to conclude that the use of a doctor as a police interrogator would violate "the unfair advantage or improper exploitation strand of the due process voluntariness doctrine," Grano states that it is fundamentally unfair, in light of "the way our society traditionally has viewed the physician-patient relationship," to provide deceptively a doctor who "intended to act against [the suspect's] interests rather than for his well-being" (p. 111).[34] The contrived nature of these explanations[35] leaves one uncomfortably suspicious that Grano has unwittingly done little more than label as "fundamentally unfair" those principles that he finds most strongly objectionable.

---

and a Written Constitution in a Democratic Society, 28 WAYNE L. REV. 1, 8–11, 25–27 (1981)). He ignores his prior criticisms because he is "talking now about second best interpretational strategies" (p. 261 n.74).

33. Letter from Abraham Lincoln to Joshua F. Speed (Aug. 24, 1855), *in* 2 THE COLLECTED WORKS OF LINCOLN 323 (Roy Basler ed., 1952–55).

34. Grano's doctor hypothetical is loosely based on Leyra v. Denno, 347 U.S. 556 (1954), a case which was resolved on more traditional voluntariness grounds based not only on the use of a "highly skilled psychiatrist" but also on the police's marathon questioning of defendant over several days despite his severe pain from a sinus attack. *Id.* at 561.

35. It was argued earlier that *Lynumn*'s finding of involuntariness is questionable. *See supra* p. 195. The weakness of Grano's conclusions in the suspect-doctor hypothetical is apparent when one contrasts it with the other two hypotheticals he posits involving police who pretend to be a defense attorney or a priest (pp. 109–10). The latter hypotheticals confirm the suspicion, noted earlier, that Grano is trying to make the voluntariness concept do too much work: what makes the lawyer and priest examples so especially troubling is that (unlike the doctor hypothetical) they implicate relationships that are clearly protected by other constitutional provisions, namely the First and Sixth Amendments. In order to resolve the doctor hypothetical to his satisfaction, Grano essentially posited a questionable constitutional right of privacy in physician-patient communications.

IV

In chapters 5 and 6 of his book, Grano persuasively argues that the Fifth and Sixth Amendments, to the extent they apply to police interrogation, do not impose any requirements beyond those of the voluntariness test (whatever its precise contours).

With respect to the Fifth Amendment, Grano reviews the separate histories of the voluntariness doctrine and the privilege against self-incrimination and concludes that "*Miranda* erred, at least from a historical perspective, in perceiving an 'intimate connection' between the privilege, which prohibited compulsory oaths and mandatory judicial questioning of the accused, and the issues pertaining to the admissibility of extrajudicial confessions" (p. 131). Even assuming that the Fifth Amendment is to be applied to police questioning, Grano rejects the extreme view that the Fifth Amendment "should make police-initiated interrogation unlawful" (p. 132). Such a view "would make the privilege in the police station coextensive with the privilege at trial," but Grano argues that police investigations should instead be governed by the different rule that applies in most nontrial situations, where "the 'privilege is merely an option of refusal, not a prohibition of inquiry.'"[36] As Grano notes, "[a]ll this leads . . . to the unremarkable conclusion that the Fifth Amendment, if properly applied to police interrogation at all, prohibits coerced or involuntary confessions" (p. 135).

Miranda departed from this approach, however, by declaring a "'right to remain silent.'"[37] But the right guaranteed by the Fifth Amendment is a right not to be *compelled* to incriminate oneself and, Grano argues, there is therefore no "right to silence" except in the limited sense that "a person who cannot lawfully be coerced into speaking can, of course, remain silent" (pp. 141–42). Indeed, taken seriously, a Fifth Amendment right to silence would imply that even noncustodial questioning "would have to be preceded by a valid waiver, a result inconsistent with *Miranda*, Fifth Amendment precedent in general, and the historical understanding that a person, in almost all contexts other than trial, must affirmatively assert the privilege or lose it" (p. 142). By limiting the Fifth Amendment to precluding the admission of *compelled* statements, Grano reaches the apt conclusion that "the Fifth Amendment actually means what it says" (p. 143).

---

36. Pp. 132, 134 (quoting 8 JOHN H. WIGMORE, A TREATISE ON THE ANGLO-AMERICAN SYSTEM OF EVIDENCE IN TRIALS AT COMMON LAW § 2268, at 388 (3d ed. 1940)) (emphasis omitted).

37. P. 141 (quoting *Miranda*, 384 U.S. at 467–68).

V

In chapter 6, Grano addresses the question whether the Sixth Amendment might be deemed to guarantee a right to counsel during police questioning, even if *Miranda* were overruled. Here, Grano's negative answer is more or less consistent with current law (p. 147). He examines the Court's interpretation of the Sixth Amendment guarantee and notes that, prior to its aberrational decision in *Escobedo*, the Court had never applied the Sixth Amendment in a preindictment police interrogation context (pp. 147–51). Subsequently, *Miranda* itself recharacterized *Escobedo* as essentially a Fifth Amendment case, and the Court has since settled upon the rule that the Sixth Amendment does not apply prior to the start of adversary judicial proceedings (pp. 152–55).[38] On the other hand, *Massiah v. United States*[39] held that, once adversarial proceedings have begun, police-initiated interrogation of a defendant without a lawyer present violates the Sixth Amendment.

Grano vigorously contends that the Sixth Amendment should not be understood as applying to police interrogation at all, even after the initiation of formal adversary proceedings (pp. 155–69). His basic point is that "counsel's help to a defendant during police interrogation is not the 'assistance' the amendment was intended to assure" (p. 155). The Sixth Amendment guarantees counsel in connection with a trial because it furthers the truth-finding function: without counsel, "many defendants with possible defenses, both legal and factual, were incapable of recognizing or presenting those defenses on their own" (p. 156). By contrast, the purpose of having a lawyer at the police station is not to promote the overall truth-finding function, but instead "to protect the defendant from the unwise choice of revealing the truth" (p. 158).

It seems, however, that in making these arguments, Grano does not fully consider their breadth. To take an extreme example, it is at least arguable that uncounseled police interrogation of a defendant during, say, an overnight break in a criminal trial might so undermine the attorney-client relationship as to impair significantly the ability to have counsel's assistance in preparing and presenting a defense. Put another way, unless one takes the untenable position that the Sixth Amendment applies only during the hours that the trial is actually in session, it is arguable that a defense attorney cannot successfully provide the "Assistance of Counsel for [the] defence" guaranteed by the Amendment if the police at all other times during the period of trial have free access to the defendant. But if all attempts at police interrogation must cease at some point between arrest and the start of the trial,

38. Moran v. Burbine, 475 U.S. 412, 428–32 (1986); United States v. Gouveia, 467 U.S. 180, 187–92 (1984).

39. 377 U.S. 201 (1964).

it is not obvious that, when stare decisis concerns are factored in, the bright-line drawn by *Massiah* should be rejected.[40] In any event, Grano's anti-*Massiah* argument is unnecessary to his ultimate attack on *Miranda*, since *Massiah*'s bright line actually helps *prevent* the Sixth Amendment from serving as a fallback source for a right to counsel during prearraignment interrogation (which includes the vast majority of police interrogation that anyone in law enforcement would care about).

VI

Having sealed off all other avenues of escape, Grano's final attack on *Miranda* is his most powerful. In the last two chapters of his book, Grano persuasively argues that the Court's inevitable recognition that *Miranda*'s rules were prophylactic—that is, that they were designed to prevent, rather than to define, constitutional violations[41]—has served to make clear the illegitimacy of the *Miranda* regime. Because the Court has repeatedly (and correctly) insisted that it lacks supervisory power over the state courts, the Court lacks authority to reverse state court judgments without finding a constitutional violation (pp. 185–91).

Grano rejects Professor Monaghan's theory that the Court is authorized to create "'a common law substructure to carry out the purposes and policies'" of the constitutional guarantees at issue,[42] reasoning that such a view is inconsistent with the well-established rule that federal courts may not impose federal common law on the states and that it would "eviscerate the structure of federalism inherent in our Constitution."[43] Nor can *Miranda* be justified as an instance is which the Court applied federal law to preclude a state from preventing the assertion of an otherwise valid federal claim: "*Miranda* does not displace state law so that a federal constitutional violation may be reached and remedied; rather, *Miranda* displaces state evidentiary law even when no federal constitutional violation has occurred" (p. 194). Finally, *Miranda* cannot be viewed as merely establish-

---

40. *Cf.* Quill Corp. v. North Dakota, 504 U.S. 298, 321 (1992) (Scalia, J., concurring in the judgment) (noting that the "'bright-line' regime" established by a decision may be a factor in favor of applying stare decisis).

41. As Grano puts it (p. 175), "prophylactic rules are not simply protective devices for constitutional provisions but more importantly... rules that may be violated without violating the Constitution."

42. P. 186 (quoting Henry P. Monaghan, *The Supreme Court, 1974 Term—Foreword: Constitutional Common Law*, 89 HARV. L. REV. 1, 18 (1975)).

43. P. 191 (citing Erie R.R. v. Tompkins, 304 U.S. 64 (1938)). To these arguments, it might be added that the power, if it exists, to prescribe prophylactic rules intended to prevent violations of the Fourteenth Amendment is lodged in Congress, not the Court. *See* U.S. CONST. amend. XIV, §5; Katzenbach v. Morgan, 384 U.S. 641 (1966).

ing a legitimate "conclusive presumption" of compulsion under certain circumstances (pp. 195–98). As Grano notes, "a conclusive presumption is not an aid to adjudication or a presumption at all; rather, a conclusive presumption is a substantive rule of law" (p. 196).

These legitimacy arguments, of course, attack *Miranda* only insofar as it applies to the states. There is, nonetheless, an equally serious legitimacy problem in *Miranda*'s continued application in federal cases as well. In response to *Miranda*, Congress enacted 18 U.S.C. § 3501, which provides that a confession "shall be admissible in evidence if it is voluntarily given" and that a confession should not be found involuntary on the sole ground that the defendant was not provided with *Miranda* warnings. Grano quotes from a 1986 report from the Justice Department's Office of Legal Policy, which noted the obvious problem: "'Applying *Miranda* [despite section 3501] . . . requires a federal court to violate an Act of Congress, though complying with the Act would involve no violation of a constitutional right of the defendant.'"[44]

Having concluded that *Miranda* cannot be justified by the due process voluntariness doctrine, the Fifth Amendment, or the Sixth Amendment, or as a prophylactic rule, Grano turns to the final step of his argument, a consideration of stare decisis. This final hurdle is by no means a small one, since few decisions are as deeply embedded in both the legal and popular culture as *Miranda*. As Grano notes, even Judge Frank Easterbrook—no advocate of the sort of legislative judicial decisionmaking that *Miranda* represents—has viewed *Miranda* as a prime candidate for the application of stare decisis.[45]

Grano's strongest argument against applying stare decisis derives from his legitimacy point. By simultaneously committing itself to the view that *Miranda* is prophylactic and the view that the Court lacks a supervisory power over the states—two flatly contradictory propositions—the Court has placed itself "'in a position where it must choose between two lines of authority.'"[46] Moreover, the bright-line nature of the *Miranda* regime provides no reason for retaining it; since voluntary but un-Mirandized statements may still be used for impeachment,[47] it is in most cases necessary in any event to make a determination of voluntariness. And the bright-line characteristics

44. P. 203 (quoting OFFICE OF LEGAL POLICY, U.S. DEP'T OF JUSTICE, "TRUTH IN CRIMINAL JUSTICE" SERIES, Rep. No. 1, *The Law of Pretrial Interrogation* 80, 103 (1986), *reprinted in* 22 U. MICH. J.L. REF. 437, 527, 549–50 (1989)).

45. P. 199 (citing Frank Easterbrook, *Stability and Reliability in Judicial Decisions*, 73 CORNELL L. REV. 422, 431, 433 (1988)).

46. P. 206 (quoting Jerold H. Israel, Gideon v. Wainwright: *The "Art" of Overruling*, 1963 SUP. CT. REV. 211, 225).

47. Harris v. New York, 401 U.S. 222, 224–26 (1971).

of the decision, when coupled with the severity of the exclusionary remedy that follows upon a *Miranda* violation, have created a shamefully formalistic regime in which the ability to bring to justice a person known to be guilty may turn on such sophistic inquiries as whether a defendant has invoked the *Miranda* right to silence as opposed to the *Miranda* right to counsel,[48] and whether the defendant has requested a lawyer with sufficient clarity[49] (pp. 206–16).

Even if one concedes, however, that *Miranda*'s current jurisprudential position is unsatisfactory, if not unstable, the question remains how to resolve the doctrinal tension. There are several conceivable options: (1) the Court could jettison the prophylactic view of *Miranda* by declaring that all *Miranda* violations are constitutional violations; (2) the Court could lay claim to a supervisory power over the states; (3) the Court could recast *Miranda*'s rigid requirements as merely establishing a rebuttable presumption of voluntariness; or (4) the Court could overrule *Miranda.*

Grano rejects the first position for several reasons. Because a renunciation of the prophylactic reading of *Miranda* would require the Court to overrule specific *holdings* that are predicated on that reading, this position would require a significant departure from the principle of stare decisis;[50] and if cases are to be overruled, one may fairly ask why the cases that reach *correct* results should be rejected. That is, if stare decisis is to be set aside in any event, there is no reason why the Court should not reject those cases (like *Miranda*) that were *wrong* as an original matter. Moreover, a nonprophylactic reading of *Miranda* would require the Court to embrace the view that an "unwarned response to even one custodial question is actually compelled" (pp. 205–06). In Grano's view, such a sweeping view of what constitutes compulsion would not only defy common sense, it would be inconsistent with precedent both before and after *Miranda* (pp. 182, 206). Finally, recasting *Miranda* in this way would lead to the seemingly self-contradictory conclusion that police interrogation is so inherently coercive that an unwarned suspect's answers are always involuntary, but not so coercive as to render the suspect's waiver of his rights involuntary (p. 182).

Grano rejects the second option—recognizing a supervisory power over state courts—because it has "the potential to destroy our system of separate federal and state courts" (p. 205). And, once again, as long as the Court would have to overrule something in order to make the law coher-

48. *Compare* Edwards v. Arizona, 451 U.S. 477, 485 (1981), *with* Michigan v. Mosley, 423 U.S. 96, 104–05 (1975).

49. Davis v. United States, 114 S. Ct. 2350, 2355 (1994).

50. Pp. 205, 297 n.42 (citing, as examples, Oregon v. Elstad, 470 U.S. 298 (1985), and New York v. Quarles, 467 U.S. 649 (1984)).

ent in this area, it might as well preserve the decisions and principles that are correct.

Grano acknowledges that he once suggested that the third option was a legitimate one; that is, he once suggested that the Court "may have had authority to create rebuttable presumption[s] in *Miranda*" (p. 294 n.176). Given that *Miranda* is deeply embedded in our legal and popular culture, it should under no circumstances be lightly overruled, and it would therefore seem that any legitimate position that can restore doctrinal coherence to this area of the law while preserving as much of *Miranda* as possible should be preferred. Grano now rejects the view that *Miranda* should be converted to a set of rebuttable presumptions, but his argument is relatively weak compared to his arguments against the preceding two options. Grano argues (p. 196) that

> [b]ecause the states in our federal system have the authority, subject only to constitutional constraints, to adopt whatever procedures and evidentiary devices they choose, it is far from obvious that the Supreme Court through the vehicle of appellate reversal should be able to force state courts to employ a rebuttable presumption they prefer not to employ.

But it is not sufficient to say that "it is far from obvious" that the Supreme Court cannot create rebuttable presumptions in this area; on the contrary, because it is far from obvious that the Court does *not* have such a power, this argument is insufficient to overcome the force of stare decisis.

The real argument against creating rebuttable presumptions is that they would be both wrong and far more harmful than preserving *Miranda* undisturbed. As to the first point, it is illogical to employ a presumption that is incorrect in the vast majority of cases. Not only does common sense suggest that a statement is not coerced simply because it was not Mirandized, one strongly suspects that an analysis of judicial behavior under *Miranda* would confirm that, in at least a very significant majority of cases, un-Mirandized statements are found to be voluntary and therefore proper grounds for impeaching a defendant. Moreover, the damage created by the rebuttable-presumption approach (if applied consistently) would likely be significant. In any case in which the "presumption" were thought not to have been sufficiently rebutted, the statement would then be deemed "involuntary" and therefore completely inadmissible, even for impeachment.[51] If those cases are large in number, the opportunities for defense perjury will have been substantially increased, since the defendant will be able to testify without fear that his prior statements will be used against him in any way. There is good reason to think that the use of such a presumption would in fact artificially inflate the number of involuntariness

51. *But cf. Elstad*, 470 U.S. at 307.

determinations by placing an unwarranted thumb on the defense side of the scale. A rebuttable presumption would thus sacrifice the important interest in accurate fact-finding with little corresponding legitimate benefit to defendants.

Having eliminated all of the other available options, Grano confronts a final objection to overruling *Miranda*, namely that overturning the decision "would have the symbolic effect of saying that the Court no longer is concerned" about police interrogation (p. 219). Grano rejects this argument because it embraces "a symbolism that a viable society, one that believes in itself and its right to punish lawlessness, can ill afford" (p. 219). Indeed, eliminating the criminal justice system's perceived symbolic solicitude for the guilty[52] is emphatically a reason in *favor* of overruling *Miranda*.

There is perhaps one last option that must be considered: why not simply ignore the tension that underlies the Court's decisions? Why not just recognize *Miranda* as an aberration in which the Court wrongly exercised a supervisory power over state courts, but nonetheless let the decision stand? There are at least two responses. First, it seems odd to invoke stare decisis to defend an incorrect answer to a question the Court has never addressed. That is, the Court has never considered whether, in light of the subsequent prophylactic reading of *Miranda* and the enactment of 18 U.S.C. § 3501, the decision can still be considered a legitimate one. That question, when the Court finally addresses it, should be answered correctly in the first instance.[53] Second, and most importantly, a decision simply to ignore the internal conflict in the Court's decisions is the jurisprudential equivalent of leaving a loaded gun lying around. As Grano aptly observes, "[t]he serious threat... is that down the road a Court more sympathetic to *Miranda* will take its unrepudiated premises seriously and eliminate police interrogation altogether" (p. 218).

VII

In sum, and despite the occasional weaknesses of the book, Professor Grano has presented a thorough, intelligent, and ultimately persuasive argu-

52. There is little doubt that the *Miranda* rules largely protect the guilty. The prohibition against coercive methods of interrogation, like the prohibition against unreasonable searches, protects us all; but a rule that excludes voluntary statements when the suspect was not given the proper warnings merely protects guilty people who were stupid enough to confess.

53. The opportunity may soon present itself. In *Davis*, 114 S. Ct. at 2357–58, Justice Scalia expressed exasperation at the government's studied refusal, for almost 25 years, to raise the question whether *Miranda* has been invalidated in federal cases by the enactment of § 3501, and he stated that the time for the Court to address this issue sua sponte "will have arrived when a case that comes within the terms of this statute is next presented to us." *Id.* at 2358.

ment for overruling *Miranda*. Even the book's flaws are instructive: it is tempting but often futile to attempt to fashion a middle ground between activism and originalism. *Miranda* should be jettisoned, not in favor of some "second best" theory of constitutional interpretation, but in favor of the constitutional *text*.

REVIEWED BY DANIEL P. COLLINS

Slaying the Dragon of Bad Originalism: Jaffa Answers Cooper

I

Robert Bork and Lino Graglia having broken their lances and retired from the field, a new champion has entered the lists. Charles (Don Carlos) Cooper has now saddled his Rosinante, charging to the rescue of the Dulcinea of Good Originalism, from the Jaffa dragon of Bad Originalism. Of course, we must suspend judgment as to which originalism is the bad, and which is the good—who is the knight and who is the dragon.

For uninstructed readers, this controversy centers upon my book, *Original Intent and the Framers of the Constitution: A Disputed Question*, reviewed by Mr. Cooper in the last issue of *The Public Interest Law Review.*[1] In it I agreed with the campaign by Attorney General Meese, and his Department of Justice, that liberal judicial activism was a great evil, and that a necessary (if not sufficient) antidote to it was a jurisprudence of original intent. My differences with the Attorney General, and those to whom he looked for guidance, centered upon the fact that by and large they were legal positivists, who denied the relevance for original intent of the natural law prin-

1. Charles J. Cooper, *Harry Jaffa's Bad Originalism*, 1994 PUB. INTEREST L. REV. 189 (reviewing HARRY V. JAFFA, ORIGINAL INTENT AND THE FRAMERS OF THE CONSTITUTION: A DISPUTED QUESTION (1994)). Other documents in this controversy are Robert Bork, *Mr. Jaffa's Constitution*, NAT'L REV., Feb. 7, 1994, at 61 (book review); *Jaffa v. Bork: An Exchange*, NAT'L REV., Mar. 21, 1994, at 56 (featuring Jaffa's reply to Bork's review, with a further response by Bork). STORM OVER THE CONSTITUTION: JAFFA ANSWERS BORK (1994) is a more complete reply to Bork's review than *National Review* would allow space to publish, with the addition of several collateral essays. Forthcoming (by the *Southern California Interdisciplinary Law Journal*) is an exchange between Lino Graglia ("Jaffa's Quarrel with Bork: Religious Belief Masquerading as Constitutional Argument") and Harry V. Jaffa ("Graglia's Quarrel with God: Atheism and Nihilism Masquerading as Constitutional Argument") from a Symposium on Natural Law and the Constitution, held at the University of Southern California Law Center on November 4–5, 1994. It has also been published, with permission, by *National Review* (Aug. 14, 1995, pp. 27–32).

ciples—largely but not exclusively enshrined in the Declaration of Independence—which guided the framers and ratifiers of the Constitution.

Nothing better illustrates the distance of legal positivism from the original intent of the framers and ratifiers than the pronouncements of Chief Justice Rehnquist. He is the philosopher-king of the legal positivist version of original intent jurisprudence (otherwise called "originalism"). In his landmark essay on "The Notion of a Living Constitution,"[2] he admonishes those who ignore

> the nature of political value judgments in a democratic society. If such a society adopts a constitution and incorporates in that constitution safeguards for individual liberty, these safeguards do indeed take on a generalized moral rightness or goodness. They assume a general social acceptance neither because of any intrinsic worth nor because of any unique origins in someone's idea of natural justice but instead simply because they have been incorporated in a constitution by the people.

To say that "safeguards for individual liberty" are not incorporated in a constitution because of "any intrinsic worth" is as much as to say that individual liberty does not possess any intrinsic worth, which in turn implies that human life does not possess any intrinsic worth. Now this is more than legal positivism, it is moral relativism and nihilism in their most naked form. It cannot by any stretch of the imagination have anything in common with the political philosophy of the generation that framed and ratified the Constitution. Yet Bork's and Cooper's "good originalism" subsists wholly within the parameters defined by Rehnquist.

The Constitution of 1787, together with the Bill of Rights, included many "safeguards for individual liberty." But it also included a number of safeguards for slavery, most notably the Fugitive Slave Clause of Article IV. By Rehnquist's "originalism," the safeguards for slavery and the safeguards for individual liberty have exactly the same moral standing. Both were incorporated into the same constitution by the same people, and both—according to Rehnquist—must have acquired the same "moral goodness and rightness" by virtue of that incorporation. This was also the position taken by John C. Calhoun, and by the states that "seceded" in 1860 and 1861.

In the balance of this reply I will show that the fact that the original Constitution did recognize a right to own slaves underscores the importance of the Declaration of Independence in enabling us to distinguish the *principles* of the Constitution from the *compromises* of the Constitution. This is some-

2. 54 Texas L. Rev. 693 (1976), *reprinted in* Taking the Constitution Seriously: Essays on the Constitution and Constitutional Law 69–70 (Gary L. McDowell ed., 1981). For a full analysis of this and collateral passages in the Rehnquist essay (including Rehnquist's discussion of *Dred Scott*, which largely parallels that of Bork), see my essay in *Original Intent and the Framers of the Constitution*, *supra* note 1, at 83–108.

thing that neither Rehnquist nor Bork (nor Calhoun) is able to do. I will show that Bork's accusation against Chief Justice Taney for introducing "substantive due process" is wholly anachronistic, and that the Borkian separation of due process from any ends or purposes degenerates into complete moral relativism.

II

Judge Bork's 1990 book *The Tempting of America: The Political Seduction of the Law* has as its central theme that liberal activist judges have invented rights which are nowhere in the Constitution, and have then invented remedies for violations of these rights. This, he says, is judicial legislation. It is an assumption of authority that violates the constitutional separation of powers, and that usurps the legislative authority that the Constitution has placed in Congress. Bork calls this substantive due process. If and when this occurs, and to the extent that it does occur, I am in full agreement with Bork.

Bork, however, asserts erroneously that substantive due process entered American constitutional law in the case of *Dred Scott v. Sandford*.[3] Bork's analysis of *Dred Scott* is the linchpin of his entire book. In it he denies that the Constitution says what it does say, in order to reach a conclusion he wishes to reach. In doing this, he lays the foundation for a results-oriented jurisprudence that does not differ in principle from that of the liberals he chastises.

In *Tempting*, Bork accuses Chief Justice Taney in *Dred Scott* of inventing a right of slave ownership that is "nowhere . . . in the Constitution."[4] On this basis Bork charges Taney with transforming the Due Process Clause of the Fifth Amendment. Although the Framers employed circuitous phrasing to avoid using the word slavery, no one before Bork has ever doubted that it is present in at least three major provisions of the Constitution: Article I, Section 2; Article I, Section 9; and Article IV, Section 2. The latter two—the Migration and Importation Clause, and the Fugitive Slave Clause—are cited by Taney as evidence that Negro slaves are recognized as chattel property by the Constitution. Accordingly it was not Taney who has read the right of slave property *into* the antebellum Constitution, but Bork who has attempted to read it *out*.

Cooper attempts to rescue Bork from his manifestly expurgated reading as follows: "Jaffa is certainly right that the original Constitution recognized

3. 60 U.S. (19 How.) 393 (1857).

4. Robert H. Bork, The Tempting of America: The Political Seduction of the Law 31 (1990).

a right of slave ownership. But Bork did not deny that the Constitution recognized a right to slave ownership; he said instead that the Constitution does not *confer* a right to slave ownership."[5] Here, however, is the crucial passage in Bork's book. "How did Taney know that slave ownership was a constitutional right? Such a right is nowhere to be found in the Constitution. He knew it because he was passionately convinced that it *must* be a constitutional right."[6] If a right is "nowhere to be found" in the Constitution, how can it be either recognized or conferred?

Cooper attempts to avoid this conclusion by quoting Bork in his exchange with me in the February 7, 1994, *National Review*: "The Constitution certainly recognized that slaves were held pursuant to the laws of some states, but the Constitution most emphatically did not guarantee such a right." What Bork recognized in 1994 (under the flail of my critique) he had not recognized in 1990, and Bork and Cooper are both disingenuous in pretending otherwise. In any event, Bork's original error is only compounded by his denial that there is any guarantee of slavery in the Constitution. Here is what Abraham Lincoln said about the Fugitive Slave Clause, in the last of his seven joint debates with Stephen Douglas, on October 15, 1858:

> I suppose most of us (I know it of myself) believe that the people of the Southern States are entitled to a Congressional fugitive slave law—*that it is a right fixed in the Constitution*.... And *as the right is constitutional* I agree that legislation shall be granted to it.... Why then do I yield support to a fugitive slave law? Because I do not understand that the Constitution, *which guarantees that right*, can be supported without it."[7]

According to Lincoln, as long as there is slave property in any of the states, there is a constitutional guarantee of the security of that property.

III

In attempting to distinguish rights recognized from rights conferred by the Constitution, Cooper places himself in a position that is, if possible, even more indefensible than Bork's. In the Fugitive Slave Clause, he says, the Constitution recognized a right of slave ownership under *state* law. But, he says, "It is not a federal constitutional right. In contrast, the Second Amendment *confers* a federal constitutional right to keep... arms.... There is no similar constitutional provision conferring a right to keep slaves."[8] This is

5. Cooper, *supra* note 1, at 208.
6. BORK, *supra* note 4, at 31.
7. 3 COLLECTED WORKS OF ABRAHAM LINCOLN 317 (Roy P. Basler ed., 1953) (emphasis added).
8. Cooper, *supra* note 1, at 208 (emphasis added).

a remarkable assertion for a former Assistant Attorney General who once headed the Justice Department's Office of Legal Counsel. The Ninth Amendment says, "The enumeration in the Constitution of certain rights shall not be construed to deny or disparage others retained by the people." The antebellum Constitution *enumerates* rights, it does not *confer* them. "The right of the people to keep and bear arms," like all other such rights—for example, the free exercise of religion, freedom of speech and of the press, freedom of peaceable assembly—is a right which the amendment says "shall not be infringed." Madison, in his speech in the House of Representatives on June 8, 1789, introducing what became the first ten amendments, invited the House "expressly [to] declare the great rights of mankind secured under this Constitution."[9] The "great rights of mankind" are *declared and secured*, they are not *conferred*. They are prior to the Constitution, they are prior to all positive law. These rights are nothing less than what the Declaration of Independence meant by the unalienable rights with which all men are endowed by their Creator.

Unlike the enumerated rights to which Madison referred, the right to own slaves, so far from arising from a natural right, is against nature and against natural law. For this reason, unlike the enumerated (and unenumerated) rights, the right of slave ownership has its origin exclusively in positive law. It can therefore be said to be "conferred" by the laws of the slave states. Without recognizing the distinction between rights originating in the natural law, and rights originating in positive law, the antebellum Constitution is a sealed book.

The Fifth Amendment says, "No person shall be . . . deprived of life, liberty, or property, without due process of law. . . ." Taney held that, because of this, no owner could be deprived of his slave property merely because he had entered a United States territory. In reaching this conclusion, however, he had pointed to both Article I, Section 9, and Article IV, Section 2, as evidence that, since Negro slaves were bought and sold like any other article of commerce, the Constitution considered them only as chattel property. What Taney said about the Due Process Clause was therefore supported in his mind by other clauses in the Constitution, and for this reason he hardly could have intended that "transformation" of the Due Process Clause with which Bork credits him.

It is Bork's thesis—endorsed by Cooper—that "the guarantee of due process [in the Fifth Amendment] is simply a requirement that the substance of the law be applied to a person through fair procedures. . . . The clause says nothing whatever about what the substance of the law must be."[10] Applied

---

9. The Mind of the Founder: Sources of the Political Thought of James Madison 162 (Marvin Meyers ed., rev. ed. 1981).

10. Bork, *supra* note 4, at 31.

to the question of the constitutionality of the Missouri law of 1820 (which excluded slavery in the remaining Louisiana Territory north of thirty-six degrees, thirty minutes), Bork's and Cooper's interpretation of the Due Process Clause would mean not only that Congress had a perfect right to pass that law, but that it also had an equal right to enact a law protecting slavery in the same territory. The Due Process Clause, according to Bork and Cooper, was perfectly neutral between freedom and slavery in the territories. That is to say, the Constitution was perfectly indifferent to whether the positive law of slavery or the natural law of freedom would ultimately prevail.

This view of the moral neutrality of the Due Process Clause towards the substantive ends of legislation is repeated like a mantra by Bork and his followers (including Cooper). It is, however, contradicted by Professor Douglas Kmiec, Cooper's successor as head of the Office of Legal Counsel. Kmiec writes of Bork's conception of the Due Process Clause that

> it is analytically silly not to recognize that, at some point, procedure is substance and that appropriate procedures must include a check against arbitrary governmental actions. To posit that the framers were willing to allow life, liberty, and property to not be safeguarded against arbitrary decision making is almost to refute the argument by its mere statement.[11]

We return to Bork's charge that Taney had transformed the Due Process Clause from a merely procedural to a substantive requirement. Bork calls this "a momentous sham." But consider the following:

> The principal antislavery arguments were proslavery arguments turned upside down. Thus the due process clause of the Fifth Amendment, to which Southerners occasionally appealed, with emphasis on the word "property," could be invoked by northern radicals . . . with emphasis on the word "liberty." "Slavery," wrote Salmon P. Chase in 1844, "never has lawfully existed in any territory of the United States since the adoption of that amendment which declares that no person shall be deprived of liberty without due process of law." This argument was incorporated into the platforms of the Liberty Party in 1844, the Free Soil Party in 1848, and the Republican Party in 1856 and 1860.[12]

What Bork calls substantive due process, so far from being a radical innovation, was a commonplace of the slavery debate, whether on one side or the other, for the greater part of a generation. In 1857, the only question was which side the Due Process Clause of the Fifth Amendment favored. Here is what the Republican Party platform of 1856 said.

---

11. The Attorney General's Lawyer: Inside the Meese Justice Department 42 (1992).

12. Don E. Fehrenbacher, The Dred Scott Case 141 (1978).

> Resolved, That the maintenance of the principles promulgated in the Declaration of Independence and embodied in the Federal Constitution, is essential to the preservation of our Republican institutions, and that the Federal Constitution, the rights of the states, and the union of the states, shall be preserved.
> Resolved, That with our Republican fathers we hold it to be a self-evident truth, that all men are endowed with the unalienable rights to life, liberty, and the pursuit of happiness, and that the primary object and ulterior designs of our federal government were to secure these rights to all persons within its exclusive jurisdiction; that, as our Republican fathers, when they had abolished slavery in all our national territory[13] [and] ordained that no persons should be deprived of life, liberty, or property without due process of law, it becomes our duty to maintain this provision of the Constitution against all attempts to violate it for the purpose of establishing slavery in any Territory of the United States, by positive legislation, prohibiting its existence or extension therein. That we deny the authority of Congress, or a Territorial legislature, of any individual or association of individuals, to give legal existence to slavery in any Territory of the United States, while the present Constitution shall be maintained.[14]

With only minor differences, the identical language appears in the Republican party platform of 1860, upon which Abraham Lincoln was elected to the presidency. If the Due Process Clause of the Fifth Amendment was declared to be substantive by the Republicans in the national election of 1856, how could it have made its "first appearance" in Taney's opinion in 1857?

In fact, Taney's use of the Due Process Clause in the interest of slavery was unusual, and probably was a direct reaction to its use in the opposite sense by the Republicans. It was more characteristic of proslavery speeches, whether in or out of Congress, to rely upon Calhoun's theory of states' rights, namely that the Constitution was a compact among the states, and that the territories were the common property of the states. From this it followed that Congress as the collective trustee of all the states had no lawful power to discriminate against any form of the property lawful in any of them. When Taney composed his opinion, he had before him not only the Republican platform of 1856, but the election returns of that year. They showed that only the division of the antislavery vote had allowed Bucha-

---

13. This has reference to the Northwest Ordinance, adopted by the Confederation Congress in July of 1787, but reenacted by the first Congress under the Constitution in 1789. The Ordinance forbade slavery in all the Northwest Territory, from which the states of Ohio, Indiana, Michigan, and Illinois were later formed.

14. Edward Stanwood, A History of Presidential Elections 205–06 (2d rev. ed. 1888).

nan's election. The slave power saw itself being overwhelmed in the political process by the growing ranks of the antislavery forces in the free states. They saw in the judicial process the last alternative to secession as a means of preserving slavery. Taney and his court were anything but independent players in the drama that culminated in *Dred Scott.*

Lincoln's "House Divided" speech of June 16, 1858—a speech which may have changed the course of events more than any in the history of free government—charged a conspiracy to extend slavery, encompassing two Presidents, a United States Senator, and the Chief Justice. Lincoln pointed to the fact that after the 1856 election, the outgoing President, Pierce, and the incoming President, Buchanan, endorsed the *Dred Scott* decision before it was announced, and called upon the public to accept it—sight unseen—as a final resolution of the slavery question.[15] So also did Senator Douglas, and some Southern leaders, all of whom knew very well what the tenor of that decision would be.[16] In the territorial laws of Utah and New Mexico that formed part of the Compromise of 1850, it was provided that any dispute as to the right of property in slaves could be appealed from the supreme court of the territory to the Supreme Court of the United States. Thus Congress itself had given the direction for a judicial resolution of the territorial question. It is nonsense to think that Taney's opinion represented a merely gratuitous judicial intrusion into the political process.

Cooper makes much of a "hypothetical case" in *Original Intent*, in which I imagined a proslavery antebellum Congress enacting a slave code for the territories. Dred Scott, having been held as a slave in a territory under this law, sues for his freedom on the ground that the law was unconstitutional. I imagined a Republican Supreme Court, with Abraham Lincoln as Chief Justice. I said I believed that such a court would have agreed with Dred Scott

---

15. Here is Buchanan in his inaugural address, three days before *Dred Scott* was announced. Concerning the question of the constitutional status of slavery in the territories, he said,

> [I]t is a judicial question, which legitimately belongs to the Supreme Court of the United States, before whom it is now pending, and will, *it is understood*, be speedily and finally settled. To their decision, in common with all good citizens, I shall cheerfully submit, whatever this may be....

10 THE WORKS OF JAMES BUCHANAN 106 (John Bassett Moore ed., 1908–1911) (emphasis added). This was cosmic hypocrisy, and it utterly contradicts those who—like Rehnquist, Bork, and Cooper—think that *Dred Scott* was mere judicial usurpation.

16. *See* FEHRENBACHER, *supra* note 12, at 306–07:

> Alexander H. Stephens informed his brother on December 15 [1856] that he was urging the Court to a prompt decision, with the full expectation that it would settle the territorial issue in the South's favor. A likely object of Stephens's influence was his fellow Georgian, Justice Wayne, and Wayne proved to be the pivotal figure in an abrupt reversal of the strategy first adopted by the Court's majority.

and set him free. Cooper declares triumphantly: "Thus, Taney's illegitimate invention—substantive due process—is no less central to Jaffa's constitutionalism than it was to Taney's. Jaffa has no problem with Taney's methodology, just with his moral values and, hence, his result."[17] In response, let us repeat—and keep repeating—the Republican platforms of 1856 and 1860. They assert without equivocation: "That we deny the authority of Congress, of a Territorial legislature, of any individual or association of individuals, to give legal existence to slavery in any Territory of the United States, while the present Constitution shall last."[18] Can Cooper—can anyone—imagine a Justice appointed to the Supreme Court by a President elected on that platform hesitating to pronounce unconstitutional a law giving "legal existence to slavery in any Territory of the United States"? Yet that is neither more nor less than what was at issue in my "hypothetical case." Bork's and Cooper's idea of the merely procedural character of the Due Process Clause in 1857 is completely anachronistic. They might as well have faulted the underground railroad for not using helicopters.[19]

---

17. Cooper, *supra* note 1, at 211–12.

18. STANWOOD, *supra* note 14, at 205–06.

19. The depths of absurdity into which Cooper's notion of due process leads him is illustrated by the following (Cooper, *supra* note 1, at 209):

> ...Jaffa thinks that Taney got it right, as a matter of Borkian originalism, in concluding that a slaveholder was entitled under the Due Process Clause to take his slaves with him into a United States territory. This raises some difficult questions for Jaffa. Is Congress's plenary legislative authority over the territories similarly limited with respect to other substances or activities that are permitted in at least some of the states? Would Congress, for example, be barred by the Fifth Amendment from outlawing the possession and use of cocaine in the territories simply because some of the states had not outlawed it? If citizens of Utah, for example, enjoyed the freedom to practice polygamy, would Congress be prohibited under the Due Process Clause from outlawing the practice? Would a prostitute from Nevada be constitutionally entitled to engage in her profession in the territories? I think that the answer to these questions is plainly no.

I answer, not as a Borkian, but as a Lincolnian originalist. Moreover, Cooper's questions are not as hypothetical as he seems to suppose. The Republican platform of 1856 also resolved that "it is both the right and the duty of Congress to prohibit in the Territories those twin relics of barbarism, polygamy and slavery." It was the *Republican* understanding that polygamy should be outlawed for the same reason as slavery. It degrades women and is inconsistent with the principle of human equality. Drug use and prostitution are, or certainly may be, judged to be inconsistent with that "transcendent law of nature and of nature's God which declares that the safety and happiness of society are the objects at which all political institutions aim, and to which all such institutions must be sacrificed." THE FEDERALIST NO. 43, at 279 (James Madison) (Clinton Rossiter ed., 1961). The legislative power, either of Congress or of a territorial legislature, flowing from the law of nature, should be competent to deal with them.

IV

A penetrating insight into Cooper's (and Bork's) "originalism" is the following:

> For Jaffa, the Declaration defines "the legal... and moral personality" of the American people... once and for all. The American people are thus enslaved to the "moral and political philosophy" of the founders, powerless to redefine their "legal and... moral personality." Any attempt by the American people to "compromise" the natural law principles of the Declaration—for example, by amending their Constitution—would conflict with the "genuine principles" of the Constitution and thus be void.[20]
>
> Jaffa illustrates his point vividly by arguing that the American people lack the "inherent authority" to repeal the Thirteenth Amendment.... for which there is no support among decent people.[21]

According to Cooper, I would "enslave" the American people to the moral and political philosophy of the Founding Fathers, that is to say, I would enslave them to the principles of freedom! This is, to say the least, a curious way of thinking for someone who is committed to a jurisprudence of original intent. I had thought that the right to redefine ourselves legally and morally—a refusal to be "enslaved" to obsolete eighteenth-century doctrines—was the heart of liberal activist jurisprudence. Why, indeed, should the Justices be "enslaved" to the Constitution at all?

Among the fundamental rights of the Declaration of Independence—cited repeatedly in *The Federalist* (and by Washington in his Farewell Address)—is the right of the people to alter or abolish their governments,

---

20. Cooper expends vast ingenuity in ridiculing the unity of the Constitution and the principles of the Declaration. "Jaffa's Constitution," he says, might be called his "Declartution."

Acts of Congress admitting new states into the Union are of the highest constitutional standing. Since the Civil War every enabling act has laid down the identical relationship of Constitution and Declaration. For example:

> That the Constitution when formed shall be republican, and not repugnant to the Constitution of the United States and the principles of the Declaration of Independence. [Nebraska, 1864]
>
> The Constitution of the State of Alaska shall always be republican in form and shall not be repugnant to the Constitution of the United States and the principles of the Declaration of Independence. [1959]
>
> The Constitution of the State of Hawaii shall always be republican in form and shall not be repugnant to the Constitution of the United States and the principles of the Declaration of Independence. [1959]

I am indebted to David M. Sonenstein for this corroboration. The constitutional guarantee of a republican form of government is to this day required by positive law to be in conformity with the natural law of the Declaration of Independence.

21. Cooper, *supra* note 1, at 197, 198.

and to change such governments in any way that to them shall seem most likely to effect their safety and happiness. It is difficult to see how this doctrine can enslave anyone.

But Cooper finds slavishness in my assertion that the American people lack the inherent authority to repeal the Thirteenth Amendment. To Cooper, that is a limitation upon their freedom. So, of course, would be a prohibition of suicide. Let us then suppose instead an amendment to change the Constitution from republican to monarchical, and designating, for example, the Kennedy family as the royal family. As in the Roman empire, all authority would be a delegation or devolution from the king or emperor. Do the people have the right to annihilate their own authority? They may, of course, have the power to do so. The German people apparently did just that in 1933. But did they have the "right" to do so? Power and right are two different things—a distinction which, however, is lost upon legal positivists.

As to repealing the Thirteenth Amendment, Cooper says that this is something "for which there is no support among decent people." But what, to a legal positivist, does decency have to do with constitutionalism? According to Rehnquist, constitutions derive whatever moral goodness—or decency—that may be attributed to them from the mere fact of being adopted, and from nothing else. As we know from *The Adventures of Huckleberry Finn*, the most despised character in the antebellum South was the "nigger stealer." No one was lower on the scale of decency. After the end of Reconstruction, the worst of epithets was "nigger lover." Legal positivism and moral relativism go hand in hand: decency is nothing but the prevailing moral fashions, for those with whom the fashions prevail, for as long as they do prevail.

For Cooper—who would not be enslaved to any permanent standards—true freedom would allow one to be proslavery at one time and antislavery at another. Let us then have no squeamishness about decency. Let us not masquerade our personal preferences behind the moral and political philosophy of the Declaration of Independence!

HARRY V. JAFFA

CONTRIBUTORS

Daniel P. Collins has been an Assistant U.S. Attorney in the Central District of California since 1992. He received his A.B. from Harvard University in 1985 and his J.D. from Stanford Law School in 1988. The views expressed in his review are wholly his own and do not reflect the position of the United States government or any agency thereof.

Michael DeBow is a professor of law at the Cumberland School of Law, Samford University. During 1983–84, he was a law clerk to Judge Kenneth W. Starr of the U.S. Court of Appeals for the District of Columbia Circuit. During the Reagan Administration, he was an attorney-advisor to Chairman James C. Miller III of the Federal Trade Commission, and a special assistant to Assistant Attorney General Douglas Ginsburg of the Antitrust Division of the U.S. Department of Justice.

Orrin G. Hatch is United States Senator from Utah. He is currently chairman of the Senate Committee on the Judiciary.

Henry Mark Holzer is Professor of Law at Brooklyn Law School, author of, among other works, *Sweet Land of Liberty?: The Supreme Court and Individual Rights*, and editor of the recently published *Speaking Freely: The Case against Speech Codes*.

James L. Huffman is Dean of Lewis and Clark Law School. He has taught there since 1973, including courses in constitutional law, natural resources law and policy, water law, jurisprudence, torts, and government liability law. Dean Clark was Bradley Resident Scholar at the Heritage Foundation in 1993, and is a graduate of Montana State University (B.S. 1967), the Fletcher School of Law and Diplomacy, Tufts University (M.A. 1969), and the University of Chicago Law School (J.D. 1972).

Harry V. Jaffa is Henry Salvatori Research Professor Emeritus at Claremont McKenna College and Claremont Graduate School and Distinguished Fellow at the Claremont Institute.

Richard Klingler is an attorney with the Washington, D.C., office of Sidley & Austin, where his regulatory and appellate practice consists principally of telecommunications, broadcasting, and constitutional issues. A graduate of Oxford University and Stanford University, he clerked for Judge Kenneth W. Starr and Justice Sandra Day O'Connor.

Albert G. Lauber is a member of Caplin & Drysdale, Chtd., Washington, D.C., where he specializes in tax and appellate litigation. He clerked for Justice Blackmun during the 1978–79 Term, and he served during the

Reagan and Bush administrations as Tax Assistant to the Solicitor General and Deputy Solicitor General. He is a graduate of Yale College, Cambridge University, and Yale Law School.

GARY LAWSON is a Professor at Northwestern University School of Law, where he has taught since 1988. He has written extensively on constitutional law, jurisprudence, federal courts, and a range of other topics. He is Senior Adviser to the Federalist Society for Law and Public Policy Studies.

NELSON LUND is Professor of Law at George Mason University School of Law and an editor of the *Supreme Court Economic Review*. He previously served in the White House as Associate Counsel to the President (1989–92) and in the Office of Legal Counsel at the United States Department of Justice (1986–87). He was a law clerk for Judge Patrick E. Higginbotham of the United States Court of Appeals for the Fifth Circuit (1985–86) and for Justice Sandra Day O'Connor (1987–88).

JEREMY RABKIN is Associate Professor of Government at Cornell University. He is the author of *Judicial Compulsions* (Basic Books, 1989) and numerous articles in scholarly journals and opinion magazines.

STEPHAN THERNSTROM is the Winthrop Professor of History at Harvard University.

MICHAEL M. UHLMANN is a senior fellow at the Ethics and Public Policy Center and Of Counsel to Pepper, Hamilton & Scheetz in Washington, D.C.

ROGER CLEGG and LEONARD A. LEO are the editors of *The Public Interest Law Review*. Mr. Clegg is the vice president and general counsel of the National Legal Center for the Public Interest, which publishes the *Review*. Mr. Leo is director of the Lawyers Division of the Federalist Society.